Critical Thinking Student's Guide
M. Neil Browne
Bowling Green State University

The Legal Environment of Business: A Critical Thinking Approach
Fifth Edition

Nancy K. Kubasek
Bartley A. Brennan
M. Neil Browne

Prentice Hall

New York   Boston   San Francisco
London   Toronto   Sydney   Tokyo   Singapore   Madrid
Mexico City   Munich   Paris   Cape Town   Hong Kong   Montreal

Editor-in-Chief: Eric Svendsen
Editorial Project Manager: Kierra Kashickey
Production Editor: Clara Bartunek
Operations Specialist: Ben Smith

Copyright © 2009 by Pearson Education, Inc., Upper Saddle River, New Jersey, 07458.
Pearson Prentice Hall. All rights reserved. Printed in the United States of America. This publication is protected by Copyright and permission should be obtained from the publisher prior to any prohibited reproduction, storage in a retrieval system, or transmission in any form or by any means, electronic, mechanical, photocopying, recording, or likewise. For information regarding permission(s), write to: Rights and Permissions Department.

Pearson Prentice Hall™ is a trademark of Pearson Education, Inc.
Pearson® is a registered trademark of Pearson plc
Prentice Hall® is a registered trademark of Pearson Education, Inc.

Pearson Education Ltd., London
Pearson Education Singapore, Pte. Ltd
Pearson Education, Canada, Inc.
Pearson Education–Japan
Pearson Education Australia PTY, Limited

Pearson Education North Asia, Ltd., Hong Kong
Pearson Educación de Mexico, S.A. de C.V.
Pearson Education Malaysia, Pte. Ltd
Pearson Education Upper Saddle River, New Jersey

Prentice Hall
is an imprint of

www.pearsonhighered.com

10 9 8 7 6 5 4 3 2 1

ISBN-13: 978-0-13-605918-9
ISBN-10: 0-13-605918-X

Table of Contents

CHAPTER 1
CRITICAL THINKING AND LEGAL REASONING

This chapter in the text sets the tone for the book. It speaks directly to you about what critical thinking is and why it is so important for you as a future business leader. Let's begin the Student Guide by establishing the pattern that we will use in every chapter. After this introductory chapter in the Student Guide, we will start with the critical thinking material and then complete each chapter with the more traditional multiple choice, true-false, short answer and matching questions. In this critical thinking material, we will provide more practice opportunities than are available from the text by itself.

A.   More Critical Thinking

1. Getting Started

A good first step in understanding more about critical thinking is to jump the hurdle associated with the term itself. To be a critical thinker sounds, at first glance, mean and just generally unfriendly. I suppose a person could learn the techniques of critical thinking and be altogether obnoxious as a result. But such a result is far from what we have in mind!

A critical thinker is first and foremost a good listener. Those of us who practice critical thinking know that we must hear an argument, and hear it well, before we can react to it in a fair-minded manner. I'm sure you remember how annoying it can be when someone reacts to you by claiming that you said something you never said. To prevent this occurrence, critical thinkers work very hard to make certain that they have found the reasoning intended by the speaker or writer. <u>Then, and only then</u>, do they evaluate the reasoning.

This respect for what others have to say is based on our awareness that none of us knows everything. We have lots to learn, and just maybe that other person who is trying to say something to us possesses some reasoning that we should make our own.

So critical thinking in this respect is cooperative thinking, borrowing from one another those arguments that make the most sense.

But critical thinking is much more than that. It is also <u>productive thinking</u>. None of us benefits from weak reasoning. Critical thinking helps us distinguish *high quality* reasoning from low quality reasoning. The basic idea is that we do not want to be misled by reasoning that has insubstantial or insufficient support. A second important step in expanding your use of critical thinking is to appreciate that critical thinking is not something that you either do or do not do. Everyone tries to evaluate; we have no alternative. But what distinguishes us as critical thinkers is the depth and skill of our thinking.

The critical thinking model in Chapter 1 is just a start in your becoming a better critical thinker, but it is a powerful start. You will notice after just a few weeks in this class that you are regularly asking better questions than you had been before. Your new skill will make you feel more eager to participate in conversations about serious business issues because you will notice that you have a lot more to contribute.

2. Expanding the Critical Thinking Model

There are a huge number of critical thinking skills; we have tried to be selective, to ask you to learn only those skills that would be especially valuable to you in a legal setting. What we are going to do in this manual is discuss and apply just two additional critical thinking skills. In other words, we are going to give you two additional tools that should enable you to have an even more impressive model of critical thinking than is available in the main text.

First, let's review the steps of the model in the text. It consists of a series of interrelated steps:

> What are the significant facts in this case or argument?
> What is the issue being disputed?
> What are the reasons and the conclusion for the opinion?
> What are the rules of law that apply to this disagreement?
> Does the legal argument contain significant ambiguity?
> What ethical norms are fundamental to the reasoning?
> How appropriate are the legal analogies?
> Is there relevant missing information?

Each of these critical thinking questions provides a highly important avenue for seeing deeper levels of legal analysis. But here are two additional critical thinking questions that this Study Guide will encourage you to ask on a regular basis. They deserve equal status with the other questions, and their use will make you an even better critical thinker.

ARE THERE ALTERNATIVE CAUSES THAT MIGHT BE RESPONSIBLE FOR THE PROBLEM ADDRESSED IN THE LEGAL DISPUTE?

ARE THERE ALTERNATIVE REASONABLE CONCLUSIONS THAT ARE CONSISTENT WITH THE REASONS?

After discussing the meaning and use of each of these questions, we will apply them to the Martha Stewart case in the first chapter of your primary text.

The search for alternative causes

When an event occurs, our curiosity usually sends us hunting for the cause of the event. We are motivated by more than curiosity though. Finding causes accomplishes multiple important tasks. First, it provides us with a hint about how to encourage or prevent the event in the future. For example, if a particular advertisement is desirable behavior, we will want to encourage even more of those advertisements. Second, finding causes enables us to understand relationships among human actions. To paraphrase a saying from ecology: We can never do merely one thing. When we make decisions, the effects go on and on, like ripples on a pond when a pebble is tossed into it.

But most importantly for a legal context, finding causes enables us to fix responsibility. We want to know whom to blame and whom to applaud, so that appropriate legal responses can be made to those assignments of responsibility. We want to be fair. The person who caused the action is the person who should bear the responsibility for the actions in question.

In the exercises that we will include in later chapters, we will often ask you to reexamine the reasoning to see whether the cause that has been identified may be an imposter. Try to develop the habit of asking: Is there another possible cause that could have led to the event in question? Again, the idea is to not necessarily buy the very first plausible cause that you hear. In the spirit of critical thinking, we wonder whether there might perhaps be another cause that is responsible.

The search for alternative reasonable conclusions

Reasons are not entirely articulate. In other words, when we provide reasons, the conclusion that flows from them is never altogether clear. Picture the situation for many jurors. They have heard identical reasons. Yet, they may well disagree about what those reasons are saying. They disagree about the conclusion that flows from the reasons.

At first glance, it might appear that people disagree about conclusions because some understand the reasoning or the issue and others do not. But as you listen more to people who disagree, you become aware that people who are highly reasonable may still disagree about what a group of reasons mean. The reasons just do not speak for themselves. Even after we understand the reasons for a claim or a decision, we still need to interpret those reasons and put them into a meaningful pattern.

Typically, a judge or an author will tell you what reasons mean. Often their story about how the reasons and the conclusion fit together makes a lot of

3

sense. We are tempted to agree right away. But critical thinkers hesitate and ask: Could those same reasons lead to a different conclusion than the one we are being offered?

<u>Applying our expanded model of critical thinking</u>

First reread the Stewart case from the United States District Court for the Southern District Of New York. The basics of the case involve Martha Stewart's and Peter Bacanovic's request for a new trial following their conviction. They claim that they were entitled to a new trial because Lawrence Stewart, an expert witness for the prosecution, allegedly perjured himself during his testimony. Because this perjury influenced the jury's opinion, the defendants argue that they are entitled to a new and fair trial. However, Judge Cedarbaum denied defendants' motion for a new trial.

Are there alternative causes that could explain Stewart's decision to sell her ImClone stock?

One of the primary issues in the initial trial involved the court's determining the reason for Martha Stewart's sale, which occurred the day before ImClone announced that the FDA did not approve its drug Erbitux. Although the court considered a couple alternative causes for why Stewart sold her ImClone stock, the court found that the primary cause for Stewart's sale of her ImClone stocks was the information that Bacanovic provided Stewart about the CEO of ImClone's attempting to sell his stocks.

One alternative cause offered by the defense was that Stewart sold her stock because of a pre-existing agreement between Stewart and Bacanovic – an agreement that involved a plan to sell Stewart's stock in the event that ImClone's stock dropped below $60 per share. When the court considered this alternative cause, the court held that while the agreement may have existed, the agreement was not the reason for the sale. Instead, the court held that the tip from Bacanovic that ImClone's CEO was trying to sell his stock was the cause for Stewart's sale. Hence, even though the expert witness Lawrence Stewart may have perjured himself about his involvement in the testing of the documents that contained the "@$60" symbol that suggested an agreement existed, Lawrence Stewart's alleged perjury was not sufficient to thwart the court-determined cause of Stewart's sale, namely that Stewart received information about the actions of ImClone's CEO. Hence, the court held that Stewart's argument for an alternative cause of her actions (i.e. the $60 agreement with Bacanovic) was one of several lies she told during an agency investigation.

This case serves as a warning to you as a future employer. Know the law so that you can provide causes for your behavior that the law respects. The defendants in this case may have won had they been able to more convincingly demonstrate that the dropping ImClone stock price was the cause of the sale, not information about the CEO of ImClone's attempts to sell all his company stocks. Alternatively, had the defendants been more aware of the laws and legal consequences of conspiracy and making false statements, perhaps they would have acted differently and received a legal result that was more pleasing to them, or perhaps they would have avoided litigation in the first place if they would have avoided their participating in questionable behavior.

Are there any other reasonable conclusions that could be drawn from the reasons in this case? In other words, could another judge have reasonably found differently, given the same court record?

First, review the reasons themselves.

1. Under Rule 33 and relevant case law, perjury is not sufficient to warrant a new trial, unless (a) the government knew about the perjury or (b) the perjured testimony was so material that the verdict would probably result in acquittal of the defendants.

2. The defendants did not demonstrate that the government knew or should have known about the perjured testimony.

3. The jury would have still convicted the defendants even if Lawrence Stewart had not testified, or even if the jury had evidence that Lawrence indeed perjured himself.

4. Defense experts agreed with Lawrence on the "most critical aspects of his scientific analysis."

As you know, Judge Cedarbaum denied the defendants' motion for a new trial. Look again at the reasons. Do the reasons shout out Judge Cedarbaum's conclusion? That question is more complicated than it looks. Certainly Judge Cedarbaum's decision makes good sense. But are there other conclusions that would also make sense in light of the reasons?

Before we look to see, stop for a moment to think about the importance of the search. If reasons had only one possible reasonable conclusion, our task would be relatively simple as careful thinkers. As soon as we stumbled upon a conclusion that made sense, we would be finished with that argument; we would have found the correct conclusion. But when we realize that reasons are more fertile than that, we have a heavy responsibility to look for multiple conclusions. As soon as we find one, we critical thinkers know it makes sense to look for still other sensible conclusions. We don't want to miss out on any of the possible interpretations of the meaning of the reasons.

So, now let's look at the list of reasons used by Judge Cedarbaum and ask ourselves whether he could not have reasonably concluded something else:

> Judge Cedarbaum could have looked at the reasons and found that while Rule 33 and certain precedents apply in this instance, "the interest of justice" places a large degree of importance not only on expediting litigation processes, but also on preventing prosecutorial misconduct. Hence, the "interest of justice" could be more greatly advanced by this prevention of misconduct than the speed with which this high-profile case is resolved. Furthermore, by the court's demanding higher standards of truthfulness from prosecutorial witnesses, the court could establish a precedent that acts as a deterrent to future acts of perjury. Therefore, one alternative conclusion is that the judge could have postponed a ruling on Stewart's motion for a new trial until a more thorough investigation of Lawrence Stewart's testimony were completed, thereafter permitting the court to make a more informed assessment of the extent to which Lawrence Stewart perjured himself and the degree to which his false testimony may have tainted the evidence.

The point to this exercise is not to suggest that all conclusions are equally valuable. On the contrary, what this critical thinking activity tries to prevent is a premature rush to accept a particular conclusion. By looking for alternative conclusions, we are able to think more about which of the alternative conclusions is most reasonable.

B.   *Learning the Basics*

Matching

1. ____ issue

    a. goal toward which reasoning moves

2. ____ conclusion

    b. incompleteness of facts

3. ____ rules of law

    c. has one or more meanings in a context of facts

4. ____ ambiguity

    d. question that causes two parties to enter into the legal system.

5. ____ norm

    e. the ability to understand the structure of an argument and apply evaluative criteria to determine the worth of the argument

6. ____ analogy

    f. prior decisions (legal precedents) that provide legal rules that those in a legal dispute defer to

7. ____ critical thinking

    g. standard of conduct that moves us toward goodness and virtue

8. ____ missing information

    h. comparison that transfers meaning from something to something else

True and False

1. ____ When you hear a conclusion, you should at once form a reaction to that conclusion.

2. ____ All forms of critical thinking focus on the quality of someone's reasoning.

3. ____ Once we understand the facts surrounding a case, we can begin to evaluate that case.

4. ____ All information that is missing from the case is important; thus, if we identify any area of missing information, we should be suspicious.

5. ____ Any reason that supports a conclusion is a good reason.

6. ____ We need to have all the facts to understand a case.

7. ____ Judges usually do not explicitly state the issue and conclusion in a case.

8. ____ Rules of law provide a framework for judges when they make a legal decision.

9. ____   We can understand what a judge means by simply reading the words of her opinion.

10. ____   Judges usually describe their primary ethical norms when writing their decision.

11. ____   Rules of law should be considered when evaluating a judge's decision but precedents should not be considered.

12. ____   When evaluating analogies, you should look only for similarities in legal precedents.

Multiple Choice

1. When you encounter an argument, you should first

   a. form a reaction to the argument
   b. identify the issue, conclusion, and reasons
   c. identify ambiguous words or phrases
   d. understand the facts surrounding the argument

2. The following elements are influential in a judge's decision:

   a. rules of law
   b. ethical norms
   c. ambiguous phrases
   d. all of the above

3. Critical thinking skills can be used

   a. when evaluating a judge's decision
   b. when reading a newspaper editorial
   c. when talking to a friend
   d. all of the above

4. It is important to identify ambiguous words or phrases in reasoning because

   a. the precise meaning of these words or phrases affects our willingness to accept or reject the conclusion
   b. we need to know the most common interpretation of these words
   c. ambiguous words inform us about that which is good or virtuous
   d. we cannot identify the relevant rules of law until we identify ambiguous words and phrases

5. Efficiency is defined as

a. possessing the capacity or resources to act as one wishes
b. providing resources in proportion to need
c. maximizing the amount of wealth in our society
d. possessing a large enough supply of goods and services such that basic needs are met

6. An issue is a

a. declarative statement about a topic
b. question
c. response to a question
d. reaction to a conclusion

7. If a judge strongly values justice, her preference for justice will

a. not affect her decisions
b. probably conflict with other values
c. suggest that she does not value freedom, efficiency, and security
d. cause her to always make just decisions

Short Answer

1. What is critical thinking?

2. Why is critical thinking important in the legal environment of business?

3. What are the eight critical thinking questions we should ask when we evaluate an argument?

4. What are the four primary ethical norms? Why is it important that we be able to identify ethical norms?

CHAPTER 2
INTRODUCTION TO LAW AND THE LEGAL ENVIRONMENT OF BUSINESS

This chapter provides an introduction to both ethical schools of thought, as well as to the legal system itself. As with all the following chapters we will begin with some additional critical thinking activities and then finish the chapter with matching, true-false, multiple choice, and short answer questions.

A.   More Critical Thinking

1. Let's begin by taking a close look at some of the reasoning in Case Problem 2-15, the case of a wife suing her husband.

Margaret Beattie v. Michael Beattie
1993

In this case we review a decision of the Superior Court granting defendant husband's motion for summary judgment in a negligence action initiated by his plaintiff wife. She is seeking damages for paralyzing injuries she sustained in an automobile accident where her husband was the driver. The trial court properly followed the prior precedents of this Court and relied on the common law doctrine of interspousal immunity ("the Doctrine") which prevents one spouse from suing the other in tort. . . . The sole issue before this Court is whether the Doctrine should be abrogated and if so to what extent.

The trial court's decision granting summary judgment is based upon the Doctrine. This antiquated doctrine was first applied by Delaware courts in the seminal case of *Plotkin v. Plotkin*. In *Plotkin*, the Superior Court adopted the Doctrine primarily on the belief that upon marriage, the identity of the wife merged with that of the husband. The Doctrine's continued existence in Delaware since 1924 has been justified as a means of promoting family harmony and discouraging collusion and fraud upon insurance companies. After most recently reviewing the Doctrine [in *Alfree*] in 1979, this Court held that "it retains sufficient merit to warrant continued adherence."

The issue is whether the Doctrine remains a viable concept in Delaware jurisprudence. The trial court's decision is supported by existing Delaware case law which recognizes the antiquated Doctrine. The validity of the Doctrine has been called into question. Accordingly, this issue poses a legal question which is subject to de novo review.

This Court refused to abrogate the Doctrine in *Alfree*, despite the renunciation of the parental immunity doctrine in *Williams v. Williams*. *Williams* held that the promotion of family harmony and the discouragement of collusive and fraudulent claims were unacceptable justifications for the parental immunity doctrine "in light of contemporary conditions and modern concepts of fairness." The *Alfree* Court declined to abrogate the Doctrine because it was then perceived that the effects would be far-reaching and the problem was "more appropriate for legislative solution than for judicial determination."

The *Alfree* Court's rationale for retaining the Doctrine included: 1) the preservation of family harmony and 2) the prevention of fraud and collusion. These were the same rationales that were rejected with regard to parental immunity in *Williams*. It is inconceivable that suits between children and parents are less likely to disrupt family harmony than interspousal suits. This is also true with respect to property claims and actions for breach of contract, which are actionable in the family context.

In our view, the Doctrine is more likely to have the effect of disrupting family harmony rather than preserving it. Denying a person compensation for injuries arising from the negligence of his or her spouse can be very disruptive (e.g., large medical bills and loss of wages often result from serious accidents). Under the Doctrine, the married couple will have to pay these huge expenses, instead of relying on insurance proceeds. This added financial burden could well promote marital discord. Any destruction of family harmony that is prevented by the Doctrine is likely to be minimal due to the prevalence of liability insurance. In addition, the Doctrine may actually promote divorces because a person who suffers an injury at the hands of his or her spouse, but who has since divorced the spouse, may maintain a tort action against the former spouse. Accordingly, it is conceivable that spouses may decide to divorce solely to bypass the restrictions of a Doctrine which putatively is designed to preserve marital harmony. Such a result is repugnant to public policy.

Because of the prevalence of liability insurance, Husband argues that collusion and fraud will increase if spouses are able to sue each other. It is true that the adversarial system may be subject to tension because it is in the defendant spouse's interest for his or her injured spouse to receive some compensation, especially when the insurance company is the "real" party being sued. Such tension could potentially lead to a threat of corruption. Although the possibility of collusion exists in various situations such as intrafamily cases and suits between friends, the judicial system is adept at ferreting out frivolous and unfounded cases. It is unnecessary and unwise to deny legitimate claims in order to prevent fraudulent and collusive suits because the judicial system contains numerous safeguards and deterrents against fraudulent claims such as perjury charges and modern discovery procedures.

The conclusion that the abrogation of the Doctrine will not lead to the destruction of family harmony or the proliferation of fraudulent suits is amply supported by empirical evidence. Delaware is the only state in the nation which recognizes the doctrine solely on common law grounds. Four other states also recognize the Doctrine, but do so pursuant to a statute or a perceived statutory prohibition of judicial abrogation of the Doctrine.

We find that the Doctrine is a relic from the common law that is no longer a viable concept and no longer meets the needs of modern society. The overwhelming majority of states in this nation have already abrogated the Doctrine without negative repercussions. Accordingly, we overrule *Alfree* and reject the Doctrine as a defense in this case.

Reversed and remanded.

a. What additional information would be helpful to you in deciding whether the Supreme Court of Delaware was correct in its analysis of the viability of the spousal immunity doctrine?

b. Can you tell from the case whether the Court's analogies were a proper basis for the decision?

c. What facts seemed especially powerful in shaping the decision of the Court?

2. Apply your critical thinking skills to this argument about the election of federal judges.

I have often wondered whether democracy should have any limits at all. But I am especially hesitant to accept anti-democratic activities by organizations that affect the lives of every one of us. There just seems to be some common sense in the link between shared participation, i.e., democracy, and fairness.

As a result of my feelings about democracy, I am especially distressed that we permit federal judges to be appointed. Here are a group of people who make the rules. They are the ones who choose which precedents to cite and which to ignore. They are the ones who establish the basic rules by which the rest of must live.

Under the current format for selecting judges, the common citizen is powerless. The judges decide; we must obey. Surely, some outstanding judges have been appointed. But what can we do about the less than wonderful ones? Again, not much of anything!

My basic argument is accountability. Judges themselves need to be judged. Did they do a good job, or did they fail? Only if we vote on their continued status as a judge can we seize control of the justice system. Then we could make certain that judges do the right thing.

a. What ideas seem particularly ambiguous in this argument for the election of judges?

b. What reasons are presented for the conclusion?

c. Is there an alternative reasonable conclusion that could be reached using the same reasons as are used in the argument?

3. Here is an argument about administrative agencies. Apply your critical thinking skills.

Most of us do not know much about administrative agencies. We need to learn more. Let's start by recognizing their importance. They make the rules by which laws are implemented. You may have mistakenly believed that Congress plays that role.

They don't; they just lay out the basic guidelines for a law, and then the bureaucrats in the agencies take over. Nowhere in the Constitution does it grant these agencies the tremendous powers that they possess. These agencies become the silent regulators of our lives, able to do as they please because their behavior is not out in the open.

The number of these agencies has exploded, and we have not noticed. I think it is time for us to wake up.

a. What is the author's conclusion? Notice that answering this question is not simple in this instance.

b. Is there a link between the conclusions in #2 and #3?

c. What missing information harms the argument about administrative agencies?

B.   Learning the Basics

Matching

1. ____ jurisprudence

    a. law concerning the relationship of government to individual citizens

2. ____ natural law school

    b. source of law is actors in the legal system and analysis of their actions

3. ____ positivist school

c. creates case law

4. ____ sociological school

d. science or philosophy of law

5. ____ American Realist school

e. statutes that govern litigation between two private parties

6. ____ Critical legal studies

f. source of law is absolute

7. ____ feminist jurisprudence

g. argues that most court decisions are best understood as efforts to promote efficient allocation of resources in society

8. ____ law and economics school

h. traditional categories of law based on a new form of communication

9. ____ legislative branch

i. statutes that prevent wrongful conduct such as murder

10. ____ executive branch

j. emphasizes critiquing belief structures that emphasize wealth and privilege

11. ____ judicial branch

k. source of law is contemporary community opinion

12. ____ criminal law

l. creates statutory law

13. ____ civil law

m. creates law by executive order

14. ____ public law

n. law concerned with enforcement of private duties between individuals

15. ____ private law

o. argues that traditional common law reflects a male emphasis on individual rights

16. ____ cyber law

p. source of law is sovereign

True and False

1. ____   Natural law school theorists believe that human law supercedes legal value judgments.

2. ____   Legal positivists believe that morals are separate from law.

3. ____   Positivism is often criticized because it is too broad; it takes into consideration too many social and ethical factors.

4. ____   Adherents to the sociological school want to create laws in conformity with the community's standards and mores.

5. ____   The sociological school is criticized because its conception of law is too static.

6. ____   Adherents of critical legal jurisprudence believe that the law reflects a cluster of beliefs that convinces human beings that the hierarchical relations that they live and work under are natural.

7. ____   Feminist jurisprudence strives to emphasize a woman's individual rights.

8. ____   Critical legal theory is the best school of jurisprudence.

9. ____   The law and economics school is criticized because no single body of principles governs economics.

10. ____   Positivism is the oldest school of jurisprudence.

11. ____   Our legal system includes three sources of law.

12. ____   When a bill becomes a statute, it has been written down and codified in the United States Code Annotated.

13. ____   The United States Supreme Court has the power of judicial review, the power to determine whether a statute is constitutional.

14. ____   Administrative law is found in the Federal Register.

15. ____   The government is the plaintiff in a civil case.

Multiple Choice

1. A judge believes that unchanging legal values can be determined by reason. In a case, the judge discovers that these legal values conflict with human law. The judge strikes down the human law. This judge most likely subscribes to

   a. the positivist school
   b. critical legal school
   c. natural law school
   d. American Realist school

2. A judge believes that case precedent and statutory law should determine the direction the law should take. She probably subscribes to the

   a. positivist school
   b. critical legal school
   c. natural law school
   d. American Realist school

3. Adherents of the sociological school seek to change law by

   a. using human reason to identify legal values
   b. critiquing hierarchical relationships
   c. educating the actors in the judicial system
   d. surveying human behavior and determining community standards

4. Both the sociological school and the American Realist school emphasize

   a. people
   b. actors in the legal system
   c. morals
   d. reason

5. Your law teacher urges you to evaluate belief structures behind laws. She claims that these belief structures have been constructed by elitists. She can be described as

   a. a feminist theorist
   b. an American realist
   c. a critical legal theorist
   d. a positivist

6. The positivist law school developed in opposition to the

a. American realist school
b. natural law school
c. sociological school
d. critical legal studies

7. Law reporters include

a. constitutional law
b. statutory law
c. administrative law
d. case law

8. When two parties disagree about the meaning of a statute, they bring their case to court for the judge to interpret. The court will usually look first at the law's legislative history to

a. find the literal meaning of the law
b. discover when the law was debated
c. determine the intent of the legislature
d. determine whether the law follows precedent

9. The executive branch creates laws through

a. executive orders
b. creating treaties
c. creating statutes
d. executive orders and treaty making

10. The purpose of criminal law is to

a. seek compensation for the plaintiff
b. punish offenders by imprisonment or fines
c. guarantee certain rights to citizens
d. enforce private duties between individuals

Short Answer

1. The legal environment of business can be defined in numerous ways. What is our definition of the legal environment of business?

2. There are many reasons for studying the legal environment of business. Give three reasons.

3. How are the sociological school and the positivist school different?

4. How are critical legal jurisprudence and feminist jurisprudence similar?

5. How is the burden of proof different for a civil and criminal case?

CHAPTER 3
THE AMERICAN LEGAL SYSTEM

In this chapter, you will learn about the actors in the legal system as well as the steps in a lawsuit. Here are some further opportunities to develop your abilities as a critical thinker. Then, we provide objective questions to help you review the chapter's basics.

A.   *More Critical Thinking*

1. The attorney-client privilege exists to encourage clients to be completely honest with their attorneys. However, how long does the attorney-client privilege last? The following case addresses this issue.

SWIDLER & BERLIN et al.
v.
UNITED STATES
1998

The U.S. asked a grand jury to subpoena handwritten notes of attorney Hamilton's conversation with the former Deputy White House Counsel, Vincent Foster, nine days before his death. The notes were part of the investigation by the Independent Counsel's Office (United States) of whether crimes were committed with the dismissed White House Travel Office employees in 1993. Hamilton moved to have the subpoena quashed, arguing that the notes were protected by attorney-client privilege even after the death of Foster. The District Court denied enforcement of the subpoenas, while the Court of Appeals of the District of Columbia reversed, declaring that the risk of posthumous revelations when confined to the criminal context would have no chilling effect on attorney-client communication. Applying a balancing test, the costs of protecting communication after death were too high, and thus a posthumous exception to privileged communication was allowed. Swindler & Berlin et al. appealed to the U.S. Supreme Court.

CHIEF JUSTICE REHNQUIST

. . . The issue presented here is the scope of [the attorney-client] privilege; more particularly, the extent to which the privilege survives the death of the client. Our interpretation of the privilege's scope is guided by "the principles of the common law . . . as interpreted by the courts . . . in the light of reason and experience.". . .

The Independent Counsel argues that the attorney-client privilege should not prevent disclosure of confidential communications where the client has died and the information is relevant to a criminal proceeding. There is some authority for this position. One state appellate court . . . and the Court of Appeals below have held the privilege may be subject to posthumous exceptions in certain circumstances. . . . But other than these two decisions, cases addressing the existence of the privilege after death uniformly presume the privilege survives. . . . Given the language of Rule 50 1, at the very least the burden is on the Independent Counsel to show that "reason and experience" require a departure from this rule.

Commentators on the law also recognize that the general rule is that the attorney-client privilege continues after death. [While these] commentators have criticized this rule, [they] clearly recognize that established law supports the continuation of the privilege and that a contrary rule would be a modification of the common law. . . . Despite the scholarly criticism, we think there are weighty reasons that counsel in favor of posthumous application. Knowing that communications will remain confidential even after death encourages the client to communicate fully and frankly with counsel. While the fear of disclosure, and the consequent withholding of information from counsel, may be reduced if disclosure is limited to posthumous disclosure in a criminal context, it seems unreasonable to assume that it vanishes altogether. Clients may be concerned about reputation, civil liability, or possible harm to friends or family. Posthumous disclosure of such communications may be as feared as disclosure during the client's lifetime.

. . . Clients consult attorneys for a wide variety of reasons, only one of which involves possible criminal liability. Many attorneys act as counselors on personal and family matters . . . [and] confidences about family members or financial problems must be revealed. . . . These confidences may not come close to any sort of admission of criminal wrongdoing, but nonetheless be matters which [sic] the client would not wish divulged.

The contention that the attorney is being required to disclose only what the client could have been required to disclose is at odds with the basis for the privilege even during the client's lifetime. In related cases, we have said that the loss of evidence admittedly caused by the privilege is justified in part by the fact that without the privilege, the client may not have made such communications in the first place. This is true of disclosure before and after the client's death. Without assurance of the privilege's posthumous application, the client may very well not have made disclosures to his attorney at all, so the loss of evidence is more apparent than real. In the case at hand, it seems quite plausible that Foster, perhaps already contemplating suicide, may not have sought legal advice from Hamilton if he had not been assured the conversation was privileged.

The Independent Counsel additionally suggests that his proposed exception would have minimal impact if confined to criminal cases, or, as the Court of

Appeals suggests, if it is limited to information of substantial importance to a particular criminal case. . . . However, there is no case authority for the proposition that the privilege applies differently in criminal and civil cases, and only one commentator ventures such a suggestion. In any event, a client may not know at the time he discloses information to his attorney whether it will later be relevant to a civil or a criminal matter, let alone whether it will be of substantial importance. Balancing ex post the importance of the information against client interests, even limited to criminal cases, introduces substantial uncertainty into the privilege's application. For just that reason, we have rejected use of a balancing test in defining the contours of the privilege.

It has been generally, if not universally, accepted, for well over a century, that the attorney-client privilege survives the death of the client in a case such as this. . . . Rule 501's direction to look to "the principles of the common law as they may be interpreted by the courts of the United States in the light of reason and experience" does not mandate that a rule, once established, should endure for all time. But here the Independent Counsel has simply not made a sufficient showing to overturn the common law rule embodied in the prevailing case law. Interpreted in the light of reason and experience, that body of law requires that the attorney-client privilege prevent disclosure of the notes at issue in this case.

Reversed Court of Appeals for petitioner - defendant Hamilton, and Swidler Berlin et al.

   a. What is the main reason that the court gives for holding that the attorney- client privilege prevents disclosure after death?

   b. Why might there be a problem with this reason? Is it a good reason?

   c. While one reason usually provides support for a conclusion, some reasons provide support for other reasons. Justice Rehnquist's opinion states, "Without assurance of the privilege's posthumous application, the client may very well not have made disclosures to his attorney at all . . ." How does this statement fit into the reasoning structure?

  2. Apply your critical thinking skills to this argument about the effectiveness of the jury system.

Criminals have the right to be tried by an unbiased jury of their peers. This process supposedly helps to ensure that a criminal receives a fair trial. However, the jury process is tainted. I can cite numerous examples of the failure of the jury system to deliver an unbiased opinion. The jury usually sides with whichever party is most sympathetic, period.

Case after case, sympathetic juries award enormous damages to allegedly "innocent" victims. Think about the McDonald's case where the woman received millions of dollars for injuries sustained from coffee burns. Fortunately, the judge reduced the award because he recognized that the award was overly excessive. Why do juries give such excessive awards?

Much research suggests that juries struggle to decide cases. For example, approximately 84 percent of juries in a 1982 study did not understand a judge's instructions in a murder case. Furthermore, in a recent survey, 79 percent of the subjects, actual jurors who heard a case in the past month, reported that they were "lost" throughout the trial. In an age of DNA testing, expert evidence, and complicated instructions, it is quite understandable that juries look to resolve a case by finding for the party that seems to be the "underdog." These jurors resolve cases by determining which party is "right" and which party is "wrong." Indeed, juror's confusion forces them to use their emotions to decide a case.

We cannot allow juries to make decisions based on their feelings. Jurors do not consider evidence; thus, their decisions are inherently flawed. The simple fact is that juries make their decisions based on sympathy. Our system is biased.

   a. What is the conclusion of this argument?

   b. The author's reasoning seems somewhat separate from the conclusion. What are the reasons provided? Do these reasons lead to the author's conclusion? What is an alternative conclusion that might make sense in light of the reasons?

   c. Based on what you learned in this chapter about juries, what words or phrases are ambiguous in the argument?

   d. What missing information could help you evaluate this argument?

B. Learning the Basics

Matching

1. ____ in personam jurisdiction

a. power of the court to hear certain kinds of cases

2. ____ original jurisdiction

b. response to allegations in plaintiff's complaint

3. ____ subject matter jurisdiction

c. process where judges and/or attorneys question potential witnesses to determine whether they can render an unbiased opinion in a case

4. ____ venue

d. lawyers practice their case before this body of individuals whose demographic make up matches that of the actual jury

5. ____ mock jury

e. power to render a decision affecting specific persons before the court

6. ____ answer

f. series of written questions sent to an opposing party, who must answer them truthfully under oath

7. ____ deposition

g. power to initially hear and decide a case

8. ____ interrogatories

h. testimony obtained before a trial because an attorney examines witnesses under oath

9. ____ voir dire

i. prescribed by statute in each state and is a matter of geographic location

True and False

1. ____   *Voir dire* is the power to determine whether a law passed by the legislature violates the United States Constitution.

2. ____   Grand juries are used only in criminal cases, whereas petit juries are used only in civil cases.

3. ____   A shadow jury is a group of individuals whose makeup matches that of the real jury, and that is present during the trial in order to give feedback to the lawyers about how well the case is going and whether the verdict is likely to favor the lawyer's client.

4. ____   Most states have now enacted long arm statutes, laws that enable a plaintiff who is dissatisfied with the trial court's decision to appeal from the trial court directly to the United States Supreme Court.

5. ____   Venue is the process of questioning potential jurors to make sure they are able to give an unbiased decision in a case.

6. ____   In order for a court to render a decision which is binding, the court must have both subject matter jurisdiction and jurisdiction over the person.

7. ____   The accessibility of a web site within a state is sufficient for the state to establish in personam jurisdiction over the owners of that web site.

8. ____   Judicial activists believe that social, political, and economic change should come primarily out of the political process.

9. ____   Federal judges are appointed by the president with the consent of the senate, whereas most state court judges are elected.

10. ____   When a tort case involves a plaintiff from Ohio and a defendant from Michigan, if the plaintiff wants the case heard in the state court, the case must be heard in that court because the plaintiff files the case and chooses the system in which the case will be heard.

Multiple Choice

1.   A lawyer is representing a client in an embezzlement case. The client tells the lawyer that he is going to have to forge his former wife's signature on a couple of legal documents in order to sell some of the property that he has in his possession. The lawyer

a.   cannot reveal that information to anyone
b.   must reveal that information in order to prevent fraud from being committed
c.   may reveal the information to prevent fraud, but doesn't have to do so
d.   must sever his relationship with the client

2.   An obese man is tried for robbing a fast food restaurant. The prosecutor uses his peremptory challenges to strike all individuals who are overweight. That use of peremptory challenges

a.   violated the defendant's equal protection rights
b.   violated the defendant's Fifth Amendment right to a jury of his peers
c.   was a valid use of peremptory challenges
d.   was not unlawful but was unnecessary because those jurors could have been excused for cause

3.   For purposes of determining jurisdiction, a corporation is a citizen of

a.   the state in which it is incorporated
b.   the state in which it does most of its business
c.   the state in which it has a physical presence
d.   both a and b

4.   In order to make a decision in a case, the court must have

a.   in rem jurisdiction and in personam jurisdiction
b.   concurrent jurisdiction and subject matter jurisdiction
c.   in personam jurisdiction and subject matter jurisdiction
d.   in rem jurisdiction and concurrent jurisdiction

5.   Venue is appropriate

a.   in the county of the plaintiff's residence
b.   in the county of the defendant's residence
c.   in the county where the dispute in issue arose
d.   all of the above

6.   One of the most crucial functions of the trial court judge is

a.   determining whether errors of law were committed by a lower court
b.   ruling on whether certain pieces of evidence are admissible
c.   reading the transcript of the trial
d.   all of the above

7.   Which of the following is a criticism offered of the adversary system?

a.   both sides bring too much evidence supporting the opposite side to the attention of the court
b.   the adversary system favors the wealthy
c.   one-shotters have a distinct advantage over repeat players
d.   because so many cases are flooding into the courts, the cost and quality of trials are decreasing

8.   Before a trial occurs, an attorney might

a.   file a reply to a counterclaim
b.   take a deposition
c.   select jurors
d.   both a and b

9.   The decision of the appellate court can take which of the following forms:

a.   affirm the decision of the lower court
b.   remand the case to the lower court for a new trial
c.   modify the remedy of the lower court
d.   all of the above

Short Answer

1.   What is a problem with the reasoning in the following statement? The adversary system is obviously the best way to achieve justice because it has been in existence since the beginning of this nation.

2.   What is the relationship between petit juries and grand juries?

3.   Provide the reasoning for the following statement: To hear a lawsuit, a court must have two types of jurisdiction, in personam and subject matter.

4.   Explain how the Class Action Fairness Act of 2005 might affect plaintiffs negatively.

CHAPTER 4
ALTERNATIVE TOOLS OF DISPUTE RESOLUTION

This chapter introduces you to methods of resolving legal disputes outside of court. This field of alternative dispute resolution (ADR) is growing in importance as our society becomes more and more litigious and trying a case in court becomes more and more expensive. We will further our study of ADR by practicing our critical thinking skills and answering objective questions covering the information from this chapter.

A. *More Critical Thinking*

1. We'll begin by returning to the *Trailmobile v. International Union of Electronic, Electrical, Salaried, Machine, and Furniture Workers* case, Case 4-1 in your primary text. You may wish to reread the case before answering the following critical thinking questions.

   a. The outcome of this case was heavily dependent on the Court's conceptualization of the issue at hand. How did Chief Judge Wollman frame the issue? What would Trailmobile have likely redefined the issue to be?

   b. What reasons does Judge Wollman provide for his framing of the issue? How are they related to the ambiguity of the phrase "just cause" in the contract signed by the disputant parties?

   c. How might Trailmobile rewrite its contract to prevent cases like this from arising in the future?

2. Apply your critical thinking skills to this argument about private jury trials.

Private jury trials may provide the solution to the problems of litigation. Litigation, although it is the oldest form of dispute resolution, is hardly a good method of resolving disputes. It is characterized as time-consuming and expensive. In an attempt to resolve civil disputes more inexpensively and efficiently, more and more people are turning to private justice providers, who are paid to arrange for a judge and jury to decide a case. Parties often turn to private justice providers because the party wants a jury to decide the case yet wants the efficiency of alternative dispute resolution methods.

One of the biggest concerns about litigation is the problem with jurors deciding cases. Jury research has demonstrated that jurors in the public courts struggle to perform their role. However, this concern is not applicable in private jury trials. Parties who chose to use a private jury typically experience jurors who are better trained and more interested in the justice system. Those who provide private juries create a database of individuals interested in serving on juries. To encourage educated people to volunteer as jurors, private justice providers pay anywhere from $60 to $150 a day, depending on the case. Furthermore, a juror might serve in a tort case involving a particular company. This same juror then might serve in a different tort case involving the same company. Therefore, parties in a private jury trial can be confident that the jurors deciding their case will make the correct decision.

Indeed, private jury trials fill in the holes of the litigation system.

    a. What is the conclusion of this argument?

    b. The author emphasizes the positive aspects of selecting a jury from a "database" of volunteer jurors. However, he seems to ignore the negative aspects of selecting jurors from a limited database. Identify some of these negative aspects.

    c. Before you can decide whether private jury trials solve the problems of the litigation system, what additional information do you need about private jury trials?

    d. Suppose the author made the following statement: Private jurors make better decisions than public jurors. What critical thinking question would you have for this author?

3. The following argument is a response to the previous argument about private jury trials:

Time-consuming. Expensive. Biased. These adjectives have all been used to describe litigation. However, most people do not realize that even if all these adjectives are true, litigation still offers the best method of dispute resolution. Why?

Alternative dispute methods are loopholes for people who want to beat the litigation system. However, parties that use alternative dispute methods soon learn that they will have to enter the litigation system. It would simply be easier for parties to begin in litigation if they are going to eventually be forced to litigate their claim.

Moreover, alternative dispute methods claim to preserve the relationship between the parties. Sure, ADR "preserves the relationship" because ADR forces parties to compromise when they should not compromise. Parties who have been wronged are expected to be more than willing to compromise with the other party. These wronged individuals would fare much better in litigation.

    a. What is the conclusion and reasons for this argument?

    b. What words are ambiguous in this argument?

B. Leaning the Basics

Matching

1. ____ private trial

    a. written agreement stating that parties want to settle their dispute by arbitration

2. ____ arbitration

    b. informal process where disputants select a party to help them reconcile their differences

3. ____ award

    c. resolution of a dispute by a neutral third party outside the judicial setting

4. ____ submission agreement

    d. settlement authority resides with senior executives of the disputing corporations in this resolution method

5. ____ mediation

    e. jury hears a case and reaches a verdict within one day

6. ____ minitrials

    f. cases are tried by a referee selected and paid by the disputants

7. ____ summary jury trials

    g. the arbitrator's decision

True and False

1. _____   Arbitration is often chosen over litigation as a dispute resolution method because it generates less publicity.

2. _____   Arbitration is commonly used as a means of resolving class action suits.

3. _____   Due to the EEOC's policy statement criticizing binding arbitration clauses for civil rights matters, all firms must now specifically exclude discrimination claims from their arbitration agreements.

4. _____   There are only two means by which parties can secure arbitration: a submission agreement and a binding arbitration clause.

5. _____   Negotiation and settlement is rarely used by disputants.

6. _____   Mediators make no final decision that resolves a dispute.

7. _____   Mediation is most commonly used to resolve collective bargaining disputes.

8. _____   Private trials do not involve juries.

9. _____   Minitrials are binding because the parties enter into a contract that encompasses the terms of the settlement.

Multiple Choice

1. Which of the following forms of alternative dispute resolution has the most limited potential use?

a.   arbitration
b.   mediation
c.   minitrials
d.   none of the above; all are equally available

2.   Typical items included in a submission agreement are:

a.   the nature of the dispute and how the arbitrator will be selected
b.   any constraints on the arbitrator's authority to settle the dispute and the time by which the arbitration must be completed
c.   both A and B
d.   none of the above

3.   The least adversarial ADR method is

a.   arbitration
b.   mediation
c.   minitrials
d.   private trial

4.   An arbitrator is authorized by the submission agreement to grant a remedy of up to $50,000. He awards the winning party $75,000. When the losing party appeals on the grounds that the arbitrator exceeded his authority,

a.   the award will be thrown out as exceeding the arbitrator's authority
b.   the award will be reduced to $50,000
c.   either a or b may occur
d.   none of the above; an arbitrator's award cannot be appealed

5.   A type of alternative dispute resolution that is available to only corporations (and not private citizens) is

a.   private trials
b.   minitrials
c.   mediation
d.   court-annexed ADR

6.   Which of the following is not an element of a summary jury trial?

a.   no witnesses appear, only attorneys summarizing their clients' positions
b.   the jury is comprised of only six persons
c.   the jury's verdict is only advisory, even though the jury is not usually aware that their verdict is not binding
d.   none of the above (All are elements.)

7. Court-annexed arbitration differs from purely voluntary arbitration in that

a. voluntary arbitration is usually binding, whereas court mandated arbitration is usually not binding
b. in most systems, the rules of evidence in the court annexed arbitrations are the same as the rules of evidence for a trial, whereas for voluntary arbitration the rules of evidence are more relaxed
c. both a and b
d. none of the above

8. Which of the following is NOT a benefit derived from using alternative dispute resolution methods?

a. less publicity
b. no precedent set
c. less expense
d. less convenient proceedings

Short Answer

1. What is inadequate about the following statement? Arbitration is the best means for resolving disputes because it is the least adversarial method available.

2. Provide the reasoning for the following statement: Mediation seems to be based on a different value assumption than most other forms of dispute resolution.

3. What is inadequate about the following statement? The federal mandate for all district courts to have alternative dispute resolution programs is good for the country because it will clear a crowded federal docket by resolving cases more efficiently.

CHAPTER 5
CONSTITUTIONAL PRINCIPLES

In this chapter, you learned various ways in which the U.S. Constitution protects individual citizens and regulates businesses. Below are several opportunities for you to improve your critical thinking skills, while also enhancing your understanding of constitutional principles.

A.   *More Critical Thinking*

1. The First Amendment guarantees freedom of speech. However, the First Amendment does not guarantee that you can say anything you wish at any time. Certain restrictions are made on your freedom of speech. The following case examines the restriction of freedom of speech as it relates to symbolic expression. Specifically, it addresses the following issue: Does the First Amendment prevent a state from interfering in an act of cross-burning, when the individual or individuals involved in the act possessed intent to intimidate?

VIRGINIA
v.
BLACK, et al.
2003

Respondent Black was leading a Ku Klux Klan meeting in Carroll County, Virginia, during which he was arrested for burning a cross, allegedly violating a Virginia statute. Similarly, respondents Elliot and O'Mara were arrested for allegedly burning a cross in the yard of an African-American, in Virginia Beach, Virginia. These three individuals were convicted separately of violating the cross-burning statute in Virginia. The statute (§ 18.2-423) states: "It shall be unlawful for any person or persons, with the intent of intimidating any person or group of persons, to burn, or cause to be burned, a cross on the property of another, a highway or other public place. Any person who shall violate any provision of this section shall be guilty of a Class 6 felony...Any such burning of a cross shall be prima facie evidence of an intent to intimidate a person or group of persons." All three respondents argued that the Virginia statute was unconstitutional. The Supreme Court of Virginia agreed, holding that the statute was facially unconstitutional. The court reasoned that the statute "is analytically indistinguishable from the ordinance found unconstitutional in *R.A.V. v. St. Paul*," and that the statute discriminates on the basis of content because the statute "selectively chooses only cross burning because of its distinctive message." However, three justices of the Supreme Court of Virginia disagreed, and the U.S. Supreme Court granted certiorari.

33
© 2009 Pearson Education, Inc. publishing as Prentice Hall

JUSTICE O'CONNOR

The First Amendment, applicable to the States through the Fourteenth Amendment, provides that "Congress shall make no law . . . abridging the freedom of speech." The hallmark of the protection of free speech is to allow "free trade in ideas" – even ideas that the overwhelming majority of people might find distasteful or discomforting. Thus, the First Amendment "ordinarily" denies a State "the power to prohibit dissemination of social, economic and political doctrine which a vast majority of its citizens believes to be false and fraught with evil consequence."...The First Amendment affords protection to symbolic or expressive conduct as well as to actual speech.

The protections afforded by the First Amendment, however, are not absolute, and we have long recognized that the government may regulate certain categories of expression consistent with the Constitution. We have consequently held that fighting words – "those personally abusive epithets which, when addressed to the ordinary citizen, are, as a matter of common knowledge, inherently likely to provoke violent reaction" – are generally proscribable under the First Amendment. Furthermore, "the constitutional guarantees of free speech and free press do not permit a State to forbid or proscribe advocacy of the use of force or of law violation except where such advocacy is directed to inciting or producing imminent lawless action and is likely to incite or produce such action."

The fact that cross burning is symbolic expression, however, does not resolve the constitutional question. The Supreme Court of Virginia relied upon *R.A.V. v. City of St. Paul*, to conclude that once a statute discriminates on the basis of this type of content, the law is unconstitutional. We disagree.

In *R.A.V.*, we held that a local ordinance that banned certain symbolic conduct, including cross burning, when done with the knowledge that such conduct would "arouse anger, alarm or resentment in others on the basis of race, color, creed, religion or gender" was unconstitutional. We held that the ordinance did not pass constitutional muster because it discriminated on the basis of content by targeting only those individuals who "provoke violence" on a basis specified in the law. The ordinance did not cover "those who wish to use 'fighting words' in connection with other ideas – to express hostility, for example, on the basis of political affiliation, union membership, or homosexuality." This content-based discrimination was unconstitutional because it allowed the city "to impose special prohibitions on those speakers who express views on disfavored subjects."

We did not hold in *R.A.V.* that the First Amendment prohibits all forms of content-based discrimination within a proscribable area of speech. Rather, we specifically stated that some types of content discrimination did not violate the

First Amendment. A ban on cross burning carried out with the intent to intimidate is fully consistent with our holding in *R.A.V.* and is proscribable under the First Amendment.

The Supreme Court of Virginia ruled in the alternative that Virginia's cross-burning statute was unconstitutionally overbroad due to its provision stating that "any such burning of a cross shall be prima facie evidence of an intent to intimidate a person or group of persons." It has, however, stated that "the act of burning a cross alone, with no evidence of intent to intimidate, will nonetheless suffice for arrest and prosecution and will insulate the Commonwealth from a motion to strike the evidence at the end of its case-in-chief." The prima facie evidence provision, as interpreted by the jury instruction, renders the statute unconstitutional.

As construed by the jury instruction, the prima facie provision strips away the very reason why a State may ban cross burning with the intent to intimidate. The prima facie evidence provision permits a jury to convict in every cross-burning case in which defendants exercise their constitutional right not to put on a defense. And even where a defendant like Black presents a defense, the prima facie evidence provision makes it more likely that the jury will find an intent to intimidate regardless of the particular facts of the case. It is apparent that the provision as so interpreted "'would create an unacceptable risk of the suppression of ideas.'"

As the history of cross burning indicates, a burning cross is not always intended to intimidate. Rather, sometimes the cross burning is a statement of ideology, a symbol of group solidarity. The prima facie provision makes no effort to distinguish among these different types of cross burnings. It does not distinguish between a cross burning done with the purpose of creating anger or resentment and a cross burning done with the purpose of threatening or intimidating a victim. For these reasons, the prima facie evidence provision, as interpreted through the jury instruction and as applied in Barry Black's case, is unconstitutional on its face.

With respect to Barry Black, we agree with the Supreme Court of Virginia that his conviction cannot stand, and we affirm the judgment of the Supreme Court of Virginia. With respect to Elliott and O'Mara, we vacate the judgment of the Supreme Court of Virginia, and remand the case for further proceedings.

a. In *R.A.V. v. City of St. Paul*, the court ruled that a city ordinance was unconstitutional, as the ordinance prohibited speakers' expressing views on "disfavored subjects." However, the Supreme Court of Virginia applied this precedent in a manner different than the way in which the U.S. Supreme Court intended. Justice O'Connor noted some of these important differences between the Supreme Court of Virginia's and the U.S. Supreme Court's applying *R.A.V.* in the *Black* case. What were these differences?

b. One of the reasons that the U.S. Supreme Court uses to reach its conclusion that Virginia's prima facie provision was unconstitutional is that juries would be more likely to find "an intent to intimidate," creating "an unacceptable risk of the suppression of ideas." What words or phrases are ambiguous in this reason?

c. Translate the *Black* conclusion into a statement of a value preference. In other words, what value is the court emphasizing at the expense of another value?

    2. After you read the argument, answer the following critical thinking questions:

The Fourth Amendment protects citizens from unreasonable search and seizures of property and person. Too many criminals are using this amendment as a loophole to escape punishment for committing crimes. How?

The following example will clearly prove my point. Police recently arrested Jonathan Jones, a repeat criminal, for the rape and murder of a 5-year-old named Sarah Tom. From 1985-1990, Jones served a jail sentence for molesting two little girls. When police discovered Sarah's body, they began to search for the murderer. Police entered Jones' apartment and found Sarah's clothing hidden in his closet. However, because the police did not have a warrant to enter Jones' apartment, the evidence was inadmissible. Jones was set free.

Our criminal justice system was created to punish criminals, not present them with excuses to walk away from their crimes. Because we force police to get a warrant before entering someone's home, many criminals can hide evidence. Let's alter the Fourth Amendment to stop protecting criminals and force them to face the consequences of their actions. If we discover evidence proving that an individual committed a crime, we should not allow the criminal to escape by classifying the evidence as inadmissible.

a. What is the conclusion? What evidence is offered in support of that conclusion?

b. The Jones case is particularly persuasive to the author. Why should you NOT be persuaded by the Jones case?

c. How does the author's use of the word "criminal" affect her argument?

B. Learning the Basics

Matching

1. ____ federalism

    a. any law that directly conflicts with the federal Constitution, laws or treaties is void

2. ____ Supremacy Clause

    b. guarantees freedom of speech and of the press

3. ____ federal supremacy

    c. includes the due process provision

4. ____ police power

    d. if the government takes private property for public use, it must pay the owner just compensation

5. ____ First Amendment

    e. the authority to govern is divided between two sovereigns

6. ____ Fourth Amendment

    f. applies almost all first ten amendments to the state governments

7. ____ Fifth Amendment

    g. empowers the legislature to regulate Commerce between foreign nations, states, and Indian tribes

8. ____ Takings clause

    h. provides that the Constitution, laws and treaties of the United States constitute the supreme law of the land

9. ____ Fourteenth Amendment

    i. the residual powers retained by the state to enact legislation to safeguard the health and welfare of its citizenry

10. ____ Commerce Clause

j. protects the rights of individuals to be secure in their persons, their homes, and their personal property

True and False

1. ____ If the federal government establishes standards for emitting water pollutants into streams, any state law that attempts to establish more stringent water pollutant standards will be struck down as unconstitutional.

2. ____ Corporate speech and commercial speech are synonyms; both are entitled to significantly less protection than purely private speech.

3. ____ Any search conducted without a warrant is unlawful, and any evidence seized cannot be admitted into a court of law.

4. ____ The takings clause allows the state or federal government to take an individual's property for any purpose, as long as they give the property owner at least 90 days notice of the taking and adequate compensation for the property.

5. ____ *United States v. Lopez* and *Brzonkala v. Morrison* (the gun control and federal rape statute cases) are examples of the commerce clause being expansively interpreted to enhance Congress' power to make law on various issues.

6. ____ The doctrine of federal preemption is used to strike down a state law that attempts to regulate an area in which federal legislation is so pervasive that it is evident that Congress wanted only federal regulation in that general area.

7. ____ Most of the first ten amendments do not apply to corporations.

8. ____ All powers not given exclusively to the federal government nor taken from the states are reserved to the states.

9. ____ The doctrine of separation of powers suggests that federal and state governments are independent branches with their own distinct powers.

Multiple Choice

1. A federal or state regulation will be considered a taking

a. if the action renders the land valueless
b. if its impact is to reduce the value of the land by 30 percent
c. if either a or b is true
d. none of the above is true

2. The U.S. Constitution

a. is the document that sets forth the responsibilities of the various branches of government
b. provides Congress, via the Commerce Clause, with the authority to regulate business
c. both a and b
d. none of the above

3. When states have enacted legislation that affects interstate commerce, the courts must decide whether to uphold or strike down this legislation. The courts

a. determine whether the state has an interest in enforcing the legislation
b. apply the following two-pronged test: a) determine whether the regulation is related to a legitimate state end and b) deciding if the burden imposed on interstate commerce is outweighed by the state interest enforcing the legislation
c. must strike down the legislation because of the Supremacy Clause
d. can choose to uphold the legislation if precedent supports upholding the legislation

4. The Takings Clause is included in

a. the First Amendment
b. the Fifth Amendment
c. the Fourth Amendment
d. the Fourteenth Amendment

5. The privilege against self-incrimination applies to

a. individuals
b. corporations
c. individuals and corporations
d. all citizens excluding government officials

39

6. Warrantless searches of corporate premises are permissible when

a. there is a substantial government interest involved in the regulation prescribing the search
b. unannounced searches are necessary to ensure the success of the regulation prescribing the search
c. there is a constitutionally adequate substitute for a warrant, such as advance notification of the relevant business that certain areas of its operation are open to periodic search and codified limitations on what government regulators can and cannot search
d. all of the above

7. If a state law directly conflicts with a federal law, it will be struck down according to

a. the Supremacy Clause
b. the principle of federal supremacy
c. the doctrine of federal preemption
d. the two-pronged test courts use

8. Due process means that

a. a criminal whose life, liberty, or property would be taken be given a fair trial
b. an accused criminal has the opportunity to face his or her accusers before an impartial tribunal
c. the laws that deprive an individual of his or her liberty or property must be fair
d. all of the above

9. The Fourteenth Amendment

a. contains the equal protection clause
b. applies the due process clause to the federal government
c. applies the entire bill of rights to the states
d. both a and c

Short Answer

1. Provide the reasoning for the following statement: The Commerce Clause can be described both as giving power to the government and taking power away from the government.

2. How can the federal government further its aims without direct regulation by statute? (Hint: What are the constitutionally permissible uses of its power of taxing and spending?)

3. What is the link between the Supremacy Clause and federal preemption?

CHAPTER 6
CYBERLAW AND BUSINESS

This chapter shows you how the development of new computer technology has affected the legal system and shows why those changes to the law are relevant to businesses. For review, we have provided additional critical thinking activities, followed by matching, true-false, multiple choice, and short answer sections.

A.   *More Critical Thinking*

1. The following case involves copyright law and its applicability to new technologies. Put your critical thinking skills in action by reading and critically evaluating the following case. Then, answer the critical thinking questions that follow.

RECORDING INDUSTRY ASSOCIATION OF AMERICA and ALLIANCE OF ARTISTS AND RECORDING COMPANIES
v.
DIAMOND MULTIMEDIA SYSTEMS INC.
2000

O'SCANNLAIN, Circuit Judge for the U.S. Ninth Circuit Court of Appeals:

In this case involving the intersection of computer technology, the Internet, and music listening, we must decide whether the Rio portable music player is a digital audio recording device subject to the restrictions of the Audio Home Recording Act of 1992.

This appeal arises from the efforts of the Recording Industry Association of America and the Alliance of Artists and Recording Companies (collectively, "RIAA") to enjoin the manufacture and distribution by Diamond Multimedia Systems ("Diamond") of the Rio portable music player. The Rio is a small device (roughly the size of an audio cassette) with headphones that allows a user to download MP3 audio files from a computer and to listen to them elsewhere. . . .

. . . Prior to the invention of devices like the Rio, MP3 users had little option other than to listen to their downloaded digital audio files through headphones or speakers at their computers, playing them from their hard drives. The Rio renders these files portable. More precisely, once an audio file has been downloaded onto a computer hard drive from the Internet or some other source (such as a compact disc player or digital audio tape machine), separate computer software provided with the Rio (called "Rio Manager") allows the user further to download the file to the Rio itself via a parallel port cable that plugs the Rio into the computer. The Rio device is incapable of affecting such a transfer, and is incapable of receiving audio files from anything other than a personal computer equipped with Rio Manager. . . .

. . . RIAA brought suit to enjoin the manufacture and distribution of the Rio, alleging that the Rio does not meet the requirements for digital audio recording devices under the Audio Home Recording Act of 1992, 17 U.S.C. § 1001 *et seq.* (the "Act"), because it does not employ a Serial Copyright Management System ("SCMS") that sends, receives, and acts upon information about the generation and copyright status of the files that it plays. RIAA also sought payment of the royalties owed by Diamond as the manufacturer and distributor of a digital audio recording device.

The district court denied RIAA's motion for a preliminary injunction, holding that RIAA's likelihood of success on the merits was mixed and the balance of hardships did not tip in RIAA's favor.

The initial question presented is whether the Rio falls within the ambit of the Act. The Act does not broadly prohibit digital serial copying of copyright protected audio recordings. Instead, the Act places restrictions only upon a specific type of recording device. Most relevant here, the Act provides that "no person shall import, manufacture, or distribute any *digital audio recording device* . . . that does not conform to the Serial Copy Management System ["SCMS"] [or] a system that has the same functional characteristics." 17 U.S.C. § 1002(a)(1), (2) (emphasis added). The Act further provides that "no person shall import into and distribute, or manufacture and distribute, any *digital audio recording device* . . . unless such person records the notice specified by this section and subsequently deposits the statements of account and applicable royalty payments." *Id.* § 1003(a) (emphasis added). Thus, to fall within the SCMS and royalty requirements in question, the Rio must be a "digital audio recording device," which the Act defines through a set of nested definitions.

The Act defines a "digital audio recording device" as "any machine or device of a type commonly distributed to individuals for use by individuals, whether or not included with or as part of some other machine or device, the digital recording function of which is designed or marketed for the primary purpose of, and that is capable of, making a *digital audio copied recording* for private use." [*Id.* § 1001(3) (emphasis added).]

A "digital audio copied recording" is defined as "a reproduction in a digital recording format of a *digital musical recording*, whether that reproduction is made directly from another digital musical recording or indirectly from a transmission." [*Id.* § 1001(1) (emphasis added).]

A "digital musical recording" is defined as *"a material object* (i) in which are fixed, in a digital recording format, *only sounds, and material, statements, or instructions incidental to those fixed sounds,* if any, and (ii) from which the sounds and material can be perceived, reproduced, or otherwise communicated, either directly or with the aid of a machine or device." [*Id.* § 1001(5)(A) (emphasis added).]

In sum, to be a digital audio recording device, the Rio must be able to reproduce, either "directly" or "from a transmission," a "digital music recording."

. . . the Act expressly provides that the term "digital musical recording" does not include *"a material object* (i) in which the fixed sounds consist entirely of spoken word recordings, or (ii) *in which one or more computer programs are fixed,* except that a digital recording may contain statements or instructions constituting the fixed sounds and incidental material, and statements or instructions to be used directly or indirectly in order to bring about the perception, reproduction, or communication of the fixed sounds and incidental material." [*Id.* § 1001(5)(B) (emphasis added).]

As noted previously, a hard drive is a material object in which one or more programs are fixed; thus, a hard drive is excluded from the definition of digital music recordings. This provides confirmation that the Rio does not record "directly" from "digital music recordings," and therefore could not be a digital audio recording device unless it makes copies "from transmissions."

. . . The district court concluded that the exemption of hard drives from the definition of digital music recording, and the exemption of computers generally from the Act's ambit, "would effectively eviscerate the [Act]" because "any recording device could evade regulation simply by passing the music through a computer and ensuring that the MP3 file resided momentarily on the hard drive." *RIAA I,* 29 F. Supp. 2d at 630. While this may be true, the Act seems to have been expressly designed to create this loophole.

Under the plain meaning of the Act's definition of digital audio recording devices, computers (and their hard drives) are not digital audio recording devices because their "primary purpose" is not to make digital audio copied recordings. *See* 17 U.S.C. § 1001(3). Unlike digital audio tape machines, for example, whose primary purpose is to make digital audio copied recordings, the primary purpose of a computer is to run various programs and to record the data necessary to run those programs and perform various tasks. The legislative history is consistent with this interpretation of the Act's provisions, stating that "the typical personal computer would not fall within the definition of 'digital audio recording device,'" S. Rep. 102-294, at 122, because a personal computer's "recording function is designed and marketed primarily for the recording of data and computer programs," *id.* at 121. Another portion of the Senate Report states that "if the 'primary purpose' of the recording function is to make objects other than digital audio copied recordings, then the machine or device is not a 'digital audio recording device,' *even if the machine or device is technically capable of making such recordings.*" *Id.* (emphasis added). The legislative history thus expressly recognizes that computers (and other devices) have recording functions capable of recording digital musical recordings, and thus implicate the home taping and piracy concerns to which the Act is responsive. Nonetheless, the legislative history is consistent with the Act's plain language - computers are *not* digital audio recording devices.

In turn, because computers are not digital audio recording devices, they are not required to comply with the SCMS requirement and thus need not send, receive, or act upon information regarding copyright and generation status. *See* 17 U.S.C. § 1002(a)(2). . . .

In fact, the Rio's operation is entirely consistent with the Act's main purpose - the facilitation of personal use. As the Senate Report explains, "the purpose of [the Act] is to ensure the right of consumers to make analog or digital audio recordings of copyrighted music for their *private, noncommercial use.*" S. Rep. 102-294, at 86 (emphasis added). The Act does so through its home taping exemption, *see* 17 U.S.C. § 1008, which "protects all noncommercial copying by consumers of digital and analog musical recordings," H.R. Rep. 102-873(I), at 59. The Rio merely makes copies in order to render portable, or "space-shift," those files that already reside on a user's hard drive. *Cf. Sony Corp. of America v. Universal City Studios*, 464 U.S. 417, 455, 78 L. Ed. 2d 574, 104 S. Ct. 774 (1984) (holding that "time-shifting" of copyrighted television shows with VCR's constitutes fair use under the Copyright Act, and thus is not an infringement). Such copying is paradigmatic noncommercial personal use entirely consistent with the purposes of the Act.

Even though it cannot directly reproduce a digital music recording, the Rio would nevertheless be a digital audio recording device if it could reproduce a digital music recording "from a transmission." 17 U.S.C. § 1001(1).

[The Court, through examining legislative history and precedent in copyright law, concludes that to "transmit" something is "to communicate it by any device or process whereby images or sounds are received beyond the place from which they are sent."]

RIAA asserts that indirect reproduction of a transmission is sufficient for the Rio to fall within the Act's ambit as a digital audio recording device. (*See* 17 U.S.C. § 1001(1): digital audio recording devices are those devices that are capable of making "a reproduction in a digital recording format of a digital musical recording, whether that reproduction is made directly from another digital musical recording or *indirectly* from a transmission" (emphasis added)). Diamond asserts that the adverb "indirectly" modifies the recording of the underlying "digital music recording," rather than the recording "from the transmission." Diamond effectively asserts that the statute should be read as covering devices that are capable of making a reproduction of a digital musical recording, "whether that reproduction is made directly[,] from another digital musical recording[,] or indirectly[,] from a transmission."

While the Rio can only directly reproduce files from a computer hard drive via a cable linking the two devices (which is obviously not a transmission), the Rio can indirectly reproduce a transmission. For example, if a radio broadcast of a digital audio recording were recorded on a digital audio tape machine or compact disc recorder and then uploaded to a computer hard drive, the Rio could indirectly reproduce the transmission by downloading a copy from the hard drive. Thus, if indirect reproduction of a transmission falls within the statutory definition, the Rio would be a digital audio recording device.

RIAA's interpretation of the statutory language initially seems plausible, but closer analysis reveals that it is contrary to the statutory language and common sense. The focus of the statutory language seems to be on the two means of reproducing the underlying digital music recording - either directly from that recording, or indirectly, by reproducing the recording from a transmission. RIAA's interpretation of the Act's language (in which "indirectly" modifies copying "from a transmission," rather than the copying of the underlying digital music recording) would only cover the indirect recording of transmissions, and would omit restrictions on the direct recording of transmissions (e.g., recording songs from the radio) from the Act's ambit. This interpretation would significantly reduce the protection afforded by the Act to transmissions, and neither the statutory language nor structure provides any reason that the Act's protections should be so limited. Moreover, it makes little sense for the Act to restrict the indirect recording of transmissions, but to allow unrestricted direct recording of transmissions (e.g., to regulate second-hand recording of songs from the radio, but to allow unlimited direct recording of songs from the radio). Thus, the most logical reading of the Act extends protection to direct copying of digital music recordings, and to indirect copying of digital music recordings from transmissions of those recordings.

[After reviewing records of Congressional debate on the Audio Home Recording Act to verify its reading of the statue, the Court concludes by arguing that] the legislative history confirms the most logical reading of the statute, which we adopt: "indirectly" modifies the verb "is made" - in other words, modifies the making of the reproduction of the underlying digital music recording. Thus, a device falls within the Act's provisions if it can indirectly copy a digital music recording by making a copy from a transmission of that recording. Because the Rio cannot make copies from transmissions, but instead, can only make copies from a computer hard drive, it is not a digital audio recording device.

For the foregoing reasons, the Rio is not a digital audio recording device subject to the restrictions of the Audio Home Recording Act of 1992. The district court properly denied the motion for a preliminary injunction against the Rio's manufacture and distribution. Having so determined, we need not consider whether the balance of hardships or the possibility of irreparable harm supports injunctive relief.

AFFIRMED.

a. What is the issue in this case?

b. The linchpin of this decision is the Court's clarification of an ambiguity in the Audio Home Recording Act. What is the ambiguity? Why did the Court decide on the particular meaning that it assigned to this ambiguity (i.e., what were its reasons?)

c. Would the Audio Home Recording Act apply to a service like Napster that connects individual users to other users to enable the sharing of MP3s over the internet?

2. Apply your critical thinking skills to this argument about copyright issues on the Internet.

Nowhere on earth is free speech more important than on the Internet, the largest free marketplace of ideas in history. In order for citizens to make informed judgements about their life and governance, it is essential that they have full and free access to information and an open forum to discuss ideas. Restrictions on either are therefore undesirable, and doubly so for a platform whose low costs of publication and use make widespread communication a realistic possibility for many whose voices would otherwise have never been heard.

It is therefore crucial that the music exchange services like Napster be preserved. Such services give relatively unknown bands a chance to get their music out to a wide audience without the huge barriers that restrict radio play or the production and marketing of CDs. Furthermore, the importance of a free interchange of ideas, including those expressed in musical form, outweighs the consideration that we should give to record company profits; if those companies' CEOs can afford one less tailored suit thanks to Napster, so be it.

a. What is the conclusion of this argument?

b. What are the reasons given by the author to support her conclusion?

c. Of the four primary ethical norms noted in your book, which does this author seem to prefer?

d. Consider the phrase: "Furthermore, the importance of a free interchange of ideas, including those expressed in musical form, outweighs the consideration that we should give to record company profits; if those companies' CEOs can afford one less tailored suit thanks to Napster, so be it." What missing information might be helpful to evaluating the validity of this statement?

B. Learning the Basics

Matching

1. ____ cyberspace

    a. a relatively new form of fraud in which an individual gathers personal information of another person for criminal purposes.

2. ____ spam

    b. a unique medium composed of e-mail, World Wide Web pages, and similar tools located in no particular geographic location but available to anyone, anywhere in the world, with access to the Internet

3. ____ fair use doctrine

    c. unsolicited "junk" e-mail, usually intended for commercial purposes

4. ____ identity theft

    d. an exception to copyright law that allows the reproduction of copyrighted materials for educational purposes, news reporting, and criticism

5. ____ cybersquatting

    e. a publicly viewable message posting forum

6. ____ denial of service attack

    f. a form of copyright infringement stemming from the registration of a domain name similar to a corporate trademark in order to resell that domain name for a high price

7. ____ bulletin board service

    g. a possible form of copyright infringement resulting from the use of unidentified connections from one web site to another

8. ____ linking

    h. disseminating proprietary information about a company to non-employees in order to influence stock choices

9. ____ insider trading

    i. a cybercrime involving the orchestrated, simultaneous access of a server by numerous computers to overload the server

True and False

1. ____ The accessibility of a web site from a state is sufficient for that state to have in personam jurisdiction over the site's owner.

2. ____ Employers may be held liable for messages in online bulletin boards that contain harassing messages created by employees.

3. ____ Warehousing is the practice of illegally purchasing corporate domain names with the intent of reselling the name to its owner for a higher price.

4. ____ Ideas and forms of expression can be protected under copyright law.

5. ____ Employees have an unambiguous right to privacy in e-mail transmissions sent over their employers' networks.

6. ____ Contributory copyright infringement is the act of inducing, causing, or materially contributing to such infringement without actually perpetrating the infringement.

7. _____ Encryption is one method of hacking, a form of cybercrime.

8. _____ Open source programming conventions have been successfully used to defend music-sharing services, like Napster.

9. _____ Pharmaceutical companies must provide information about the harmful effects of their drugs in advertising to consumers.

Multiple Choice

1. A state may shut down an internet gambling site when

   a. the server holding the site is within its boundaries
   b. the site is accessible within the state
   c. never
   d. none of the above

2. A corporation is responsible for its employees actions in cyberspace <u>outside the workplace</u> though vicarious liability when

   a. any civil rights case is brought against the firm
   b. the corporation derives substantial benefit from the outside venue
   c. the corporation is located in certain states where vicarious liability statutes have been passed
   d. none of the above

3. In the *Napster* case from your primary text, contributory copyright infringement occurred whenever

   a. Napster's actions encouraged or assisted infringers, and Napster had knowledge that infringing material was available on its system
   b. individuals visited the site
   c. Napster unknowingly permitted infringing behavior through peer-to-peer file-sharing software
   d. all of the above

4. The Supreme Court struck down the Communications Decency Act on the argument that

   a. a "compelling state interest" was involved in the case
   b. the statute was not a "time, place, and manner regulation"
   c. the statute was not overbroad and vague
   d. all of the above

5.   Direct-to-consumer marketing has begun to replace physician-oriented marketing in the pharmaceutical industry, causing the Courts to reconsider the validity of the

a.   intermediary liability doctrine
b.   producer immunity doctrine
c.   pharmaceutical-physician privilege doctrine
d.   none of the above

6.   Which of the following are options presented under the Electronic Signatures in Global and National Commerce Act as means of individual identification?

a.   information that is unique to a customer, such as a mother's maiden name
b.   a third party who holds the identity of the two parties, making sure that only the two parties have access to view and sign the contract
c.   encryption software used to protect transmissions
d.   all of the above

Short Answer

1. Give an argument against allowing firms like AnswerThink to subpoena information about users from online services like Yahoo as described in the text.

2. When can a company be held liable for the behavior of its employees on-line?

CHAPTER 7
WHITE COLLAR CRIME AND THE BUSINESS COMMUNITY

This chapter introduces you to criminal law and the way our legal system handles white-collar criminals. For review, we have provided additional critical thinking activities, followed by the usual matching, true-false, multiple choice, and short answer sections.

A.   *More Critical Thinking*

1. Put your critical thinking skills in action by reading and critically evaluating the following case. Then, answer the critical thinking questions that follow.

NATIONAL ORGANIZATION FOR WOMEN, INC., et al.,PETITIONERS
v.
JOSEPH SCHEIDLER et al.
1994

In this action, petitioner health care clinics . . . alleged, among other things, that respondents, a coalition of antiabortion groups called the Pro Life Action Network (PLAN) and others, were members of a nationwide conspiracy to shut down abortion clinics through a pattern of racketeering activity . . . in violation of the Racketeer Influenced and Corrupt Organizations (RICO) chapter of the Organized Crime Control Act of 1970. . . . This District Court dismissed the case [, finding] that the clinics failed to state a claim under §1962(c)–which makes it unlawful "for any person employed by or associated with any enterprise engaged in, or the activities of which affect, interstate or foreign commerce, to conduct or participate . . . in the conduct of such enterprise's affairs through a pattern of racketeering activity or collection of unlawful debt"– because they did not allege a profit generating purpose in the activity or enterprise. . . . The Court of Appeals affirmed, agreeing that there is an economic motive requirement implicit in §1962(c)'s enterprise element.

CHIEF JUSTICE REHNQUIST:

We turn to the question of whether the racketeering enterprise or the racketeering predicate acts must be accompanied by an underlying economic motive. Section 1962(c) makes it unlawful "for any person employed by or associated with any enterprise engaged in, or the activities of which affect, interstate or foreign commerce, to conduct or participate, directly or indirectly, in the conduct of such enterprise's affairs through a pattern of racketeering activity or collection of unlawful debt." Section 1961(1) defines "pattern of racketeering activity" to include conduct that is "chargeable" or "indictable" under a host of state and federal laws. RICO broadly defines "enterprise" . . . to "include[e] any individual, partnership, corporation, association, or other legal entity, and any union or group of individuals associated in fact although not a legal entity." Nowhere in either § 1962(c), or in the RICO definitions in § 1961, is there any indication that an economic motive is required.

The phrase "any enterprise engaged in, or the activities of which affect, interstate or foreign commerce" comes the closest of any language in subsection (c) to suggesting a need for an economic motive. Arguably an enterprise engaged in interstate or foreign commerce would have a profit seeking motive, but the language in § 1962(c) does not stop there; it includes enterprises whose activities "affect" interstate or foreign commerce. Webster's Third New International Dictionary 35 (1969) defines "affect" as "to have a detrimental influence on–used especially in the phrase affecting commerce." An enterprise surely can have a detrimental influence on interstate or foreign commerce without having its own profit seeking motives.

The Court of Appeals also relied on the reasoning of *United States v. Bagaric* to support its conclusion that subsection (c) requires an economic motive. In upholding the dismissal of a RICO claim against a political terrorist group, the *Bagaric* court relied in part on the congressional statement of findings which prefaces RICO and refers to the activities of groups that "'drain billions of dollars from America's economy by unlawful conduct and the illegal use of force, fraud, and corruption.'" The Court of Appeals for the Second Circuit decided that the sort of activity thus condemned required an economic motive.

We do not think this is so. Respondents and the two courts of appeals, we think, overlook the fact that predicate acts, such as the alleged extortion, may not benefit the protestors financially but still may drain money from the economy by harming businesses such as the clinics which are petitioners in this case.

We also think that the quoted statement of congressional findings is a rather thin reed upon which to base a requirement of economic motive neither expressed nor, we think, fairly implied in the operative sections of the Act.

In *United States v. Turkette*, we faced the analogous question of whether "enterprise" as used in §1961(4) should be confined to "legitimate" enterprises. Looking to the statutory language, we found that "[t]here is no restriction upon the associations embraced by the definition: an enterprise includes any union or group of individuals associated in fact." Accordingly, we resolved that § 1961(4)'s definition of enterprise "appears to include both legitimate and illegitimate enterprises within its scope; it no more excludes criminal enterprises than it does legitimate ones." We noted that Congress could easily have narrowed the sweep of the term "enterprise" by inserting a single word,

53
© 2009 Pearson Education, Inc. publishing as Prentice Hall

"legitimate." Instead, Congress did nothing to indicate that "enterprise" should exclude those entities whose sole purpose was criminal.

The parallel to the present case is apparent. Congress has not, either in the definitional section or in the operative language, required that an "enterprise" in §1962(c) have an economic motive.

The Court of Appeals also found persuasive guidelines for RICO prosecutions issued by the Department of Justice in 1981. The guidelines provided that a RICO indictment should not charge an association as an enterprise, unless the association exists "'for the purpose of maintaining operations directed toward an economic goal . . .'" Whatever may be the appropriate deference afforded to such internal rules, for our purposes we need note only that the Department of Justice amended its guidelines in 1984. The amended guidelines provide that an association in fact enterprise must be "directed toward an economic or other identifiable goal."

We therefore hold that petitioners may maintain this action if respondents conducted the enterprise through a pattern of racketeering activity. The questions or whether the respondents committed the requisite predicate acts, and whether the commission of these acts fell into a pattern, are not before us. We hold only that RICO contains no economic motive requirement.

The judgment of the Court of Appeals is accordingly reversed.

    a. What is the issue in this case?

    b. For what reasons did the Supreme Court invalidate the decision of the Court of Appeals?

    c. What important words or phrases are ambiguous?

2. Now demonstrate your critical thinking skills by applying them to the following argument:

What's all this I've been hearing about requiring harsher sentences for white-collar crimes? Honestly, that's the looniest idea I've heard since Looney Toons!

If anyone needs to be punished more harshly, it's those street criminals. They're the ones who will sneak up behind you on the street or break into your home to rob you. When such things happen, not only do you feel bad that you lost money or possessions, you lose your sense of security. Nobody could place a dollar amount on the luxury of feeling secure. Clearly, street crimes are much more traumatic to victims than white-collar crimes.

Why would you want to lock up white-collar criminals any longer? Almost without exception, they get caught once and then stop committing crimes. That just goes to show that small sentences get the job done. On the other hand, look at all the street criminals who return to prison. There are lots more of them. If any group needs harsher sentences, they do.

It's time that our society wakes up and punishes the real criminals. Honestly, fraud and embezzlement cannot even be compared to crimes such as burglary, armed robbery, rape, assault, arson, and murder. These latter crimes violate not only people's property, but also their rights.

    a. What reasons does the author give for opposing harsher sentences for white-collar crimes?

    b. What reasonable alternative conclusions might a reader draw from these reasons?

    c. How solid is the author's evidence? What missing information would improve the evidence?

    d. What words or phrases are significantly ambiguous?

    e. What is the relationship between the issue and the author's reasons?

B.   *Learning the Basics*

Matching

1. _____ bench trial

    a. defense used when the idea for the crime was not the defendant's, but instead the idea was put in the defendant's mind by a police officer or other government official

2. _____ plea bargaining

    b. the secretive and wrongful taking and carrying away of the property of another with the intent to permanently deprive the owner of its use or possession

3. ____ duress

    c. the giving or receiving of money or other valuable items for the purpose of swaying the decision of an individual who occupies a position of trust, such as a government official

4. ____ strict liability offenses

    d. the case is heard by a judge because the defendant has declined a jury trial

5. ____ larceny

    e. the wrongful conversion of the property of another by one who is lawfully in possession of that property

6. ____ embezzlement

    f. defense used when a person is forced to commit a wrongful act by a threat of immediate bodily harm or loss of life

7. ____ bribery

    g. crimes in which an individual intentionally uses some sort of misrepresentation to gain an advantage over another

8. ____ entrapment

    h. a process of negotiation between the defense attorney and the public prosecutor or district attorney

9. ____ criminal fraud

    i. crimes for which no state of mind is required

True and False

1. _____ The responsible corporate officer doctrine increases the number of circumstances under which a manager may be found guilty for committing a white-collar crime.

2. _____ White-collar criminals are more likely than street criminals to have a college degree and to be committing the crime with the assistance of at least one other person.

3. _____ Computer viruses are one of the biggest business problems, costing billions of dollars in damages every year.

4. _____ White-collar criminals are generally sentenced more severely than other criminals.

5. _____ An important difference between an indictment and an information is that the former is handed down by a grand jury for a felony, whereas the latter is handed down by a magistrate for a misdemeanor.

6. _____ Whistleblower statutes allow private citizens to bring actions against their employers for fraud against the government.

7. _____ RICO allows individuals or businesses who are injured as a result of a pattern of criminal activity to sue the perpetrator of the illegal acts for treble damages.

8. _____ A plea of nolo contendre is another name for a plea of not guilty.

9. _____ In a felony case, the grand jury decides whether the defendant should be indicted.

10. _____ All federal employees who act as whistleblowers are protected by the Whistleblower Protection Act.

Multiple Choice

1. Which of the following laws allow private law suits that financially punish those who commit certain kinds of white-collar crime?

a. RICO
b. False Claims Act
c. both a and b
d. none of the above

2. Which of the following is NOT an affirmative defense to a criminal charge?

a. entrapment
b. mistake of fact
c. duress
d. none of the above

3.   The Federal Sentencing Guidelines

a.   were developed in part in response to a public perception that judges were not imposing harsh enough penalties on white-collar criminals
b.   state the fines judges now impose are a product of a "base fine" and a "culpability score"
c.   both a and b
d.   none of the above

4.   A defendant enters a plea at the

a.   first appearance
b.   arraignment
c.   indictment
d.   information

5.   Which of the following is NOT an act of criminal fraud?

a.   defalcation
b.   false token
c.   forgery
d.   none of the above

6.   When a person is lawfully in possession of the property of another, but converts that property for his own use, the person has engaged in

a.   entrapment
b.   larceny
c.   embezzlement
d.   bribery

7.   Which is not an alternative to prison used to punish white-collar criminals?

a.   fines
b.   occupational disqualification
c.   house arrest
d.   none of the above

8.   Although the procedures may differ from state to state, criminal proceedings generally begin with

a.   the arrest of the defendant
b.   the reading of the Miranda rights

c.   the filing of the criminal complaint against the defendant
d.   the booking of the defendant

Short Answer

1.   Name four reasons why a corporation's personnel and operating procedures can encourage white-collar crime by its employees. Name one way that the managers can work to discourage such behavior.

2.   Give two arguments for and two arguments against holding corporations criminally liable.

CHAPTER 8
ETHICS, SOCIAL RESPONSIBILITY, AND THE BUSINESS MANAGER

This chapter introduces you to the role of ethics in business. Should business managers be required to consider social responsibility when making decisions? What ethical theories are used to guide business decisions? Business ethics is a particularly fertile ground for practicing your critical thinking skills.

A.   More Critical Thinking

1. The following case discusses the decision to disbar an attorney who was involved in covert felonious activities that were authorized by the President of the United States. Practice your critical thinking skills by reading it and answering the questions that follow.

In Re Krogh
1975

JUDGE ROSELLINI:

Egil Krogh, Jr., was admitted [to practice] law in the state of Washington on September 20, 1968. On February 4, 1974, he was suspended as a result of his having been convicted of a felony. [Krogh now appeals the disciplinary board's decision to disbar him.]

The information referred to in the complaint charged that while the respondent was an officer and employee of the United States Government. . . . and acting in his official capacity, in conjunction with others who were officials and employees of the United States Government, the defendant unlawfully, willfully and knowingly did combine, conspire, confederate and agree with his co-conspirators to injure, oppress, threaten and intimidate Dr. Lewis J. Fielding . . . . in the free exercise and enjoyment of a right and privilege secured to him by the Constitution and laws of the United States, and to conceal such activities. It further charged that the co-conspirators did, without legal process, probable cause, search warrant or other lawful authority, enter the offices of Dr. Fielding in Los Angeles County, California, with the intent to search for, examine and photograph documents and records containing confidential information concerning Daniel Ellsberg, and thereby injure, oppress, threaten and intimidate Dr. Fielding in the free exercise and enjoyment of the right and privilege secured to him by the fourth amendment to the Constitution of the United States, to be secure in his person, house, papers and effects against unreasonable searches and seizures. . . . To all of these allegations, the respondent had pleaded guilty.

Both the hearing panel and the disciplinary board found that moral turpitude was an element of the crime of which respondent was convicted. The panel found that he has a spotless record except for the incident involved in these proceedings; that he is outstanding in character and ability; that his reputation is beyond reproach; that he acted, although mistakenly, out of a misguided loyalty to [President Nixon]; that the event was an isolated one, and that in all probability there would be no repetition of any such error on his part. The panel further found that the respondent had accepted responsibility and had made amends to the best of his ability; that he testified fully and candidly and that his attitude in the proceeding was excellent. The panel concluded that in this case which it found to be distinguishable from all other cases, the respondent apparently followed the order of a "somewhat distraught President of the United States" under the guise of national security to stop by all means further security leaks.

Th[e] rule [that attorneys are disbarred automatically when they are found guilty of a felony] still governs the disposition of such disciplinary proceedings in a number of jurisdictions. However, under our disciplinary rules, some flexibility is permitted, and the court retains its discretionary power to determine whether, on the facts of the particular case, the attorney should be disbarred.

The question before us then, is: Should the respondent, who has been convicted of a felony involving moral turpitude, be disbarred?

[The respondent's] testimony reveals that when it was suggested that he violate not only the laws but the constitutional rights of his fellow citizens, he accepted the proposition without any misgivings as to its legality, accepting as a tenable proposition the notion that whatever was ordered by his superiors should be done. Such an attitude on the part of an attorney, particularly one who has accepted a position of responsibility in the office of the President of the United States, manifests at once a fundamental unfitness to serve as an officer of the courts.

We find it difficult to believe that the respondent was not aware that the activities in which he was engaging were at least questionable under the law.
. . . Apparently it did not occur to the respondent to look at the Constitution, the statutes, or the case law to ascertain whether his project was unlawful.

The respondent's conduct cannot be excused on the ground of ignorance. Here, not only did the respondent fail to question the propriety of his own acts at the time they were committed; for two years thereafter his mind and conscience remained at rest. His interest in the quality of his acts was not aroused until it appeared that his conduct could no longer be kept secret.

We cannot accept the assumption that attorneys . . . can ordinarily be expected to abandon the principles which they have sworn to uphold, when asked to do so by a person who holds a constitutional office. Rather than being overawed by the authority of one who holds such an office . . . the attorney who is employed by such an officer should be the most keenly aware of the Constitution and all of its provisions, the most alert to discourage the abuse of power. In such a position those powers of discernment and reason, which he holds himself out as possessing, perform their most important function. If, when given a position of power himself, he forgets his oath to uphold the Constitution and laws of the land and instead flaunts the constitutional rights of other citizens and holds himself above the law, can we say to the public that a person so weak in his dedication to constitutional principles is qualified to practice law?

That the reputation and honor of the bar have suffered severe damage as a result is now a matter of common knowledge. We find it difficult to believe that the respondent was not aware, when he authorized the burglary of Dr. Fielding's office, that if his conduct became known, it would reflect discredit upon his profession.

For the reasons set forth herein, we must conclude that the respondent, in spite of his many commendable qualities and achievements, has shown himself to be unfit to practice law.

The recommendation of the disciplinary board is **approved**, and the respondent's name shall be stricken from the roll of attorneys in this state.

  a. What ethical norm is central to the court's decision in this case?

  b. What fact seems especially powerful in shaping the court's reasoning?

  c. What reasons does the court provide for upholding the respondent's disbarment?

  2. Look back at the case of *Pavlik v. Lane* in your primary text to answer the following questions.

  a. How can the court's argument be justified in terms of a rule utilitarian ethical system? An act utilitarian ethical system?

  b. How can the court's argument be justified in terms of a humanist ethical system?

c. How can the court's reasoning be understood in the framework of a deontological ethic?

B.   *Learning the Basics*

Matching

1. ____ business ethics

   a. argues that an act is ethically correct if it brings net happiness to society

2. ____ social responsibility of business

   b. actions are good or bad depending on whether they contribute to improving inherent human qualities

3. ____ consequentialist theory of ethics

   c. study of what makes up good and bad ethical behavior

4. ____ utilitarianism

   d. one should focus on the general rule that exemplifies net happiness for the whole society

5. ____ act utilitarianism

   e. concern by business about its activities and their impact on groups outside the business

6. ____ rule utilitarianism

   f. uses the principle of utility to focus on an individual's action at one point in time

7. ____ deontological theory of ethics

   g. rules and principles determine whether actions are ethically good or bad

8. ____ humanist theory of ethics

   h. judge acts as ethically good or bad based on whether they have achieved desired results

True and False

1. _____ The consequential theory of ethics is best exemplified by the utilitarian school of thought.

2. _____ When verifying whether an act is ethically good or bad, act utilitarians focus on the process while rule utilitarians focus on the consequences of an act.

3. _____ Advocates of deontology do not consider consequences.

4. _____ Someone who subscribed to the humanist theory of ethics would argue that the bribing of a foreign official is ethical.

5. _____ Corporations are not influenced by individual codes of conduct.

6. _____ Professionals are not required to obey the professional code of conduct; instead, professional codes of conduct provide suggestions that guide a professional's behavior.

7. _____ Those advocating a managerial theory of social responsibility argue that all business entities must be held responsible for their actions and sanctioned appropriately when necessary.

8. _____ Ethical considerations aren't really necessary in business; business transactions are in a separate sphere from ethical considerations.

Multiple Choice

1. What factors caused an outcry of public concern about the social responsibility of business?

a. the complexity and interdependence of a post industrial society
b. political influence
c. philosophical differences about the obligations of businesses
d. all of the above

2. A business manager pays a bribe to a foreign official to secure a production contract. This manager believes that her act is ethically correct because it will bring jobs and spending to her community. The theory of ethics that best describes her thinking is

a. the humanist theory of ethics
b. the deontological theory of ethics
c. the profit-oriented theory of social responsibility
d. utilitarianism

3. On the first day of your new job, your manager tells you to always obey the golden rule when making business transactions. The theory of ethics that best describes her thinking is

a. the humanist theory of ethics
b. the deontological theory of ethics
c. the profit-oriented theory of social responsibility
d. utilitarianism

4. Business professionals may be influenced by numerous codes of ethics. Which code of ethics does NOT influence an individual's business decisions?

a. corporate ethical codes
b. industry ethical codes
c. social responsibility ethical codes
d. professional codes of ethics

5. Which of the following is a characteristic of a professional group?

a. pre-licensing mandatory university educational training
b. licensing exam requirements
c. a set of written ethical standards enforced by the group
d. all of the above

6. Which of the following is a theory of social responsibility?

a. regulation theory
b. professional ethical theory
c. corporate officer theory
d. all of the above

7.   The profit-oriented theory of social responsibility

a.   argues that business entities are distinct organizations that exist to increase profits for shareholders
b.   suggests that businesses should be judged on the criteria of economic efficiency and growth in productivity and technology
c.   both a and b
d.   none of the above

8.   A business person who advocates a managerial theory of social responsibility

a.   argues that the firm must have clear ethical standards and a sense of social responsibility for its unintended acts
b.   wants to maximize short term profits
c.   must not be persuaded by claims of interest groups
d.   focuses on increasing profits for stockholders

Short Answer

1.   Of the theories of social responsibility that you have learned, which does it appear that the R.J. Reynolds corporation subscribes to given its Joe Camel advertising campaign as described in your primary text? Why did you choose that one, and not one of the other options?

2.   In the *Bates v. State Bar of Arizona* case, how would the court's decision have changed if it were revealed that Bates and O'Steen were posting deliberately misleading advertisements about their legal clinic's prices?

CHAPTER 9
THE INTERNATIONAL LEGAL ENVIRONMENT OF BUSINESS

As a future business manager, you need to be aware of the effect of international law on your business. This chapter will increase your understanding of the impact of international legal systems on global business.

A.   More Critical Thinking

1. How do international treaties interact with constitutional law? The following case addresses this issue:

BREARD v.GREENE
U. S. SUPREME COURT
April 14, 1998
Per Curiam.

Angel Francisco Breard [was] scheduled to be executed by the Commonwealth of Virginia [that] evening at 9:00 p.m. Breard, a citizen of Paraguay, came to the United States in 1986, at the age of 20. In 1992, Breard was charged with the attempted rape and capital murder of Ruth Dickie. At his trial in 1993, the State presented overwhelming evidence of guilt, including semen found on Dickie's body matching Breard's DNA profile and hairs on Dickie's body identical in all microscopic characteristics to hair samples taken from Breard. Breard chose to take the witness stand in his defense. During his testimony, Breard confessed to killing Dickie, but explained that he had only done so because of a satanic curse placed on him by his father-in-law. Following a jury trial in the Circuit Court of Arlington County, Virginia, Breard was convicted of both charges and sentenced to death. On appeal, the Virginia Supreme Court affirmed Breard's convictions and sentences, and we denied certiorari.

Breard then filed a motion for habeas relief under 28 U.S.C. ' 2254 in Federal District Court on August 20, 1996. In that motion, Breard argued for the first time that his conviction and sentence should be overturned because of alleged violations of the Vienna Convention on Consular Relations (Vienna Convention), April 24, 1963, [1970] 21 U. S. T. 77, T.I.A.S. No. 6820, at the time of his arrest. Specifically, Breard alleged that the Vienna Convention was violated when the arresting authorities failed to inform him that, as a foreign national, he had the right to contact the Paraguayan Consulate. The District Court rejected this claim, concluding that Breard procedurally defaulted the claim when he failed to raise it in state court and that Breard could not demonstrate cause and prejudice for this default. The Fourth Circuit affirmed. Breard has petitioned this Court for a writ of certiorari.

It is clear that Breard procedurally defaulted his claim, if any, under the Vienna Convention by failing to raise that claim in the state courts.

Nevertheless, in their petitions for certiorari, both Breard and Paraguay contend that Breard's Vienna Convention claim may be heard in federal court because the Convention is the "supreme law of the land" and thus trumps the procedural default doctrine. This argument is plainly incorrect for two reasons.

First, while we should give respectful consideration to the interpretation of an international treaty rendered by an international court with jurisdiction to interpret such, it has been recognized in international law that ... the procedural rules of the forum State govern the implementation of the treaty in that State. This proposition is embodied in the Vienna Convention itself, which provides that the rights expressed in the Convention "shall be exercised in conformity with the laws and regulations of the receiving State," provided that "said laws and regulations must enable full effect to be given to the purposes for which the rights accorded under this Article are intended." It is the rule in this country that assertions of error in criminal proceedings must first be raised in state court in order to form the basis for relief in habeas. Claims not so raised are considered defaulted. By not asserting his Vienna Convention claim in state court, Breard failed to exercise his rights under the Vienna Convention in conformity with the laws of the United States and the Commonwealth of Virginia. Having failed to do so, he cannot raise a claim of violation of those rights now on federal habeas review.

Second, although treaties are recognized by our Constitution as the supreme law of the land, this status is no less true of provisions of the Constitution itself, to which rules of procedural default apply. We have held "that an Act of Congress . . . is on a full parity with a treaty, and that when a statute which is subsequent in time is inconsistent with a treaty, the statute to the extent of conflict renders the treaty null." The Vienna Convention-which arguably confers on an individual the right to consular assistance following arrest-has continuously been in effect since 1969. But in 1996, before Breard filed his habeas petition raising claims under the Vienna Convention, Congress enacted the Antiterrorism and Effective Death Penalty Act (AEDPA), which provides that a habeas petitioner alleging that he is held in violation of "treaties of the United States" will, as a general rule, not be afforded an evidentiary hearing if he "has failed to develop the factual basis of [the] claim in State court proceedings." Breard's ability to obtain relief based on violations of the Vienna Convention is subject to this subsequently-enacted rule, just as any claim arising under the United States Constitution would be. This rule prevents Breard from establishing that the violation of his Vienna Convention rights prejudiced him. Without a hearing, Breard cannot establish how the Consul would have advised him, how the advice of his attorneys differed from the advice the Consul could have provided, and what factors he considered in electing to reject the plea bargain that the State offered him. That limitation, Breard also argues, is not justified because his Vienna Convention claims were so novel that he could not have discovered them any earlier.

For the foregoing reasons, we **deny the petition for an original writ of habeas corpus**, the motion for leave to file a bill of complaint, the petitions for certiorari, and the accompanying stay applications filed by Breard and Paraguay.

    a. What is the issue in this case?

    b. What reasons does the court offer?

    c. What ethical norms are fundamental to the courts reasoning in this case?

2. Read the following argument and answer the critical thinking questions.

Allowing China to gain Permanent Normal Trade Relations status with the United States was a grave error that the U.S. will regret in the near future.

Trade with China isn't good for business: China exports far more to the United States than the U.S. exports in return. Why should the U.S. allow another country to reap the rewards of a trade relationship that is guaranteed to bankrupt the American economy? Yet the United States gave away its only protection against such exploitation -- tariffs and other trade barriers -- by offering the Chinese government the fullest trade concessions possible. Piracy of intellectual property within China only reinforces the claim that trade with China will only undermine American business interests.

Far from expanding and promoting trade with China, the U.S. should revoke its trade concessions and oppose China's entry into the WTO.

    a. What are the author's conclusion and reasons?

    b. What evidence does the author provide to support his argument?

    c. Do you see any problems with this evidence?

    d. Is there relevant missing information?

B.   Learning the Basics

Matching

1. ____ country analysis

2. ____ culture

3. ____ common law

4. ____ Romano-Germanic Civil law

5. ____ public international law

6. ____ private international law

7. ____ international trade

8. ____ international licensing

9. ____ international franchising

10. ____ expropriation

a. primary reliance is on case law and precedent

b. law that governs the relationships between the nation-states

c. a contractual agreement by which a company makes its intellectual property available to a foreign party in return for compensation

d. learned norms of a society that are based on values, beliefs and attitudes

e. the taking of private property by the host country either for political or economic reasons

f. permits a licensee of a trademark to market the licensor's goods or services in a particular nation

g. examines political variables and dissects a nation's economic performance

h. exporting goods and services from a country and importing goods and services into a country

i. allows a government expropriating foreign-owned private property to claim immunity from the jurisdiction of courts in the owner's country

j. primary reliance is on codes and statutory law

11. ____ sovereign immunity doctrine

     k. law that governs relationships between private parties involved in transactions across national borders

True and False

1. ____ The type of government of a country will not influence how international firms conduct business in that country.

2. ____ Islamic law governs the behavior of people in each caste.

3. ____ Trade is considered the least risky means of doing international business.

4. ____ The Foreign Sovereign Immunities Act shields foreign governments from U.S. judicial review of their acts.

5. ____ The act of state doctrine holds that each sovereign nation is bound to respect the independence of every other sovereign state.

6. ____ Currency controls, as well as import and export controls, are typically used in the United States to protect foreign companies from destroying the U.S market.

7. ____ The World Trade Organization has the power to enforce the new trade accord that evolved out of seven rounds of GATT negotiations.

8. ____ NAFTA, like the European Union, is intended to create a common market between Canada, the United States, and Mexico.

9. ____ When an international dispute arises, the parties may turn to arbitration or litigation to resolve the dispute.

Multiple Choice

1. When conducting international business, a business manager must consider

   a. political, economic, and legal dimensions
   b. social and political dimensions
   c. economic and business dimensions
   d. historical, political, and legal dimensions

2. An economic factor that especially impacts business investment

   a. availability of indisposable income
   b. availability of workers
   c. the existence of an appropriate transportation infrastructure
   d. type of government

3. Socialist law

   a. is based on the teaching of Karl Marx
   b. encourages collectivization of property
   c. is primarily concerned with hereditary categories
   d. both a and b

4. Sources of international law can be found in

   a. custom
   b. international organizations
   c. treaties between nations
   d. all of the above

5. Foreign direct investment may take the following form:

   a. a multinational corporation creates a wholly or partially owned and controlled foreign subsidiary in the host country
   b. a multinational corporation enters into a joint venture with an individual, corporation, or government agency of the host country
   c. both a and b
   d. none of the above

6. A large multinational corporation may create foreign subsidiaries to

   a. dispense their knowledge in foreign nations
   b. acquire foreign resources

c. create distance between their customers
d. reduce production efficiency

7. Bilateral investment treaties

a. oblige the host government to show fair and nondiscriminatory treatment to investors from the other country
b. are a risk of international business
c. both a and b
d. none of the above

8. In times of financial crisis, the United States and other exporters might hedge against exchange risks by contracting with a bank. What is the hedging process?

a. Exporters refuse to perform any transactions with the foreign nation and deal only with the bank.
b. Exporters enter into a contract with the bank that gives the exporter insurance that the foreign nation will fulfill the contract.
c. In return for a fee, the bank assumes the risk of currency fluctuation by guaranteeing the exporter a fixed number of dollars in exchange for the foreign currency it receives.
d. all of the above

9. The European Union

a. wants to create a common market
b. has created uniform agricultural, environmental, and labor legislation
c. has eliminated tariff and nontariff barriers
d. both a and b

Short Answer

1. Identify similarities and differences in Common law and Romano-Germanic Civil law.

2. What is a problem with the claim in the following statement? International trade is the best method of engaging in international business.

CHAPTER 10

THE LAW OF CONTRACTS AND SALES I

This chapter will improve your understanding of contracts. As a business manager, you will encounter contracts on a regular basis. Hence, it is important that you gain a clear understanding of the law regulating contracts.

A.   More Critical Thinking

1. The main ethical norm underlying contract law is security. Courts want to provide parties with security that their bargained-for agreements will be upheld. The following case gives you the opportunity to evaluate the reasoning in a breach of contract case.

   Reread *The Private Movie Company, Inc. v. Pamela Lee Anderson, et al.* in your primary textbook.

   a. What was the judge's conclusion?

   b. How did the facts shape the reasoning in this case?

   c. You discover that Pamela Lee Anderson has posed in Playboy magazine.   Moreover, nude pictures of her are numerous on the Internet. Her main concern in the negotiation with The Private Movie Company was the removal of scenes with "nudity and sexual conduct." In light of the pictures in Playboy and on the Internet, what do you now think about her argument?

2. Read the following argument regarding contracts.

Let me tell you a story about my friend, Jerry. After hearing this story, I'm sure that you will agree with me that we need to change contract law.

Jerry entered into a contract with Elaine. Elaine wanted to rent Jerry's house, and she planned to eventually buy his house. She signed a lease to rent the house from Jerry for one year. However, Jerry told her that he would deduct the rent payments from the final sale price of the house. Elaine agreed to the deduction. Nine months later, Elaine told Jerry that she did not think she could afford to buy the house.

Jerry ran a "for sale" advertisement in the newspaper, and soon another party made an offer on Jerry's house. This offer was $5,000 more than the final sale price that Jerry had given to Elaine. During the nine months that Elaine lived in Jerry's house, she made numerous improvements that raised the value of the house by $3,500. Jerry verbally agreed to sell the house to the outside party. However, Elaine became very furious when Jerry told her that he sold the house she had planned to buy. Elaine had just received a large promotion and was now financially able to buy the house. Elaine sued Jerry for breach of contract. When Jerry told the outside party that he may not be able to sell them the house, they brought a suit against Jerry for breach of contract.

Jerry had two lawsuits against him for the same house. Furthermore, my lawyer told me that Jerry will probably have to pay damages in both cases. Contract law is just too complicated for the ordinary citizen to understand. Jerry is really worried about these cases. Without such complex standards for a contract, his life would be much happier. Citizens are going to make business transactions, and the courts need to understand that people make mistakes. Courts should relax their standards to allow for more mistakes in contracts.

    a. What is the conclusion of this argument?

    b. What evidence does the author provide for this conclusion?

    c. Can you create an alternative conclusion based on the evidence offered?

B. *Learning the Basics*

Matching

1. ____ express contract

2. ____ implied contract

3. ____ unilateral contract

4. ____ bilateral contract

5. ____ executed contract

a. exchange of a promise for an act

b. contract for which all the terms have been performed

c. contract established by the conduct of a party rather than by the party's written or oral words

d. court-imposed agreement to prevent unjust enrichment of one party when the parties had not really agreed to an enforceable contract

e. an error made by only one party to a contract

6. ____ quasi-contract

    f. any wrongful act or threat that prevents a party from exercising free will when executing a contract

7. ____ consideration

    g. exchange of oral or written promises between parties that are enforceable in a court of law

8. ____ duress

    h. present transfer of an existing right

9. ____ unilateral mistake

    i. exchange of one promise for another

10. ____ assignment

    j. bargained for exchange of promises in which a legal detriment is suffered by the promisee

True and False

1. _____ The very first question one must ask before figuring out whether a contract exists is, "What was the offer?"

2. _____ A good is a tangible, moveable object.

3. _____ To prove a case of undue influence, the plaintiff must be able to show that the defendant threatened to harm her if she did not sign the contract.

4. _____ If Julie promises to hold an offer open for three weeks, she can still withdraw the offer at any time unless she made that promise in writing.

5. _____ The standard of performance is higher under the UCC than it is under the common law.

6. _____ Contracts by insane people are void.

7. _____ Judges will not rescind a contract if a mistake has occurred.

8. _____ To be considered enforceable, a contract must be in writing.

9. _____ If Michael Jordan agrees to play basketball for three years for the Chicago Bulls, the contract must be in writing.

10. _____ Newspaper ads are generally considered to be offers.

Multiple Choice

1. A contract is void if

a. made by someone adjudicated insane
b. made under duress
c. procured by fraud
d. all of the above

2. Contract law is shaped by

a. state courts
b. federal courts
c. statutory law from state and federal legislatures
d. all of the above

3. A reward is an example of

a. a unilateral offer
b. an offer for a bilateral contract
c. avoidable offer
d. none of the above

4. A contract must be in writing if the contract involves

a. an interest in land
b. an agreement to pay the debts of another
c. both a and b
d. none of the above
5. In order for an offer to be valid, it must meet certain requirements. Which of the following is NOT a requirement for a valid legal offer?

a. The offer must show objective intent to enter into the contract.
b. The offer must be definite.
c. The offer must be legal.
d. The offer must be communicated to the party intended by the offeror

6. You decide to sell your house, so you place an ad in the newspaper. However, before anyone responds to your ad, your house catches fire and burns to the ground. The offer is

a. valid
b. terminated
c. executed
d. void

7. You offer to sell your roommate a computer for $500. The next morning she says that she will pay you $450 for the computer. This situation fulfills which requirement(s) of a legal contract?

a. legal offer
b. legal acceptance
c. both a and b
d. none of the above

8. You had too much alcohol to drink last night, but you vaguely remember making an agreement with an acquaintance to sell him your new car for $100. This morning, when the acquaintance came to your house to pick up the car, you tell him that you were drunk and do not wish to sell your car. He threatens to take you to court. The court will

a. disaffirm the contract
b. examine the degree of your intoxication at the time of the agreement
c. affirm the contract and force you to sell your car
d. ask you if you received the money for the car when you were drunk

9. While signing a written contract, two parties make an oral agreement that contradicts the written contract. A court would most likely

a. consider the oral agreement a supplement to the written agreement
b. not allow the oral agreement as evidence
c. give greater weight to the oral agreement than the written contract
d. none of the above

Short Answer

1. Why is the following statement problematic? The most important element of the contract is the offer.

2. What is a link between fraud and duress?

3. What is inadequate about the following statement? All contracts can be classified as implied or express and unilateral or bilateral, and some can be classified as executed or executory.

CHAPTER 11
THE LAW OF CONTRACTS II

This chapter will sharpen your thinking about contracts. You will learn more about the specific ways that a contract is discharged. Here are some critical thinking and review exercises designed to further your understanding of contracts law and to provide practice opportunities for your growing critical thinking skills.

A.   *More Critical Thinking*

1. The following case gives you another opportunity to practice your critical thinking skills in the context of contracts.

THOMAS v. I.N.S,
1994

In 1983, Thomas, who had lived in the United States for thirty years but was not a citizen, pleaded guilty to conspiracy to possess cocaine for sale, and was sentenced to seven years' imprisonment. At the government's urging, he was released from prison after about two years because of his cooperation in a major narcotics investigation. Thomas and an Assistant United States Attorney entered into a cooperation agreement that consisted of a formal "letter of agreement" on the letterhead of the "United States Attorney _ Mountain States Drug Task Force." Thomas traded information to the United States Attorney for a promise that "the government" would not oppose his application for discretionary relief from deportation. The government nevertheless did oppose his application. The Immigration and Naturalization Service argues that it was not bound by the United States Attorney's promise.

KLEINFELD, Circuit Judge:

It has long been the law that the government's failure to keep a commitment which induces a guilty plea requires that judgment be vacated and the case remanded. A cooperation agreement is analogous to a plea agreement. The government is held to the literal terms of the agreement, and ordinarily must bear responsibility for any lack of clarity . . . . Enforcement of the agreement requires that the person making the promise be authorized, and that the promisee rely on the promise to his detriment.

The INS argues that "the Service was not a party to the agreement, nor is it bound by the agreement, nor does the agreement specify that INS would not oppose the alien's request." The INS correctly points out that the record does not show the INS was ever consulted about whether the government should make the agreement, or even advised that the agreement existed. The INS also

80
© 2009 Pearson Education, Inc. publishing as Prentice Hall

argues that the United States Attorney lacked authority to enter into an agreement on its behalf.

[However], Thomas was entitled to performance by the government of its promise. "The staff lawyers in a prosecutor's office have the burden of 'letting the left hand know what the right hand is doing' or has done. That the breach of the agreement was inadvertent does not lessen its impact." The United States Attorney should have written to whomever in the Department of Justice would be responsible for seeing that the promise he made on the government's behalf would be performed by the INS. The BIA should have reversed and remanded for a new hearing in which the government would not oppose Thomas's motion for relief from deportation.

The agreement plainly and unambiguously spoke to the issue of deportation and expressly bound the INS. In the first paragraph, the agreement says that "Government," designated as the promisor, "includes its departments, officers, agents, and agencies." The eighth paragraph bound "[t]he Government," so defined, not to oppose motions for "relief from deportation to the ... U.S. Immigration Service." Motions for relief from deportation are made and heard before the INS, and opposed by INS lawyers, so this particular promise, to mean anything, had to mean that the INS would not oppose such a motion. The letter making the promise is on "United States Attorney _ Mountain States Drug Task Force" letterhead, with the seal of the Department of Justice on the top. There is no question the agreement purported to bind the INS not to oppose Thomas's application for relief from deportation.

The most substantial issue raised by the government is whether the United States Attorney possessed the requisite authority to bind the INS . . . . [T]he United States Attorney's promise that the government would not oppose Thomas's 212(c) application is binding on the INS if the United States Attorney had either an express grant of authority to make such a promise, or his authority for making the promise is incidental to some other express grant of authority.

We have found no express limitation on the United States Attorneys' power to bind the INS. . . . We have found no express grant of authority to United States Attorneys to bind the "government" not to oppose motions for relief from deportation to the INS. We must therefore decide whether their authority to 11prosecute for all offenses against the United States," implies such authority. It does, under ordinary principles of agency law.

The authority to "prosecute" implies the power to make plea agreements incidental to prosecution. . . . Cooperation agreements subsequent to conviction are less common than plea agreements, but so customary and closely related that no one, so far as we know, has ever raised a question of whether United States Attorneys can make cooperation agreements on behalf of the government. Many criminal cases involve aliens, and the convictions affect deportability, so deportability will commonly be a concern of defense counsel, affecting the terms of the agreement.

A United States Attorney's authority to commit the government not to oppose a motion for relief from deportation as part of a plea bargain is incidental to his statutory authority to prosecute crimes. The implication arises from several factors. First, deportation commonly arises from the context of criminal prosecution. It is likely to be a central issue in many criminal cases involving aliens. Second, the terms of a plea or cooperation agreement will commonly affect deportation. The attorneys will negotiate the offenses of conviction and sentences partly by considering the effects of these determinations on deportation. Third, there is no reason why, in the absence of regulations or orders to the contrary, we should doubt that Congress implied this grant of authority. Both the United States Attorneys and the Immigration and Naturalization Service are within the same Department. United States Attorneys are very high officials. They are appointed by the President and confirmed by the Senate to high positions in which they exercise authority in criminal cases tersely stated as "prosecute" in an independent and broad statutory conferral.

The language [in the United States Attorneys' Manual] implies that a United States Attorney does have authority to promise relief from deportation if the agreement is approved by the Criminal Division. The United States Attorney made the agreement. If he followed his manual, then the agreement was approved, and he acted with express authority.

We shall not invent an excuse for the government to break its promise. If they have an excuse, let them prove it.

The case is **REMANDED** for proceedings not inconsistent with this opinion.

We *reverse*, with directions that Thomas have a new proceeding in which the government does not oppose his motion for 212(c) relief.

    a. Identify the issue and conclusion of this argument.

    b. What reasons did the court offer for its conclusion?

    c. What ethical norm does the court seem to emphasize with its decision?

2. Apply your critical thinking skills to the following argument:

Judges should start offering punitive awards for breach of contract cases. Punitive damages are awarded for the sole purpose of deterring the defendant and others from doing the same act again. Last year, over 8,000 breaches of contract occurred. Our courtrooms are flooded with enough cases. Businesses know that they can get away with breaching their contracts. However, if we start imposing punitive damages, these businesses will alter their behavior.

This change would specifically affect those businesses that make it a practice to breach a contract whenever necessary. People are losing faith in the security of a contract. A survey of 100 first-year business students suggested that contracts are little respected and rarely followed in business.

    a. What is the conclusion and reasons offered in this argument?

    b. The author cites a survey of 100 first-year business students who suggested that contracts are little respected and rarely followed in business. Do you see any problems with this evidence?

    c. What additional information do you need to evaluate this argument?

B. Learning the Basics

Matching

1. ____ accord and satisfaction

    a. when an unforeseeable event makes a promisor's performance objectively impossible

2. ____ condition precedent

    b. the canceling of a contract

3. ____ condition subsequent

    c. a particular event that must take place in order to give rise to a duty of performance

4. ____ impossibility of performance

    d. place the injured party in the position that it would have been in had the terms of the contract been performed

5. ____ commercial impracticability

e. awards for the sole purpose of deterring the defendant and others from doing the same act again

6. ____ compensatory damages

f. parties agree to rescind an original agreement and substitute a new one for it

7. ____ punitive damages

g. a situation where performance is impractical because of unreasonable expense, injury, or loss to one party

8. ____ rescission

h. a particular future event that, when following the execution of a contract, terminates the contract

9. ____ liquidated damages

i. correction of terms in an agreement so that they reflect the true understanding of the parties

10. ____ reformation

j. parties agree to pay so much a day for every day beyond a certain date that the contract is not completely performed

True and False

1. _____ If there is substantial but not complete performance of a contract, the courts will usually find breach of contract.

2. _____ If Kathy makes a contract with Matt to buy a painting and Matt's house burns down while the painting is still inside, Matt is still responsible for fulfilling the contract.

3. _____ Punitive damages are infrequently awarded in contract cases.

4. _____ If Dennis Rodman signs a contract to play exclusively for the Chicago Bulls, the court may grant an injunction to prevent him from playing for other teams.

5. _____ The substantial performance doctrine applies to the sale of goods.

6. _____ If an unforeseen event occurs that makes the fulfillment of a contract financially impractical, the contract may be rescinded by mutual mistake.

7. _____ If Michael contracted to buy 100 loaves of bread from a baker at $2 a loaf to be delivered by December 22, he has the right to buy the bread from another source if the 100 loaves are not delivered by December 22.

8. _____ In cases of fraud or duress, the courts will usually award reformation.

9. _____ The Uniform Commercial Code specifies that a buyer has the right to, for any reason, reject the goods he contracted to purchase.

Multiple Choice

1. A contract may be discharged by

a. performance
b. precedent
c. mutual agreement
d. both a and c

2. The impossibility of performance defense is used in which circumstance?

a. death or illness of a promisor
b. change of law that makes the promised performance legal
c. destruction of the subject matter
d. all of the above

3. When dollar damages are inadequate or impractical as a remedy in a contract case, the injured party may turn to

a. equitable remedies
b. rescission and reformation
c. liquidated damages
d. both a and b

4.   The Convention on Contracts for the Sale of International Sale of Goods (CISG)

a.   has been incorporated into United State federal law
b.   covers all contracts for the sale of goods in countries that have ratified it
c.   is subject to state laws dealing with contracts
d.   both a and b

5.   Substantial performance consists of which of the following elements?

a.   completion of all the terms of the agreement
b.   an honest effort to complete all the terms of the agreement
c.   willful departure from the terms of the agreement
d.   all of the above

6.   Legal remedies for breach of contract include

a.   compensatory damages and rescission
b.   reformation and liquidated damages
c.   punitive damages and compensatory damages
d.   specific performance and nominal damages

7.   The government entered into a contract with Fix-It Construction, who was supposed to build a new capital building. However, Fix-It Construction was two weeks late completing the building. The government can

a.   rescind the contract
b.   collect liquidated damages

c.   collect nominal damages
d.   reform the contract

8.   Under the Uniform Computer Information Transaction Act (UCITA),

a.   no contracts can be valid without an in-person signing
b.   a contract requiring a fee of over $100 needs to be *authenticated* before it is enforceable
c.   a seller can control the right of use by the buyer, unlike most normal UCC contracts
d.   none of the above

9.   Which of the following are rights of the seller specified under the Uniform Commercial Code for goods contracts when the buyer breaches the contract?

a.   the right to recover ten times the purchase price if the seller is unable to resell the goods
b.   the right to recover damages
c.   the right to force the buyer to accept the goods
d.   both a and b

Short Answer

1.   What is a connection between impossibility of performance and commercial impossibility?

2.   What is a link between legal remedies and equitable remedies?

Chapter 12
THE LAW OF TORTS

This chapter examines tort law, claims that involve injury to person or property. As with previous chapters, we provide some additional critical thinking practice with matching, true-false, multiple choice, and short answer questions.

A.   *More Critical Thinking*

1. You have probably seen television programs that discuss unsolved murder mysteries. Such programs often include interviews with attorneys, investigators, and family members of the victim. But how does the tort of defamation affect what a broadcaster is able to include in these kinds of programs? The following is a case in which the court applies a state's laws of defamation to statements made as part of a televised program.

RAMSEY

v.

FOX NEWS NETWORK

2005

JUDGE PHILLIP S. FIGA

Six-year-old JonBenet Ramsey was brutally murdered in her home on the night of December 25, 1996 or in the early morning hours of December 26. Her parents, along with her brother Burke, were in the house at the time, of the murder. No one has ever been charged with the crime. Six years later, during the period of December 25-27, 2002, Defendant Fox News Network, L.L.C. ("Fox News") broadcast a report noting the sixth anniversary of the murder of JonBenet Ramsey and the state of the criminal investigation. A transcript of the broadcast, as set forth verbatim in Plaintiffs' Response to the Motion to Dismiss, is attached this opinion. Most pertinent is the following statement from the broadcast uttered by Fox News reporter Carol McKinley:

> Detectives say they have had good reason to suspect the Ramseys. The couple and JonBenet's nine year old brother, Burke, were the only known people in the house the night she was killed. JonBenet had been strangled, bludgeoned and sexually assaulted, most likely from one of her mother's paintbrushes. The longest ransom note most experts have ever seen -- three pages -- was left behind. Whomever killed her spent a long time in the family home, yet there has never been any evidence to link an intruder to her brutal murder.

Plaintiffs originally filed this case in the Northern District of Georgia on February 17, 2004.... U.S. District Judge Thomas W. Thrash, Jr. transferred the case to this district by order dated July 6, 2004. The transfer was made pursuant to 28 U.S.C. § 1404(a), which states: "For the convenience of parties and witnesses, in the interest of justice, a district court may transfer any civil action to any other district or division where it might have been brought."

The first question that the Court must address is whether Georgia or Colorado defamation law applies. This is not necessarily a minor issue. If Colorado, rather than Georgia, law were to apply, plaintiffs might well be subject to a higher proof standard and might obtain a higher damages award.

In Colorado, the "actual malice" standard of *New York Times Co. v. Sullivan* is extended to situations like the one under consideration here where "a defamatory statement has been published concerning one who is not a public official or a public figure, but the matter involved is of public or general concern."

Under this higher standard, a person claiming defamation must prove with "convincing clarity" that the alleged defamatory statement was made with "actual malice" -- that is, with knowledge that the statement was false or with reckless disregard of whether it was false or not. (If a private individual were involved and the matter were not one of "public or general concern," under Colorado law such an aggrieved plaintiff would merely have to proof that the defamer was negligent.)

In contrast, under Georgia law someone who is not a public figure claiming defamation need only prove negligence on the part of the defamer, even if the matter involving the private person is a matter of public or general concern. Here, plaintiffs claim they are not public figures for purposes of this action.

This Colorado Court must look to Georgia's choice of law rules to see which state's law applies here. This is because a court sitting in diversity that has a case transferred to it from another district must apply the choice of law rules of the transferor court.

The next question is whether the broadcast is capable of defamatory meaning as against plaintiffs.... Defamation is a communication holding an individual up to contempt or ridicule that causes the individual to incur injury or damage. To be defamatory, a statement need only prejudice the plaintiff in the eyes of a substantial and respectable minority of the community. A television broadcast of defamatory matter is defamation by libel.

Plaintiffs, as Fox News points out, have asserted a claim of defamation *per se.* That is, on its face and without extrinsic proof, the statement is unmistakably recognized as injurious and specifically directed toward the plaintiffs. To determine defamation *per se,* the Court must examine the statement itself without the aid of inducements, colloquialisms, innuendoes or explanatory circumstances. A statement constitutes defamation *per se* if it imputes a criminal offense. Defamation per se is actionable without pleading or proof of special damages.

Defamation *per se* differs from defamation *per quod,* which requires innuendo or extrinsic evidence to establish its defamatory nature. Special damages, that is specific monetary losses (which exclude injuries to a plaintiffs reputation or feelings not resulting in quantifiable monetary loss), must be pled and proved in a defamatory *per quod* case. Here, plaintiffs have only pled a defamation case based on defamation *per se,* and the analysis of the motion to dismiss proceeds accordingly.

To determine defamation**,** the Court must view the broadcast as a whole rather than dwell upon specific parts of the broadcast. The Court must give each part its proper weight and the entire broadcast the meaning that people of average intelligence and understanding would give it. In determining whether words are defamatory, the Court is to give them their ordinary and popular meaning.

Applying the above legal standards to the contents of the Fox News broadcast reveals a lack of defamatory meaning in this *per se* case as a matter of law. Taking the broadcast as a whole, it did not hold up any member of the Ramsey family to public contempt or ridicule or accuse any of them of participating in the murder their youngest family member. The broadcast was not a particularly unfair or unreasonable recapitulation of recent events on or about the sixth anniversary of the murder.

The broadcast goes on to state that "the Ramseys have successfully sued tabloid and mainstream media for defamation. Former employees have sued the Ramsey's for the same reason. But still no one stands responsible for the six year-old murder of the little beauty princess." All true, and while the broadcast does not exonerate plaintiffs from any involvement in the murder, it need not in order to avoid being defamatory. Moreover, reporting that plaintiffs have successfully sued for defamation suggests that plaintiffs have been falsely accused of complicity in the crime. Importantly, a major thrust of the broadcast was to report "a recent major development," that the Boulder Police Department "long suspicious of the Ramseys, has turned the case over to District Attorney Mary Keenan, to bring fresh eyes' to the investigation." Plaintiffs' own counsel in this case, Lin Wood, Esq., appears in the broadcast stating: "This is new day in this investigation. The days of the Ramseys being the focus of the investigation . . . those days are over." Clearly the broadcast reflects that the investigation is moving in a new direction, one in which none of the plaintiffs is being accused or suspected of being involved.

The Colorado Supreme Court has observed that "in order to insure uninhibited, robust, and wide-open' debate on matters of public concern, a statement of opinion relating to matters of public concern which does not contain a provably false factual connotation,' or which cannot reasonably [be] interpreted as stating actual facts about an individual,' continues to receive full constitutional protection."

Because of the respect accorded expression in matters of public concern under the First Amendment, in this type of case the existence of a material fact must be established with convincing clarity. Plaintiffs did not establish any such material fact here.

Of course, those who broadcast publicly must accept some responsibilities of basic decency towards others as embodied in our Nation's defamation laws.

Fox News, however, did not shirk those responsibilities here. While the December 2002 broadcast appears to plaintiffs not to have been "fair and balanced" towards them, it was not defamatory. The Court therefore GRANTS Defendant's Motion to Dismiss Plaintiffs' Amended Complaint Pursuant to F.R.C.P. 12(b)(6) and DISMISSES this case with prejudice.

    a. What reasons did the court offer to support its conclusion that Fox's broadcast did not include defamatory statements?

    b. What facts were particularly important in shaping the court's reasoning?

    c. What ethical norm is most highly esteemed by the court on the basis of the reasoning in this case?

2. Read the following conversation and answer the critical thinking questions below.

Lynne: Did you know that the Texas cattlemen sued Oprah Winfrey for criticizing beef? On her talk show, Oprah had a guest who talked about the dangers associated with beef. After listening to the guest, Oprah said, "It has just stopped me cold from eating another burger." These crazy cattlemen suggested that Oprah's statement caused the beef industry to drop approximately 36 million dollars. They wanted Oprah to pay them about $13 million! I know a lot of people adore

Oprah, but get real! Do they really think that people will not eat meat just because Oprah says that she will not? This tort case is just another example of on overload of cases in the courts.

Nikki: I think the cattlemen are justified in bringing a case. Look at the influence of Oprah's Book Club. Approximately once a month, Oprah announces the title of the book to be featured in her Book Club. Oprah then asks the author of the book and selected "Oprah" viewers to dinner to discuss the book. Parts of the dinner/discussion are shown on the Book Club show. At the time of her first book club show, the book, THE DEEP END OF THE OCEAN, had 100,000 copies in print. After Oprah discussed it, there were three million more copies. If she can convince three million people to buy a book, she certainly could convince people not to eat beef. The cattlemen should be awarded the $13 million.

a. Nikki provides evidence that is contrary to Lynne's conclusion. What is this evidence?

b. Can you think of an alternative cause that could account for Nikki's evidence?

c. Lynne states that the beef industry revenue dropped approximately 36 million dollars, and they claimed that Oprah was responsible. What alternative causes could explain the drop in the beef industry?

d. What additional information would be helpful in evaluating the cattlemen's claim against Oprah?

B. Learning the Basics

Matching

1. ____ intentional tort

a. civil wrong that involves a failure to meet the standard of care a reasonable person would meet and because of that failure, harm to another resulted

2. ____ negligent tort

b. publication of a defamatory statement in a permanent form

3. ____ defamation

c. the right to make any statement, true or false, about someone and not be liable for defamation

4. ____ libel

    d. a privacy tort that consists of using a person's name or likeness for commercial gain without the person's permission

5. ____ slander

    e. failure to live up to a standard of care that a reasonable person would meet to protect others from an unreasonable risk of harm

6. ____ absolute privilege

    f. intentional publication of a false statement that is harmful to the plaintiff's reputation

7. ____ conditional privilege

    g. spoken defamatory statement

8. ____ appropriation

    h. intentionally defaming a business product or service.

9. ____ negligence

    i. civil wrong that involves taking some purposeful action that the defendant knew, or should have known, would harm the person, property, or economic interest of the plaintiff

10. ____ disparagement

    j. the right to make a false statement about someone and not be liable for defamation provided that the statement was made without malice

True or False

1. ____ Negligence per se is used to allow the jury to infer negligence based on the fact that an accident of the type in question would ordinarily not occur unless someone else were negligent.

2. ____ Punitive damages may be awarded in contract and tort cases, whereas liquidated damages are available only in contract cases.

3. ____ Conversion differs from trespass to personalty in the extent of control the tortfeasor exerts over the property and the way the damages are calculated.

4. ____ The two major defenses to defamation are truth and privilege.

5. ____ The primary goal of tort law is to punish individuals who commit acts that cause harm to the public health, safety, or morals.

6. ____ The most commonly awarded type of damages in intentional tort cases is an award for punitive damages.

7. ____ Res ipsa loquitur is the doctrine that a plaintiff is using when she points out that the defendant would not have injured her if he had not been driving at a speed that violated the speed limit.

8. ____ A defendant will not be held liable for defamation as long as she believes that the statement she is making about the plaintiff is true.

9. ____ A defendant who steals another's car and then strips off all the valuable parts of the car to sell them will be liable for conversion, whereas the defendant who steals another's car, but gets caught within the week and subsequently returns the car to the plaintiff would be liable to trespass to personalty.

10. ____ If Sam is invited to a party at Joe's house, but refuses to later leave when Joe asks him to, Sam is most likely to be found to have committed the tort of intentional infliction of emotional distress.

Multiple Choice

1. Which need NOT be proven to win a battery case?

a. an offensive contact
b. fear or apprehension on the part of the plaintiff
c. both a and b must be proven
d. neither a nor b must be proven

2. To use the defense of assumption of risk, a defendant must show that plaintiff

a. voluntarily encountered known risk
b. unreasonably encountered known risk
c. suffered harm related to risk assumed
d. all of the above

3. In general, a plaintiff

a. would prefer to be in a state that uses the rule of contributory negligence
b. would prefer to be in a state that uses the rule of pure comparative negligence
c. would prefer to be in a state that uses the modified contributory negligence rule
d. does not care which state he or she is in, because the plaintiff gets to choose which rule the court should apply

4. Jim is employed by Dr. Johnson as his research assistant. Jim has a contract to work for Dr. Johnson for one year at a salary of $200/week. Dr. Johnson bragged to his colleagues about how good his new assistant was and how he was so glad to have Jim under contract for such a low wage. Dr. Mauer contacted Jim and offered him $250/week to quit his job with Dr. Johnson and come work for Dr. Mauer. Jim quits and goes to work for Dr. Mauer. Dr. Mauer

a. has probably committed the tort of unfair compensation
b. has probably committed the tort of unreasonable interference with contract
c. has probably committed the tort of disparagement
d. has committed no tort because of the doctrine of employment at will

5. Which of the following elements is NOT necessary to prove assault?

a. defendant threatened to commit some sort of immediate, offensive bodily contact against the plaintiff
b. the plaintiff was fearful of the bodily contact
c. as a result of that fear, the plaintiff sustained substantial, compensable injuries
d. none of the above; all are necessary elements of the tort

6.   If a plaintiff is 60 percent responsible for the injuries that she suffered in an accident, she will get the largest recovery in a state that uses the defense of

a.   contributory negligence
b.   modified comparative negligence
c.   pure comparative negligence
d.   both a and c

7.   Which of the following does NOT constitute a trespass against realty?

a.   riding your bike across your neighbor's lawn
b.   throwing your football onto your neighbor's lawn
c.   refusing to leave your neighbor's party when he tells you to leave
d.   none of the above

8.   A person can be sued for defamation when he or she

a.   states an opinion about someone that could be damaging to their character
b.   makes a false claim about a public figure without "actual malice"
c.   makes false statements about a private figure that are damaging to that person's character without "actual malice"
d.   none of the above

Short Answer

1.   What is inadequate about the following statement? The most important element in proving a negligence case is proving the duty of care that the defendant owed the plaintiff.

2.   Provide the reasoning for the following statement: Tort law fulfills many important functions.

3.   Make a connection between assault and battery.

CHAPTER 13
PRODUCT AND SERVICE LIABILITY LAW

In this chapter, you will learn about the law that protects consumers from defective and dangerous products. Critical thinking practice activities as well as objective review questions follow.

A. *More Critical Thinking*

1. How do courts resolve cases in which a potentially defective product causes an injury? Who should be responsible for injuries when a person is injured by a defective product? Reread the case of *Welge v. Planters Lifesavers Co.* in your primary text and answer the following critical thinking questions to help clarify these key legal concepts.

   a. What is Judge Posner's conclusion?

   b. How did the facts of the case shape the judge's reasoning?

   c. What ethical norm seems to guide Judge Posner's reasoning?

   d. One of the new critical thinking questions you learned in chapter 1 was "Are there any alternative causes that might be responsible for the problem addressed in the legal dispute?" Should you apply this question to this case? Why or why not?

   e. Do you agree with Judge Posner's decision? Should sellers be responsible for the consequences of selling a defective product even if the defect was introduced without any fault on the seller's part? State your conclusion and at least one reason to support that conclusion.

2. Read the following argument and answer the following critical thinking questions.

Since the 1960s, approximately two million women have received breast implants. Many of these women have experienced a variety of symptoms that could be grouped as connective tissue disease. These women experience severe weakness and fatigue, and they argue that the breast implant is the cause of the disease. One hypothesis that attempts to explain these health problems is that the silicone leaks from the implant and causes an autoimmune reaction in the body. Consequently, these women have brought product liability claims against the manufacturers of the implants. Fortunately, juries have recognized that the manufacturers are liable for designing and selling these dangerous products. In one case, a jury gave a woman with silicone breast implants an award of $25 million dollars.

However, women are starting to have problems bringing product liability cases against implant manufacturers. Several research studies claim to find no link between breast implants and disease. Many legal scholars are suggesting that women with breast implants should not be able to recover damages based on the lack of evidence linking the breast implants to disease. However, in the largest class action suit ever, the implant manufacturers agreed to set aside $4.25 billion dollars for women with breast implants. Clearly, they are admitting their guilt.

The breast implant cases are just like the DES cases. DES is a drug that was given to pregnant women for the purpose of preventing miscarriages. Thirty years after it was introduced, the Food and Drug Administration ordered manufacturers to stop marketing and promoting DES. Furthermore, the manufacturers were told to warn physicians and pregnant women not to use the drug because of dangers to unborn children. Scientific research had demonstrated that DES can cause cancer in daughters exposed to it before birth. Daughters who have cancer are able to recover damages from the DES manufacturer. Similarly, we should certainly hold breast implant manufacturers responsible for the illness. The hundreds of thousands of women with the autoimmune disease cannot be wrong; breast implants cause disease in a woman's body. Make the implant manufacturers pay for their suffering.

a. What are the conclusion and reasons of this argument?

b. What evidence does the author offer in support of her argument?

c. The author suggests that breast implants are quite harmful to women's health. What additional information do you need before you can decide to agree or disagree with this statement?

d. The author makes an analogy about the effects of DES and breast implants. Why might we hesitate to accept this analogy?

A. *Learning the Basics*

Matching

1. ____ statute of limitations

    a. disavowal of liability for breach of warranty by the manufacturer or seller of a good in advance of the sale of the good

2. ____ state-of-the-art defense

    b. warranty that automatically arises out of a transaction

3. ____ express warranty

    c. statute that bars actions arising more than a specified number of years after the cause of action arises

4. ____ implied warranty

    d. an attempt to justify one's negligent behavior by alleging that limitations of scientific knowledge impeded the production of a safer product

5. ____ disclaimer

    e. a statute that bars actions arising more than a specified number of years after the product was purchased

6. ____ market share liability

    f. warranty that is clearly stated by the manufacturer or seller

7. ____ statute of repose

    g. warranty that a good is reasonably fit for ordinary use

8. ____ implied warranty of merchantability

    h. theory of recovery in liability cases according to which damages are apportioned among all the manufacturers of a product based on their market share at the time the plaintiff's cause of action arose

True or False

1. ____ The three theories of recovery used in product liability cases are negligence, breach of warranty, and strict product liability.

2. ____ The abolition of the privity limitation opened the door for claims under strict product liability.

3. ____ To bring a successful negligence case for failure to warn, the plaintiff must demonstrate that the defendant knew or should have known that, without reasonable warning, the product would be dangerous in its normal use or in any reasonable foreseeable use.

4. ____ If a plaintiff fails to act reasonably, the defendant in a product liability case can use the plaintiff's failure as a defense.

5. ____ The statute of repose is used by a defendant in a product liability case to demonstrate that his negligent behavior was reasonable, given the available scientific knowledge existing at the time the product was sold or reproduced.

6. ____ The Uniform Commercial Code provides the basis for recovery against a manufacturer or seller on the basis of breach of warranty.

7. ____ Strict liability is applied most frequently to malpractice cases.

8. ____ The three rules used by states to define the parameters of an accountant's liability to third parties is the Ultramares Doctrine (stating that accountants are liable to those in privity with the accountant), the law in the Restatement of Torts (extending liability to those known to be relying on the accountant's work), and reasonable foreseeability (which further extends liability to those who could reasonable be foreseen as relying on the accountant's work

Multiple Choice

1. Which of the following is NOT a negligent action leading to product liability cases?

a. negligent failure to warn
b. negligent testing or failure to test
c. negligent manufacturing
d. none of the above (all lead to product liability cases)

2. Which of the following is a defense available to defendants in a product liability case?

a. state-of-the-art defense
b. modified comparative negligence
c. statute of limitations
d. all of the above

3. Which of the following types of warranties provide the basis for a product liability action?

a. implied warranty of merchantability
b. warranty of consideration for private use
c. warranty of extraordinary use
d. both a and b

4. Teresa was thinking about buying a trampoline for her daughter, who weighed 125 pounds. Teresa asked the seller if the trampoline would safely support her daughter, and the seller said that the trampoline would support up to 150 pounds. After buying the trampoline, Teresa's daughter was injured when the trampoline collapsed while the daughter was playing on it. Teresa can bring a product liability action against the seller on the basis of

a. implied warranty of fitness
b. breach of an express warranty
c. warranty of ordinary use
d. all of the above

5. Sarah was injured when reasonably using a product. When she spoke to a lawyer about filing a product liability case against the manufacturer of the product, her lawyer pointed out a disclaimer written in small print on the bottom of the product. Sarah protested that she never saw the disclaimer. The defendant's use of this disclaimer as a defense

a. will limit the defendant's liability
b. is of no significance in this case
c. will most likely be rejected by the court
d. will force Sarah to drop her case

6. To succeed in a strict liability action, the plaintiff must prove that

a. the product was defective when sold
b. the defective composition rendered the product unreasonable dangerous
c. the product was the cause of the plaintiff's injury
d. all of the above

7. You are jogging on a street when a passing car's brakes fail. You are hit by this car and sustain a variety of injuries. You

a. have no claim against anyone involved in the accident
b. can bring a claim against the seller of the defective automobile
c. can recover damages through bystander liability
d. both b and c

8. Assumption of the risk and product misuse are defenses that can be used in

a. negligence-based actions
b. strict liability actions
c. both a and b
d. none of the above

Short Answer

1. What are the standards that a good must meet to reach the standard of merchantability?

2. What two tests are used to determine whether a product is so defective as to be unreasonably dangerous? Define these tests. How are these tests different?

CHAPTER 14
LAW OF PROPERTY: REAL, PERSONAL, AND INTELLECTUAL

This chapter introduces you to laws regulating and protecting various forms of property. To further your understanding of this important area in the legal environment of business, we will provide you with some more critical thinking exercises. Then, we conclude with objective questions.

A.   More Critical Thinking

We'll begin by returning to the *Qualitex v. Jacobson* case, which was briefly mentioned in your primary text's discussion of trademarks. Read the case excerpt below before answering the following critical thinking questions.

Qualitex Company v. Jacobson Products Company
United States Supreme Court
1995

For years, the plaintiff, Qualitex Company, colored the dry-cleaning press pads it manufactured a special shade of green-gold. When Jacobson Products, a competitor, started coloring its pads the same shade of green-gold, Qualitex sued Jacobson Products for trademark infringement. The defendant challenged the legitimacy of the trademark, arguing that color alone could not be registered as a trademark.

The district court found in favor of the plaintiff, but the Ninth Circuit reversed, holding that color alone could not be registered as a trademark. The plaintiff appealed to the U.S. Supreme Court.

Justice Breyer
The Lanham Act gives a seller or producer the exclusive right to "register" a trademark, to prevent his or her competitors from using that trademark. Both the language of the Act and the basic underlying principles of trademark law would seem to include color within the universe of things that can qualify as a trademark. The language of the Lanham Act describes that universe in the broadest of terms. It says that trademarks "include[d] any word, name, symbol, or device, or any combination thereof." Since human beings might use as a "symbol" or "device" almost anything at all that is capable of carrying meaning, this language, read literally, is not restrictive. The courts and the Patent and Trademark Office has [*sic*] authorized for use as a mark a particular shape (of a Coca-Cola bottle), a particular sound (of NBC's three chimes) and even a particular scent (of plumeria blossoms or sewing thread). If a shape, a sound, and a fragrance can act as symbols why, one might ask, can a color not do the same?

A color is also capable of satisfying the more important part of the statutory definition of a trademark, which requires that a person "us[e]" or "inten[d] to use" the mark

To identify and distinguish his or her goods, including a unique product, from those manufactured or sold by others and to indicate the source of the goods, even if that source is unknown.

True, a product's color is unlike "fanciful," "arbitrary," or "suggestive" words or designs, which almost automatically tell a customer that they refer to a brand. The imaginary word "Suntost," or the words "Suntost Marmalade," on a jar of orange jam immediately would signal a brand or a product "source"; the jam's orange color does not do so. But, over time, customers may come to treat a particular color on a product or its packaging (say, a color that in context seems unusual such as pink on a firm's insulating material or red on the head of a large industrial bolt) as signifying a brand. And, if so, that color would have come to identify and distinguish the goods—i.e., "to indicate" their "source"—much in the way that descriptive words on a product (say, "Trim" on nail clippers or "CarFreshener" on deodorizer) can come to indicate a product's origin. In this circumstance, trademark law says that the word (e.g., "Trim"), although not inherently distinctive, has developed "secondary meaning." ("Secondary meaning" is acquired when "in the minds of the public, the primary significance of a product feature ... is to identify the source of the product rather than the product itself"). Again, one might ask, if trademark law permits a descriptive word with secondary meaning to act as a mark, why would it not permit a color, under similar circumstances, to do the same?

It would seem, then, that color alone, at least sometimes, can meet the basic legal requirements for use as a trademark. It can act as a symbol that distinguishes a firm's goods and identifies their source, without serving any other significant function. The green-gold color acts as a symbol. Having developed secondary meaning (for customers identified the green-gold color as Qualitex's), it identifies the press pads' source. And, the green-gold color serves no other function. Accordingly, unless there is some special reason that convincingly militates against the use of color alone as a trademark, trademark law would protect Qualitex's use of the green-gold color on its press pads.

Respondent Jacobson Products says that there are four special reasons why the law should forbid the use of color alone as a trademark. We shall explain why we find them unpersuasive.

Jacobson says that, if the law permits the use of color as a trademark, it will produce uncertainty and unresolvable court disputes about what shades of a color a competitor may lawfully use. Because lighting will affect perceptions of protected color, competitors and courts will suffer from "shade confusion" as they try to decide whether use of a similar color on a similar product does, or does not, confuse customers and thereby infringe on a trademark.

We do not believe that color, in this respect, is special. Courts traditionally decide quite difficult questions about whether two words or phrases or symbols are sufficiently similar, in context, to confuse buyers. They have had to compare, for example, such words as "Bonamine" and "Dramamine" (motion-sickness remedies); "Huggies" and "Dougies" (diapers); "Cheracol" and "Syrocol" (cough syrup); "Cyclone" and "Tornado" (wire fences); and "mattres" and "1-800-mattres" (mattress franchisor telephone numbers). Legal standards exist to guide courts in making such comparisons. We do not see why courts could not apply those standards to a color, replicating, if necessary, lighting conditions under which a colored product is normally sold. Indeed, courts already have done so in cases where a trademark consists of a color plus a design, i.e., a colored symbol such as a gold stripe (around a sewer pipe), a yellow strand of wire rope, or a "brilliant yellow" band (on ampules).

Jacobson argues that colors are in limited supply. If one of many competitors can appropriate a particular color for use as a trademark, and each competitor then tries to do the same, the supply of colors will soon be depleted.

This argument is unpersuasive, however, largely because it relies on an occasional problem to justify a blanket prohibition. When a color serves as a mark, normally alternative colors will likely be available for similar use by others. Moreover, if that is not so—if a "color depletion" or "color scarcity" problem does arise—the trademark doctrine of "functionality" normally would seem available to prevent the anticompetitive consequences that Jacobson's argument posits.

The functionality doctrine forbids the use of a product's feature as a trademark where doing so will put a competitor at a significant disadvantage because the feature is "essential to the use or purpose of the article" or "affects [its] cost or quality." For example, this Court has written that competitors might be free to copy the color of a medical pill where that color serves to identify the kind of medication (e.g., a type of blood medicine) in addition to its source. And, the federal courts have demonstrated that they can apply this doctrine in a careful and reasoned manner, with sensitivity to the effect on competition. Lower courts have permitted competitors to copy the green color of farm machinery (because customers wanted their farm equipment to match) and have barred the use of black as a trademark on outboard boat motors (because black has the special functional attributes of decreasing the apparent size of the motor and ensuring compatibility with many different boat colors).

Where a color serves a significant nontrademark function, courts will examine whether its use as a mark would permit one competitor (or a group) to interfere with legitimate (nontrademark-related) competition through actual or potential exclusive use of an important product ingredient. That examination should not discourage firms from creating aesthetically pleasing mark designs, for it is open to their competitors to do the same. But, ordinarily, it should prevent the anticompetitive consequences of Jacobson's hypothetical "color depletion" argument, when, and if, the circumstances of a particular case threaten "color depletion."

Jacobson points to many older cases—including Supreme Court cases—in support of its position. These Supreme Court cases, however, interpreted trademark law as it existed before 1946, when Congress enacted the Lanham Act. The Lanham Act significantly changed and liberalized the common law to "dispense with more technical prohibitions," most notably, by permitting trademark registration of descriptive words (say, "U-Build-It" model airplanes) where they had acquired "secondary meaning." The Lanham Act extended protection to descriptive marks by making clear that (with certain explicit exceptions not relevant here), "Nothing ... shall prevent the registration of a mark used by the applicant which has become distinctive of the applicant's goods in commerce." This language permits an ordinary word, normally used for a nontrademark purpose (e.g., description), to act as a trademark where it has gained "secondary meaning." Its logic would appear to apply to color as well.

Jacobson argues that there is no need to permit color alone to function as a trademark because a firm already may use color as part of a trademark, say, as a colored circle or colored letter or colored word. This argument begs the question. One can understand why a firm might find it difficult to place a usable symbol or word on a product and, in such instances, a firm might want to use color, pure and simple, instead of color as part of a design.

Reversed in favor of Plaintiff, Qualitex Company.

   a. What reasons did Jacobson give for disallowing the use of colors as trademarks?

   b. How does the Court rebut each of these reasons?

   c. What primary ethical norm is elevated by the Court's decision?

1.   Now, let's sharpen our critical thinking skills by applying them to the following argument about land rights.

I thought this was a free country. Apparently, I was wrong. Federal administrative agencies have recently trampled on citizens' property rights by telling them how they are allowed to use their land. I ask you, my fellow citizens, "How can we be free if we lack the freedom to decide what to do with our own property?"

Take the United States Fish and Wildlife Service for example. All of the rules and regulations on the treatment of endangered species that they have passed have stolen land from citizens. Now, people cannot build homes on their land or even farm their land in some instances because the land qualifies as potential habitat for an endangered species. Such regulation is insane. It takes away possible uses of the property, which in turn makes the land less valuable on the market. In this sense, property owners are punished for circumstances beyond their control.

It is absolutely ridiculous for us to implement policies that treat the well-being of a kangaroo rat as more important than those of human beings. Kangaroo rats don't pay taxes, but people do. I think the government should do a better job of looking out for the interests of its customers.

Everyone knows that the freedom to own property is of the utmost importance in a free society. If we are to remain free, we must shed these regulative shackles of tyranny placed on us by the federal government. Only when people are given the right to choose how to use what belongs to them will we be true to the ideals upon which our great nation was founded.

a. What are the issue and conclusion of this argument?

b. Look at the third paragraph. What analogy does the author implicitly make? How appropriate is this analogy?

c. What additional information would help you to assess the quality of this argument?

B. Learning the Basics

Matching

1. ____ real property

    a. an irrevocable right to use some portion of another's land for a specific purpose

2. ____ fixture

    b. promises by the owner, generally included in the deed, to use or not to use the land in particular ways

3. ____ fee simple absolute

    c. item that is initially a piece of personal property but is later attached permanently to the realty and is treated a part of the realty

4. ____ conditional estate

    d. the exclusive legal right to reproduce, publish, and sell the fixed form of expression of an original creative idea

5. ____ easement

    e. grants the holder the exclusive right to produce, sell, and use a product, process, invention, or machine for a fixed period

6. ____ adverse possession

    f. the right to own and possess the land, subject to a condition whose happening will terminate the estate

7. ____ restrictive covenants

    g. the right to own and possess the land against all other, without conditions

8. ____ trademark

    h. acquiring ownership of realty by openly treating it as one's own, with neither protest nor permission from the real owner, for a statutorily established period of time

9. ____ patent

    i. land and everything permanently attached to it

10. ____ copyright

    j. a distinctive mark, word, design, picture, or arrangement used by the producer of a product that tends to cause consumers to identify the product with the producer

True or False

1. ____ The fair use doctrine is a case against a charge of copyright infringement.

2. ____ There is no protection for intellectual property outside this country.

3. ____ A free-standing coffeemaker is an example of real property while a built-in coffeemaker is personal property.

4. ____ When most people talk about owning property, they usually have in mind a conditional estate.

5. ____ The two types of deeds that are used to transfer ownership of property are a general warranty deed and a quitclaim deed.

6. ____ Communities place restrictions on the use of property through zoning laws.

7. ____ For a valid gift to occur, the following elements must occur: delivery, consideration, and acceptance.

8. ____ When one party transfers possession of personal property to another to be used in an agreed-upon manner for an agreed-upon time period, this relationship is called a bailment.

9. ____ One who has a leasehold is entitled to exclude all others, including the property owner, for the period of the lease.

10. ___ Under the Trade Related Aspects of International Property Rights (TRIPS) treaty, a nation may issue compulsory licenses to force production of a patented product.

Multiple Choice

1. Which of the following considerations in a trademark infringement case was eliminated by the Federal Trademark Dilution Act of 1995?

a. the strength of the senior user's mark
b. the goodwill of the junior user
c. the likelihood of consumer confusion
d. none of the above

2. Which is NOT a criterion for a work to receive a copyright?

a. it must be set out in a tangible medium of expression
b. it must be original
c. it must be creative
d. none of the above

3. If I create a new invention, I can protect my invention

a. with a patent
b. as a trade secret
c. through either a or b
d. none of the above

4. Ownership of land includes

a. water rights
b. mineral rights
c. both a and b
d. none of the above

5. Which of the following statements is true regarding life estates?

a. A life estate is the present right to possess and own land in the future.
b. The use of a life estate may be more restricted than that of a fee simple absolute.
c. both a and b
d. none of the above

6. An easement may arise through

a. express agreement
b. prescription
c. necessity
d. all of the above

7. In order to transfer property, the owner must follow the proper procedures. Which of the following are the steps of voluntary transfer of real property?

a. execution, delivery, acceptance, and recording
b. offer, acceptance, delivery, recording
c. execution, offer, delivery, and acceptance
d. acceptance, execution, conveyance, and specification

8. For twenty years, John has been living in a house he built on a piece of land that he believed he owned. However, the real owner recently sent John a letter stating that John owed him money for living on his land for twenty years. John will probably not have to pay the real owner because of

a. adverse possession
b. a restrictive covenant
c. condemnation
d. zoning

9. Condemnation is a process that may occur because

a. an owner has misused the land
b. the government can exercise its right of eminent domain
c. the owner enters into restrictive covenants
d. it advocates a private interest

10. Which of the following is NOT a type of co-ownership?

a. tenancy in common
b. joint tenancy
c. executed tenancy
d. tenancy in the entirety

Short Answer

1. How are trade secrets and patents similar and different?

2. The government may constitutionally exercise eminent domain to take private property for a public purpose. Why is "public purpose" ambiguous?

This chapter introduced you to agency law, the body of statutes regulating relationships in which one person acts on another's behalf. To review the chapter, we'll start by giving you some extra critical thinking exercises and then conclude with matching, true-false, multiple choice, and short answer questions.

A.   *More Critical Thinking*

1. Here is a Supreme Court case that clarifies an employer's liability when one of its employees allegedly sexually harasses other employees.

FARAGHER v. CITY OF BOCA RATON
1998

JUSTICE SOUTER:

Between 1985 and 1990, . . . petitioner Beth Ann Faragher worked part time and during the summers as an ocean lifeguard for the Marine Safety Section of the Parks and Recreation Department of respondent, the City of Boca Raton, Florida (City). During this period, Faragher's immediate supervisors were Bill Terry, David Silverman, and Robert Gordon. In June 1990, Faragher resigned.

In 1992, Faragher brought an action against Terry, Silverman, and the City, asserting that Terry and Silverman created a "sexually hostile atmosphere" at the beach[.] The complaint contained specific allegations that Terry once said that he would never promote a woman to the rank of lieutenant, and that Silverman had said to Faragher, "Date me or clean the toilets for a year." Asserting that Terry and Silverman were agents of the City, and that their conduct amounted to discrimination in the "terms, conditions, and privileges" of her employment, Faragher sought a judgment against the City for nominal damages, costs, and attorney's fees.

The District Court ruled that there were three justifications for holding the City liable for the harassment of its supervisory employees. First, the court noted that the harassment was pervasive enough to support an inference that the City had "knowledge, or constructive knowledge" of it. Next, it ruled that the City was liable under traditional agency principles because Terry and Silverman were acting as its agents when they committed the harassing acts. Finally, the court observed that Gordon's knowledge of the harassment, combined with his inaction, "provides a further basis for imputing liability on [sic] the City."

A panel of the Court of Appeals reversed the judgment against the City. Although the panel had "no trouble concluding that Terry's and Silverman's conduct . . . was severe and pervasive enough to create an objectively abusive work environment," it overturned the District Court's conclusion that the City was liable. The panel ruled that Terry and Silverman were not acting within the scope of their employment when they engaged in the harassment, that they were not aided in their actions by the agency relationship, and that the City had no constructive knowledge of the harassment by virtue of its pervasiveness or Gordon's actual knowledge.

A "master is subject to liability for the torts of his servants committed while acting in the scope of their employment." This doctrine has traditionally defined the "scope of employment" as including conduct "of the kind [a servant] is employed to perform," occurring "substantially within the authorized time and space limits," and "actuated, at least in part, by a purpose to serve the master," but as excluding an intentional use of force "unexpectable by the master."

Courts of Appeals have typically held, or assumed, that conduct similar to the subject of this complaint falls outside the scope of employment. For this reason, courts have likened hostile environment sexual harassment to the classic "frolic and detour" for which an employer has no vicarious liability.

The proper analysis here . . . calls not for a mechanical application of indefinite and malleable factors set forth in the Restatement [of Agency], but rather an enquiry [sic] into the reasons that would support a conclusion that harassing behavior ought to be held within the scope of a supervisor's employment, and the reasons for the opposite view.

We . . . agree with Faragher that in implementing [the statute outlawing sexual harassment] it makes sense to hold an employer vicariously liable for some tortious conduct of a supervisor made possible by abuse of his supervisory authority, and that the aided-by-agency-relation principle embodied in § 219(2)(d) of the Restatement provides an appropriate starting point for determining liability for the kind of harassment presented here. Several courts, indeed, have noted what Faragher has argued, that there is a sense in which a harassing supervisor is always assisted in his misconduct by the supervisory relationship.

The agency relationship affords contact with an employee subjected to a supervisor's sexual harassment, and the victim may well be reluctant to accept the risks of blowing the whistle on a superior. When a person with supervisory authority discriminates in the terms and conditions of subordinates' employment, his actions necessarily draw upon his superior position over the people who report to him, or those under them, whereas an employee generally cannot check a supervisor's abusive conduct the same way that she might deal with abuse from a coworker. When a fellow employee harasses, the victim can walk away or tell the offender where to go, but it may be difficult to offer such responses to a supervisor, whose "power to supervise -- [which may be] to hire and fire, and to set work schedules and pay rates -- does not disappear...when he chooses to harass through insults and offensive gestures rather than directly with threats of firing or promises of promotion." Recognition of employer liability when discriminatory misuse of supervisory authority alters the terms and conditions of a victim's employment is underscored by the fact that the employer has a greater opportunity to guard against misconduct by supervisors than by common workers; employers have greater opportunity and incentive to screen them, train them, and monitor their performance.

We believe that the judgment of the Court of Appeals must be reversed. The District Court found that the degree of hostility in the work environment rose to the actionable level and was attributable to Silverman and Terry. It is undisputed that these supervisors "were granted virtually unchecked authority" over their subordinates, "directly controlling and supervising all aspects of [Faragher's] day-to-day activities." It is also clear that Faragher and her colleagues were "completely isolated from the City's higher management." The City did not seek review of these findings.

The judgment of the Court of Appeals for the Eleventh Circuit is **reversed**, and the case is remanded for reinstatement of the judgment of the District Court.

   a. What is the issue in this case? Remember, issues are stated in question form.

   b. What is the relevant rule of law? What important word or phrase in this rule is ambiguous?

   c. What reasons does the Court give for holding employers liable for harassing acts of supervisors?

   2. Now, test your ability to critically evaluate an argument by reading and assessing the following argument on different types of agency relationships.

The only agency relationships that the courts should recognize are those created by agreement. Agency relationships are like contracts. There must be a meeting of the minds in order for a contract to be valid, and this standard ought also to apply to agency relationships.

Agency relationships created by implied authority, ratification, or estoppel all originate with either an ambiguous agreement or a false statement. In the first instance, the ambiguity surrounding the agreement prevents both parties from knowing if there has been a meeting of the minds. This situation may be likened to two people who speak different languages negotiating a contract. Each will never know if the other is willing to grant her desires.

The second scenario violates a notion that civilized human beings hold very dear: that we should tell the truth. By allowing agency relationships that began with one party's telling a lie, we encourage dishonesty. People are motivated to lie about their agency relationships out of hope that the other party will accept the lie. It's the same as telling all of your friends that you are engaged to someone in order to pressure that person into accepting your proposal for marriage.

Finally, by allowing such relationships the opportunity to become legally valid, we are merely opening the door for more lawsuits. Our courts' dockets are already full; we should work to reduce the courts' workload, not to increase it. To create a better society, we must treat agency relationships like other contracts.

   a. The author of this passage relies heavily on analogies in his reasoning. Locate these analogies and evaluate how reasonable they are. (Remember, the way to evaluate an analogy is to state ways in which the two things being compared are similar, and then to state ways in which they are different.)

   b. What is the author's conclusion and with what reasons does he support it?

   c. What is the evidence for these reasons?

   d. Is there any additional information that would aid you in your task of evaluating this argument?

   e. What ethical norm is the driving force behind this argument?

B. *Learning the Basics*

Matching

1. ____ agency

a. legal bar to either alleging or denying a fact because of one's previous words or actions to the contrary

2. ____ apparent authority

b. doctrine imposing liability on a principal for torts committed by an agent who is employed by the principal and is subject to the principal's control

3. ____ estoppel

c. relationship in which the agent is hired by the principal to do a specific job but is not controlled with respect to physical conduct or details of work performance

4. ____ principal-agent relationship

d. relationship formed through oral or written agreement

5. ____ employer-employee relationship

e. relationship in which the principal gives the agent expressed or actual authority to act on the former's behalf

6. ____ employer-independent contractor relationship

f. obligation of the principal to reimburse the agent for any losses the agent incurs while acting on the principal's behalf

7. ____ indemnity

g. fiduciary relationship between two parties in which one part acts on behalf of the other and is subject to the control and consent of the other

8. ____ respondeat superior

h. relationship in which an agent who works for pay and is subject to the control of the principal may enter into contracts on the latter's behalf

9. ____ expressed agency

    i. relationship in which the principal is estopped from denying that someone is her agent after leading a third party to believe the person is her agent

10. ____ implied authority

    j. relationship in which customs and authority circumstances, rather than a detailed formal agreement, determine the agent's authority

True or False

1. ____   Minors are unable to act as agents.

2. ____   According to the Statute of Frauds, all agency agreements must be in writing.

3. ____   An agent is required to carry out only reasonable and lawful instructions of his principal.

4. ____   In undisclosed principal-agent relationships, both the principal and the agent are liable to the third party with whom they contract.

5. ____   Principals may be held liable for any torts committed by their agents.

6. ____   A legal doctrine used to establish an agency relationship is called a power of attorney.

7. ____   Agents are not allowed to employ or discharge employees unless they are explicitly given power to do so in their contracts.

8. ____   Even if an agent lies about his representing a principal, that relationship may become legally valid.

9. ____   If a principal breaks his duty of cooperation, the agent may sue for breach of contract.

10. ____   Agency law is uniform across national boundaries.

Multiple Choice

1. Which of the following is NOT a method through which an agency relationship may be formed?

    a. implied authority
    b. respondeat superior
    c. expressed authority
    d. apparent authority

2. Which of the following is NOT a duty owed by a principal to an agent?

    a. estoppel
    b. safe working conditions
    c. compensation
    d. cooperation

3. The duties of an agent to her principal are loyalty, obedience, performance, and _____.

    a. compensation.
    b. safe working conditions.
    c. accounting
    d. estoppel.

4. What is a question that a court will answer in order to determine whether an agent is acting within the scope of her employment when she committed a tort?

    a. Was the agent acting in the principal's interest?
    b. Was the identity of the principal identified?
    c. Was the agent authorized by the principal to be where she was at the time of the commission of the tort?
    d. both a and c

5. Who may terminate a principal-agent relationship?

    a. only the principal
    b. only the agent
    c. either party
    d. both parties must agree to terminate the relationship

6. Which of the following is NOT a condition upon which a principal-agent relationship may be terminated by law?

a. bankruptcy of the principal
b. bankruptcy of the agent
c. death of either party
d. insanity of either party

7. Occurs when a person misrepresents himself or herself as an agent and the principal accepts the unauthorized act.

a. estoppel
b. agency by implied authority
c. a material mistake of fact
d. agency by ratification

8. I am authorized by Tom Snooze, a well-known actor, to negotiate a contract to purchase a pig farm. The party with whom I am negotiating knows that I represent someone, but he does not know who. What kind of principal is Mr. Snooze?

a. disclosed principal
b. undisclosed principal
c. partially disclosed principal
d. none of the above

9. Principals can be liable for criminal acts of their agents when

a. the criminal acts are only misdemeanors.
b. the criminal acts are first degree felonies
c. the principal had reason to know that the acts were taking place
d. none of the above

10. If Freddy Falcon hires me to build him a nest, but has no authority over the details of the construction, what kind of relationship exists?

a. principal-agent relationship
b. principal-independent contractor relationship
c. employer-employee relationship
d. estopped agency relationship

Short Answer

1. Explain a relationship between principal-agent relationships and employer-independent contractor relationships.

2. Explain a problem with the following statement: "Principals should never be held liable for the actions of their agents. After all, the agent, not the principal, is the one who committed the crime."

CHAPTER 16
LAW AND BUSINESS ASSOCIATIONS

This chapter provides an introduction to different forms of business associations and how the different forms are treated legally. To deepen your understanding of these important topics, we have provided additional critical thinking exercises, as well as a section of objective questions.

A. *More Critical Thinking*

1. Chapter 16 of your primary text discusses the fiduciary duty that directors and managers owe to the shareholders. Do these agents also owe a fiduciary duty to their employees? The following case examines this issue. It also provides more critical thinking practice. To test your critical thinking ability, read the opinion and answer the questions that follow.

SAFFORD v. PAINEWEBBER, INC.
1990

JUDGE FELDMAN

Plaintiff Charles Safford was employed by defendant PaineWebber as an investment executive and stock broker [.] After his termination from employment, plaintiff was investigated by the Chicago Board of Options Exchange. The investigation was allegedly prompted by defendant's statements on the "U-5 form" that it sent to the National Association of Securities Dealers. As a result of the investigation, the C.B.O.E. accepted an offer of settlement in a letter dated May 4, 1987, in which plaintiff agreed to a five day suspension. On September 4, 1987, plaintiff filed suit in state court against F. J. Schultz, plaintiff's former superior at PaineWebber, alleging that he made defamatory statements about plaintiff during the investigation to the effect that plaintiff was involved in child pornography and that he was having an affair with his former secretary. . . .

Upset by the circumstances of his resignation from PaineWebber and the investigation by the C.B.O.E., plaintiff filed this suit against PaineWebber... alleging several theories of recovery. Plaintiff claims that defendant made false accusations in the U-5 form which are defamatory and constitute an invasion of privacy; that defendant intentionally and negligently breached a fiduciary duty owed to plaintiff to insure that he was in compliance with all relevant securities regulations; that the actions taken by defendant constitute an unfair trade practice; and that defendant is jointly and solidarily liable with F. J.

Schultz for his defamatory statements about pornography and sexual misconduct. . . . PaineWebber now moves for summary judgment.

Plaintiff's second claim is that defendant breached its fiduciary duty to plaintiff to supervise and insure that he was in compliance with all applicable securities regulations. Defendant seeks summary judgment on plaintiff's breach of fiduciary duty claim on the ground that defendant owed plaintiff no fiduciary duty.

A fiduciary in Louisiana is "a person holding the character of a trustee, or a character analogous to that of a trustee, with respect to the trust and confidence involved in it and the scrupulous good faith and candor which it requires." One is said to act in a fiduciary capacity when the business which he transacts "is not his own or for his own benefit, but for the benefit of another person, as to whom he stands in a relation implying and necessitating great confidence and trust on the one part and a high degree of good faith on the other part."

Defendant argues that there is no support in the law for a fiduciary duty owed by an employer to an employee. The Court agrees. Plaintiff maintains that defendant's fiduciary duty to plaintiff arises out of its statutory obligation to oversee plaintiff's compliance with federal regulations, but the cases cited by plaintiff do not support this contention. For instance, *Plaquemines Par. Com'n Council v. Delta Development Co., Inc.* refers only to the duties owed by public officers to the public and by attorneys to their clients; it does not support the notion that an employer owes a fiduciary duty to its employees. Nor does *ODECO v. Nunez* impose a fiduciary duty here. In that case, the defendant acted in conflict with his employer by forming his own company and using his position with his employer to enhance his private business. After noting that an employee has a duty not to act contrary to the business interest of his employer, the court held that the employee had breached his contractual duty of fidelity and loyalty to his employer. Finally, *United Companies Mtg. v. Estate of McGee* establishes only that an intermediary who negotiates a transaction between two parties is held to a fiduciary obligation to perform his duties faithfully for both parties.

The relationship between the disputants in this case is not similar to those relationships found in the case literature mentioned which give rise to fiduciary obligations. PaineWebber may have a statutory obligation to safeguard its employees' compliance with the relevant securities regulations, but that obligation does not have the characteristics of a fiduciary duty. PaineWebber is not in a unique position of trust, as is a public official or an attorney, nor is it acting for the benefit of plaintiff so that it must be faithful to plaintiff's financial or business interests. Plaintiff himself is obligated to comply with all securities regulations. Indeed, if PaineWebber has any duty, it would seem to run in favor of those agencies charged with supervision of the securities industry.

Because plaintiff has failed to establish that defendant owed him a fiduciary duty, defendant's motion for summary judgment must be granted as a matter of law on plaintiff's claim for breach of fiduciary duty.

    a. What facts are especially powerful in shaping the court's reasoning?

    b. What is the relevant rule of law cited by the court?

    c. What evidence does the plaintiff provide to support his case? How does the court react to this evidence? Is the court's reaction an example of good critical thinking?

  2. Now, critically evaluate this argument about corporations.

Corporations should be outlawed. They have harmed our society in far more ways than they have helped it. After all, we have corporations to thank for all of the sweatshops, old-boy networks, and underpaid workers. And let's not forget about the pollution. It's always those big chemical corporations and industrial plants that are filling the air we breathe and the water we drink with pollutants. It's a miracle that our life expectancy is greater than fifty years!

Just look at what corporations today do. They put poisonous products on the market, and then use million-dollar marketing schemes to trick the public into buying them. Take cigarettes for example. For decades, the big tobacco corporations have been lying to the public and paying off our government officials. They've invested millions into covering up the fact that cigarettes kill. Hundreds of thousands of innocent Americans have died because of the lengths to which these corporations have gone just to make money.

Additionally, corporations don't know how to treat their workers. A recent survey showed that workers at corporations were five times as unhappy as were sole proprietors. Another study demonstrated that 87 percent of on-the-job accidents happened to people who worked at corporations. If we'd just get rid of these corporations, Americans would be much safer at work.

We don't have these kinds of problems with partnerships or sole proprietorships. When's the last time you've heard of a small "mom & pop" store that severely polluted the environment or killed people with its products?

Furthermore, the capitalist ideas that our economy is built upon do not support corporations. Capitalism is based upon the idea that all competing businesses will be "mom & pop" stores. Even the founder of capitalism stated that he didn't trust businessmen, and that in order for his ideas to work, the businesses would have to be small.

Our founding fathers would probably roll over in their graves if they knew that our country is being run by these large corporations. It's time that we return to the ideas on which our economy is based. All businesses should be either sole proprietorships or partnerships. The time has come for corporations to join the ranks of the dinosaurs.

   a. What reasons does the author give for his conclusion?

   b. What important information is omitted from the author's reasoning?

   c. What reasonable alternative conclusions might a reader draw from these reasons?

   d. How persuasive is the author's evidence?

B. Learning the Basic

Matching

1. ____ corporation

    a. business whose stock is traded on at least one national securities exchange

2. ____ common stock

    b. ownership in a corporation that gives the owner special preferences related to dividends or the distribution of assets

3. ____ winding-up

    c. prevents corporate officers, directors, and agents from taking advantage of opportunities that should belong to the business.

4. ____ preferred stock

    d. treated legally as a single "person"

5. ____ fiduciary duty

e. ownership in a corporation that entitles its owner to vote for the corporation's board of directors, to receive dividends, and to receive net assets upon liquidation of the corporation

6. ____ corporate opportunity doctrine

f. business that does not restrict its operations to a single country

7. ____ closely held corporation

g. obligation placed on parties who control the property of other parties

8. ____ publicly held corporation

h. states that corporate officers and directors are not liable for honest mistakes that arose from business judgment

9. ____ business judgment rule

i. business whose stock is not traded nationally, but is held by a small group of people

10. ____ multinational

j. process of completing all unfinished transactions paying off debts, dividing remaining profits, and distributing assets before a partnership dies

True or False

1. ____   All partnerships must originate with a written agreement.

2. ____   The laws governing closely held corporations are identical to the laws governing publicly held corporations.

3. ____   Debentures are long-term corporate loans secured by a lien or mortgage on corporate assets

4. ____   The proxy system provides managers with a greater degree of control over a corporation than they would have in its absence.

5. _____ Any time a transaction involving a conflict of interest occurs, the transaction will be voided.

6. _____ Corporations are created according to state, rather than federal, law.

7. _____ Both corporations and partnerships have perpetual existence.

8. _____ A corporation's officers and managers are responsible for the actual management and day-to-day operations of the corporation.

9. _____ The primary purpose of syndicates is to finance large purchases.

10. _____ Employees who receive stock options can trade their rights to the shares.

11. _____ Courts agree that franchisees who market on the internet are violating the territorial clauses of their franchise agreements.

Multiple Choice

1. Limited liability corporations

a. are taxed like publicly held corporations
b. are companies whose members are personally liable for all the debts, obligations, and liabilities of the LLC
c. are created by the delivery of articles of organization to the secretary of the state of the state of organization for filing, and comes into existence at the time of filing
d. none of the above

2. Carrie and Mike created a partnership called the Tiger Publishing Company. Stu invested in the company, but does not take part in its management functions. What kind of company is this?

a. publicly held corporation
b. general partnership
c. limited partnership
d. joint stock company

3.	The business form that is organized and operated like a corporation, but is taxed like a partnership is a

a.	publicly held corporation.
b.	limited liability limited partnership.
c.	Subchapter S corporation.
d.	professional corporation.

4.	Generally, the issuing corporation can buy _____ back for a prespecified amount.

a.	capital structure
b.	preferred stock
c.	stock options
d.	consideration

5.	The _____ own(s) a corporation.

a.	shareholders
b.	CEO
c.	Board of Directors
d.	managers

6.	In which of the following business forms are owners subject to full liability?

a.	corporations
b.	sole proprietorships
c.	general partnerships
d.	both b and c

7.	A _____ is a not-for-profit organization formed by individuals to market products.

a.	charity
b.	cooperative
c.	joint-stock company
d.	joint venture

8. According to the RMBCA, corporations are managed under the direction of the _____.

a. Board of Directors
b. preferred stockholders
c. CEO
d. both a and c

9. Which of the following is not a form of debt-financing?

a. notes
b. debentures
c. common stock
d. bonds

11. In _____ partnerships, the partners are not jointly and separately liable when a large judgment is found against the firm in a malpractice suit.

a. limited liability
b. limited liability limited
c. general
d. both a and b

Short Answer

1. Explain the differences between a limited liability corporation and a publicly held corporation.

2. What are three different kinds of preferred stock, and what are the differences among them?

CHAPTER 17

THE LAW OF ADMINISTRATIVE AGENCIES

This chapter introduces you to an especially important area of the law, administrative law. Federal administrative agencies create regulations that affect the operations of businesses in every industry. Hence, administrative law is of extreme importance to the business manager. We offer some additional critical thinking exercises and some objective questions to conclude your study of administrative law.

A. *More Critical Thinking*

1. The following case offers you an opportunity to critically evaluate the opinion of a federal judge in an administrative law case. Read the case with a critical eye, and answer the questions that follow.

HECLA MINING COMPANY v. UNITED STATES ENVIRONMENTAL PROTECTION AGENCY; THOMAS P. DUNNE, ADMINISTRATOR
1993

JUDGE FERGUSON:

This case is a challenge brought pursuant to the Administrative Procedures Act (APA) by Hecla Mining Company (Hecla) to decisions of the Environmental Protection Agency (EPA) made pursuant to §§ 304(l)(1)(B) and (C) of the Clean Water Act. The district court dismissed the action. We affirm for the reason that the challenged decisions of the EPA do not constitute the final agency action which is necessary to state a cause of action under the Act.

Hecla operates the Lucky Friday Mine located along the Coeur d'Alene River in Idaho. In its mining process, toxic pollutants are discharged into the river.

The Clean Water Act prohibits the discharge of any pollutants from a point source unless the discharge complies with the terms of a National Pollutant Discharge Elimination Systems ("NPDES") permit. The EPA has granted authority to 39 states to issue these permits. Idaho is not one of them. The Clean Water Act was amended by the Water Quality Act of 1987, which placed greater emphasis on attaining state water quality standards. In order to attain water quality standards for toxic pollutants, § 304(1) requires states to submit to the EPA lists of, inter alia, (1) the state's navigable waters that, after the application of technology based controls, are not expected to meet prescribed water quality standards (the B list), and (2) those point sources discharging toxic pollutants that are responsible for impairing the achievement of water quality standards for the waters on List B (the C list).

The State of Idaho submitted its B and C lists to the EPA. Upon receipt of the lists, the EPA issued a proposed decision approving in part and disapproving in part the Idaho lists because they were under-inclusive. The EPA then initiated a 120-day public comment period regarding the possible addition of waters and point sources to the Idaho lists. The EPA, after the public comment period, issued a proposal to amend Idaho's B list to include the South Fork of the Coeur d'Alene River and include the Lucky Friday Mine on the C list. Following a public comment period on its proposal, the EPA issued a decision adding the river and the mine to the appropriate lists.

Hecla in this action contends that the EPA exceeded its authority when, after it approved Idaho's B and C lists, it unilaterally amended them. It contends that the decision of the EPA to include the South Fork of the Coeur d'Alene River and the Lucky Friday Mine on Idaho's lists is final agency action because the decisions are final. It asserts that the river and mine are on the lists and that is a final decision.

We hold that the decision to include the river and mine on the lists is not the final agency action necessary to state a cause of action under § 704 of the APA. Finality of an agency action turns on whether the action was a definitive statement of the agency's position, had a direct and immediate effect on the day-to-day business of the complaining party, had the status of law and whether immediate compliance with the decision is expected.

We concur with the Third and Fourth Circuits in concluding that EPA listing decisions do not constitute final agency action. Both circuits have held that listing decisions are merely preliminary steps in the § 304(l) process.

In this case, the final agency decision that will require action on the part of Hecla is the issuance of a final NPDES permit. Until such a permit is issued there is no definitive statement on the EPA's position and no rules are established with which immediate compliance is required. Administrative agency action that serves only to initiate proceedings does not have the status of law or a direct and immediate effect on the day to day business of the complaining party.

The judgment of the district court dismissing the action is affirmed.

    a. What ambiguous word or phrase is really the same as the issue of this case?

    b. For what reasons does this court uphold the judgment of the district court?

c. Evaluate these reasons.

2. An argument about formal and informal rulemaking follows. Read it and apply your critical thinking skills to it.

In order for our administrative agencies to be more effective, we ought to require them to use formal rulemaking. To continue to allow agencies to use the informal rulemaking process is to undermine the democratic principles that we hold so dear.

Representative democracy is based on the notion that our elected officials will represent the views of the people. When the ideas and opinions of the people are not expressed, or are expressed but then ignored, the ideal of representative democracy is not realized. In such instances, our form of government is more like an autocracy because the government is able to rule at its whim free of responsibility to the citizens.

Formal rulemaking requires a full public hearing in which the testimony is printed in an official transcript. It also requires the publication of formal findings. These features ensure that the agency will listen to the opinions of the people. Additionally, the printed records of testimony and factual findings guarantee the people an opportunity to make sure that the agency's reasoning in each decision is sound.

Informal rulemaking does not provide this guarantee that the agency's officials will be responsive to the public's desires. Informal rulemaking requires only the publication of the proposed rule in the Federal Register. Afterward, interested parties are able to submit written arguments for or against the rule. However, how can we be sure that the agency will adequately consider this written testimony? If the head of the agency disagrees with what you write, he may tell you that your letter "must have gotten lost in the mail." Clearly, it is too easy for agency officials to ignore the public in the process of informal rulemaking.

Many people argue that we should continue to allow informal rulemaking because it is more convenient to the agencies than formal rulemaking. Well, I suppose it would also be more convenient for the heads of the agencies to imprison people with ideas different from theirs. Ladies and gentlemen, isn't the preservation of our freedom in this democratic society worth a small inconvenience to federal agencies? Indeed it is, as anyone with an elementary understanding of democracy could tell you.

a. Which primary ethical norm is downplayed by this argument?

b. What reasons does the author give for rejecting informal rulemaking?

c. What are some problems with the author's evidence?

d. What additional information would be helpful in assessing the validity of the author's argument?

B. *Learning the Basics*

Matching

1. ____ procedural rule

    a. a rule that governs the internal processes of an administrative agency

2. ____ substantive rule

    b. combines some of the aspects of formal and informal rulemaking

3. ____ consent order

    c. a rule that creates, defines, or regulates the legal rights of administrative agencies and the parties they regulate

4. ____ executive power

    d. power delegated by Congress to an administrative agency to adjudicate cases through administrative proceedings

5. ____ judicial power

    e. any rule that directly or indirectly affects an administrative agency

6. ____ hybrid rulemaking

    f. an agreement by a business to stop an activity an administrative agency alleges to be unlawful and to accept the remedy the agency imposes

7. ____ exempted rulemaking

    g. proceeding that occurs when dealing with military and foreign affairs

8. ____ administrative law

h. the power delegated by Congress to an administrative agency to investigate whether the rules enacted by the agency have been properly followed by business and individuals

True or False

1. ____ The first step in informal rulemaking is publication of the proposed rule in the Federal Register, whereas the first step in informal rulemaking is formal hearing.

2. ____ The President of the United States can appoint and remove heads of independent administrative agencies.

3. ____ An enabling statue delegates to the agency congressional legislative power.

4. ____ Administrative law judges are assigned to specific administrative agencies.

5. ____ Congress has the power to terminate an agency.

6. ____ Exempted rulemaking is the most common form of rulemaking.

7. ____ A hearing before an administrative law judge resembles a judicial proceeding because there is a jury.

8. ____ If a losing party does not agree with an administrative law judge's decision, it may appeal to the full commission or to the head of an executive department.

9. ____ A city council could create an administrative agency.

10. ____ Administrative agencies can investigate potential violations of rules or statues because they have judicial power.

Multiple Choice

1.   The President of the United States

a.   appoints heads of executive agencies
b.   appoints heads of independent agencies
c.   both a and b
d.   none of the above

2.   The Administrative Procedure Act (APA)

a.   establishes the standards and procedures federal administrative agencies must follow in their rulemaking and adjudicative functions
b.   is the legislation that allows the creation of administrative agencies
c.   both a and b
d.   none of the above

3.   An executive administrative agency

a.   is located within a department of the executive branch of government
b.   can remove heads and appointed members at any time
c.   both a and b
d.   none of the above

4.   Administrative agencies perform the following function:

a.   rulemaking
b.   adjudication
c.   administrative activities
d.   all of the above

5.   Which of the following is NOT a reason for an appellate court to strike down agency regulations?

a.   constitutional delegation of legislative authority in the enabling act was too vague and not limited
b.   an act of agency was not approved by Congress
c.   an agency violated a constitutional standard
d.   an act of agency was beyond the scope of power granted to it by Congress

6.   Which of the following is NOT a reason for growth of administrative agencies?

a.   need for expertise
b.   prevention of overcrowding in courts

c.   expeditious solutions to national problems
d.   deregulation of industry

7.   The power of administrative agencies is limited by the executive branch through

a.   the power of the President to appoint heads of the agencies
b.   the power of the Office of Management and Budget to recommend a fiscal year budget for each agency
c.   both a and b
d.   none of the above

8.   If a party loses at the full-commission or agency-head level in an adjudicative proceeding and wishes to appeal, the party must

a.   publish its appeal in the Federal Register
b.   file a motion for appeal with the appropriate federal circuit court of appeals
c.   select an administrative law judge to hear the case
d.   none of the above

9.   State and local administrative agencies often have authority over

a.   workmen's compensation claims
b.   public universities
c.   zoning regulations
d.   all of the above

Short Answer

1.   Briefly identify each step in formal and informal rulemaking.

2.   What are the executive and legislative checks on administrative agencies?

CHAPTER 18
THE EMPLOYMENT RELATIONSHIP

A. *More Critical Thinking*

1. Read the following case and answer the questions that follow in order to polish your critical thinking skills.

METROPOLITAN STEVEDORE COMPANY v. JOHN RAMBO
1997

Respondent Rambo, injured while doing longshore work for petitioner Metropolitan Stevedore Company, received a compensation award under the Longshore and Harbor Workers' Compensation Act (LHWCA or Act), [because] he had sustained permanent partial disability. After Rambo acquired new skills as a longshore crane operator and began making about three times his pre-injury earnings, Metropolitan moved to modify his LHWCA award. Despite an absence of evidence that Rambo's physical condition had improved, the Administrative Law Judge (ALJ) ordered his benefits discontinued because of his increased earnings. The Benefits Review Board affirmed, but the Ninth Circuit reversed on the ground that LHWCA §22 authorizes modification of an award only for changed physical conditions. This Court in turn reversed in *Metropolitan Stevedore Co. v. Rambo*, holding that the Act's fundamental purpose is economic, to compensate employees for wage earning capacity lost because of injury; where that capacity has been reduced, restored, or improved, the basis for compensation changes and the statutory scheme allows for modification, even without any change in physical condition. On remand, the Ninth Circuit again reversed the order discontinuing compensation. . . . It held that the order discontinuing benefits was based on the ALJ's over-emphasis on Rambo's current status and failure to consider his permanent partial disability's effect on his future earnings, and remanded the case for entry of a nominal award.

JUSTICE SOUTER

The LHWCA authorizes compensation not for physical injury as such, but for economic harm to the injured worker from decreased ability to earn wages. The Act speaks of this economic harm as "disability," defined as the "incapacity because of injury to earn the wages which the employee was receiving at the time of injury in the same or any other employment."

We may summarize [the Act's] provisions and their implications this way. Disability is a measure of earning capacity lost as a result of work related injury. By distinguishing between the diminished capacity and the injury itself, and by defining capacity in relation both to the injured worker's old job and to

136

other employment, the statute makes it clear that disability is the product of injury and opportunities in the job market. Capacity, and thus disability, is not necessarily reflected in actual wages earned after injury, and when it is not, the fact finder under the Act must make a determination of disability that is "reasonable" and "in the interest of justice," and one that takes account of the disability's future effects.

The practical effect of denying any compensation to a disabled claimant on the ground that he is presently able to earn as much as (or more than) before his injury would run afoul of the Act's mandate to account for the future effects of disability in fashioning an award, since those effects would not be reflected in the current award and the one year statute of limitations for modification after denial of compensation would foreclose responding to such effects on a wait and see basis as they might arise. On the other hand, trying to honor that mandate by basing a present award on a comprehensive prediction of an inherently uncertain future would, as we have seen, almost always result in present over or under compensation. And it would be passing strange to credit Congress with the intent to guarantee fairness to employers and employees by a wait and see approach in most cases where future effects are imperfectly foreseeable, but to find no such intent in one class of cases, those in which wage earning ability does not immediately decline.

There is moreover an even more fundamental objection to Metropolitan's proposed options. They implicitly reject the very conclusion required to make sense of the combined provisions limiting claims and mandating consideration of future effects: that a disability whose substantial effects are only potential is nonetheless a present disability, albeit a presently nominal one. It is, indeed, this realization that points toward a way to employ the wait and see approach to provide for the future effects of disability when capacity does not immediately decline. It is simply "reasonable" and "in the interest of justice" (to use the language of §8(h)) to reflect merely nominal current disability with a correspondingly nominal award. Ordering nominal compensation holds open the possibility of a modified award if a future conjunction of injury, training, and employment opportunity should later depress the worker's ability to earn wages below the pre-injury level, turning the potential disability into an actual one. It allows full scope to the mandate to consider the future effects of disability, it promotes accuracy, it preserves administrative simplicity by obviating cumbersome inquiries relating to the entire range of possible future states of affairs, and it avoids imputing to Congress the unlikely intent to join a wait and see rule for most cases with a predict the future method when the disability results in no current decline in what the worker can earn.

Our view, as it turns out, coincides on this point with the position taken by the Director of the Office of Workers' Compensation Programs (OWCP), who is charged with the administration of the Act, and who also construes the Act as permitting nominal compensation as a mechanism for taking future effects of disability into account when present wage earning ability remains undiminished. The Secretary of Labor has delegated the bulk of her statutory authority to administer and enforce the Act, including rulemaking power, to the Director, . . . and the Director's reasonable interpretation of the Act brings at least some added persuasive force to our conclusion[.]

We therefore hold that a worker is entitled to nominal compensation when his work related injury has not diminished his present wage earning capacity under current circumstances, but there is a significant potential that the injury will cause diminished capacity under future conditions.

We therefore **vacate the Ninth Circuit's judgment** insofar as it directs entry of an award of nominal compensation and remand for further proceedings consistent with this opinion.

     a. Which primary ethical norm(s) does the Court's decision support?

     b. What reasons does the Court give for allowing accident victims whose earnings are not harmed by their disability to continue collecting compensation?

     c. What missing information would help in our task of evaluating these reasons?

    2. Next, let's critically evaluate this argument about family leave.

It's about time that the United States gets with the program and guarantees new parents time away from work. The U.S. is the only major industrialized nation without some form of paid leave for new mothers or new fathers. We're behind the times, and we need to catch up.

Newborn children need a lot of care. Studies show that the amount of time that parents spend with their children during infancy has a profound effect on how the child turns out. Infants whose parents spend only minimal time with them tend to grow up to be poorly socialized, as well as a host of other problems. People with such psychological problems are generally very unproductive workers. In this sense, businesses have something to gain from giving parents time to spend with their children: good workers for the future. Additionally, very few jobs pay enough for parents to take much time off from work without pay. Many Americans live from one check to the next, and thus the Family Medical Leave Act does not help them. After all, what good does the right to unpaid leave do you if you need money?

We could learn a lot from Sweden. A Swedish mother and father are allowed to take off up to nine months of work between the two of them after a baby is born. Not only are their jobs protected while they are away from work, they also receive 90 percent of their usual wages during the time that they're away. The Swedish system shows that paid parental leave works, and it is a model for the United States to follow.

    a. What are the issue and conclusion of this argument?

    b. What significant words and phrases are ambiguous?

    c. What additional information would be helpful in evaluating the worth of the author's argument?

    d. Which primary ethical norm is elevated by this argument? Which is downplayed?

B. Learning the Basics

Matching

1. ____ workers' compensation laws

    a. occurs whenever an accident hospitalizes five or more workers or causes a death

2. ____ Family and Medical Leave Act

    b. agency responsible for setting and enforcing standards for occupational health and safety

3. ____ Occupational Safety and Health Act

    c. occurs when OSHA learns of a hazard that can be expected to cause physical harm or death

4. ____ Occupational Safety and Health Administration

    d. laws that provide financial compensation to covered employees, or their dependents, when employees are injured on the job

5. ____ imminent danger inspections

   e. act designed to provide a workplace free from recognized hazards that are likely to cause death or serious harm to employees

6. ____ catastrophe and fatality investigations

   f. law designed that workers facing a medical catastrophe or certain specified family responsibilities would be able to take needed time off from work without pay

True or False

1. ____ The most pervasive law regulating wages and hours is the Davis-Bacon Act.

2. ____ Workers' compensation laws are purely state laws.

3. ____ If you are injured when running an errand for your employer on the way to or from work, you cannot receive workers' compensation benefits because you were not injured at your place of employment.

4. ____ The Occupational Safety and Health Administration enforces the Occupational Safety and Health Act through unannounced inspections and levying fines against violators.

5. ____ Employers cannot listen to phone conversations of employees.

6. ____ Michael, a manager at a factory, believes that one of his workers is working under the influence of drugs; thus, he can legally make the worker take a drug test.

7. ____ All states exclude a worker from receiving state unemployment compensation if the employee voluntarily quit.

8. ____ Federal employees have more worker privacy rights than private workers.

9. ____ An employer is not permitted to discriminate in hiring on the basis of a pre-employment drug test when the result of the test is proven false.

Multiple Choice

1. To recover workers' compensation benefits, an injured party must show that

a. she or he is an employee, as opposed to being an independent contractor
b. the injury occurred on the job
c. both the injured party and employer are covered by the state workers' compensation statute
d. all of the above

2. You work at a family owned restaurant that employs thirty people. The Family and Medical Leave Act

a. provides that you may take a leave from work when your aunt is ill
b. does not apply to your place of employment
c. allows you to take a leave of absence for illness
d. both a and c

3. If an employer fails to comply with the Family and Medical Leave Act, the plaintiff could recover damages for

a. unpaid wages or salary
b. lost benefits
c. denied compensation
d. all of the above

4. The creation of which agency was NOT authorized under the Occupational Safety and Health Act?

a. the Occupational Safety and Health Review Commission
b. the National Institute for Occupational Safety and Health
c. the Association for Occupational Safety and Health
d. the Occupational Safety and Health Administration

5. What categories of violations are possible under OSHA?

a. serious, harmful, and flagrant
b. nonserious, harmful, and willful
c. willful or repeat, serious, and nonserious
d. harmful, willful or repeat, and flagrant

6. The Electronic Communications Act

a. prohibits intentional interception of electronic communications
b. allows employers to monitor employee telephone conversations in the ordinary course of their employment
c. both a and b
d. none of the above

7. The Consolidated Omnibus Budget Reconciliation Act of 1985 provides that

a. no employee can be fired without just cause
b. employees who lose their jobs can be covered by their previous employer's medical, dental, or optical benefits under the employer's policy by paying the premiums
c. publicly held corporations may opt out of state worker's compensation programs
d. none of the above

Short Answer

1. Describe two advantages and disadvantages (from the workers' perspective) of the workers' compensation program.

2. The Family and Medical Leave Act states that employers must give eligible employees up to 12 weeks of leave during any 12-month period for five family-related occurrences. What are these occurrences?

3. What is the typical inspection procedure for an OSHA inspection?

CHAPTER 19
LAWS GOVERNING LABOR-MANAGEMENT RELATIONS

This chapter introduces you to the laws governing employee organizing and the collective bargaining process. We'll begin our review of the chapter by critically evaluating a Supreme Court Justice's opinion in a labor law case and a short argument. Then, we'll conclude with objective review questions.

A. More Critical Thinking

1. Test your critical thinking skills by reading this opinion from a case before the Supreme Court and answering the questions that follow.

Allentown Mack v. NLRB
1998

JUSTICE SCALIA:

Under longstanding precedent of the National Labor Relations Board, an employer who believes that an incumbent union no longer enjoys the support of a majority of its employees has three options: to request a formal, Board-supervised election, to withdraw recognition from the union and refuse to bargain, or to conduct an internal poll of employee support for the union. The Board has held that the latter two are unfair labor practices unless the employer can show that it had a "good faith reasonable doubt" about the union's majority support. We must decide whether the Board's standard for employer polling is rational and consistent with the National Labor Relations Act, and whether the Board's factual determinations in this case are supported by substantial evidence in the record.

Allentown challenges the Board's decision in this case [, claiming] that the record evidence clearly demonstrates that it had a good-faith reasonable doubt about the union's claim to majority support.

The Board held Allentown guilty of an unfair labor practice in its conduct of the polling because it "had not demonstrated that it held a reasonable doubt, based on objective considerations, that the Union continued to enjoy the support of a majority of the bargaining unit employees." We must decide whether that conclusion is supported by substantial evidence on the record as a whole.

The question presented for review is whether, on the evidence presented to the Board, a reasonable jury could have found that Allentown lacked a genuine, reasonable uncertainty about whether Local 724 enjoyed the continuing support of a majority of unit employees. In our view, the answer is no.

The Board adopted the ALJ's finding that 6 of Allentown's 32 employees had made statements which could be used as objective considerations supporting a good-faith reasonable doubt as to continued majority status by the Union... The Board seemingly also accepted (though this is not essential to our analysis) the ALJ's willingness to assume that the statement of a seventh employee (to the effect that he "did not feel comfortable with the Union and thought it was a waste of $35 a month,") supported good-faith reasonable doubt of his support for the union -- as in our view it unquestionably does. And it presumably accepted the ALJ's assessment that "7 of 32, or roughly 20 percent of the involved employees" were not alone sufficient to create "an objective reasonable doubt of union majority support". . . . But there was much more.

For one thing, the ALJ and the Board totally disregarded the effect upon Allentown of the statement of an eighth employee . . . who said that "he was not being represented for the $35 he was paying." The ALJ, whose findings were adopted by the Board, said that this statement "seems more an expression of a desire for better representation than one for no representation at all." It seems to us that it is, more accurately, simply an expression of dissatisfaction with the union's performance -- which could reflect the speaker's desire that the union represent him more effectively, but could also reflect the speaker's desire to save his $35 and get rid of the union. The statement would assuredly engender an uncertainty whether the speaker supported the union, and so could not be entirely ignored. But the most significant evidence excluded from consideration by the Board consisted of statements of two employees regarding not merely their own support of the union, but support among the work force in general. Kermit Bloch, who worked on the night shift, told an Allentown manager "that the entire night shift did not want the Union." The ALJ refused to credit this, because "Bloch did not testify and thus could not explain how he formed his opinion about the views of his fellow employees." Unsubstantiated assertions that other employees do not support the union certainly do not establish the fact of that disfavor with the degree of reliability ordinarily demanded in legal proceedings. But under the Board's enunciated test for polling, it is not the fact of disfavor that is at issue (the poll itself is meant to establish that), but rather the existence of a reasonable uncertainty on the part of the employer regarding that fact. On that issue, absent some reason for the employer to know that Bloch had no basis for his information, or that Bloch was lying, reason demands that the statement be given considerable weight.

Another employee who gave information concerning overall support for the union was Ron Mohr, who told Allentown managers that "if a vote was taken, the Union would lose" and that "it was his feeling that the employees did not want a union." The ALJ again objected irrelevantly that "there is no evidence with respect to how he gained this knowledge." In addition, the Board held that Allentown "could not legitimately rely on [the statement] as a basis for doubting the Union's majority status" . . . This basis for disregarding Mohr's statements is wholly irrational.

It must be borne in mind that the issue here is not whether Mohr's statement clearly establishes a majority in opposition to the union, but whether it contributes to a reasonable uncertainty whether a majority in favor of the union existed. We think it surely does. Allentown would reasonably have given great credence to Mohr's assertion of lack of union support, since he was not hostile to the union, and was in a good position to assess anti-union sentiment. Mohr was a union shop steward for the service department, and a member of the union's bargaining committee; according to the ALJ, he "did not indicate personal dissatisfaction with the Union." It seems to us that Mohr's statement has undeniable and substantial probative value on the issue of "reasonable doubt."

Accepting the Board's apparent (and in our view inescapable) concession that Allentown received reliable information that 7 of the bargaining-unit employees did not support the union, the remaining 25 would have had to support the union by a margin of 17 to 8 -- a ratio of more than 2 to 1 -- if the union commanded majority support. The statements of Bloch and Mohr would cause anyone to doubt that degree of support, and neither the Board nor the ALJ discussed any evidence that Allentown should have weighed on the other side. The most pro-union statement cited in the ALJ's opinion was Ron Mohr's comment that he personally "could work with or without the Union," and "was there to do his job." Giving fair weight to Allentown's circumstantial evidence, we think it quite impossible for a rational fact finder to avoid the conclusion that Allentown had reasonable, good-faith grounds to doubt -- to be uncertain about -- the union's retention of majority support.

We conclude that . . . the Board's factual finding that Allentown Mack Sales lacked [a reasonable] doubt is not supported by substantial evidence on the record as a whole. The judgment of the Court of Appeals for the D. C. Circuit is therefore reversed, and ***the case is remanded with instructions to deny enforcement.***

    a. What is the relevant rule of law in this case?

    b. As with many cases, ambiguity in a rule or statute was the cause of this legal action. What important ambiguity is really the point of contention in this case?

    c. What reasons does the Court give for reversing the Court of Appeals?

2. Now, sharpen your critical thinking ability by applying your skills to the following argument about unions.

It's about time that the National Labor Relations Act was repealed. Unions have absolutely no place in our society. Our economy is supposed to be based on competition, right? Well, then why do we let workers come together to corner the market on labor? The collective bargaining process completely undermines our economy.

It's clear that a double standard exists here. We give workers the green light to band together and bargain collectively. However, at the same time, we prevent businesses from doing the same thing. Any time two businesses try to work together, they must clear endless legal hurdles that result from laws banning collective action between businesses. This inconsistency reeks of injustice.

Furthermore, unions are hardly necessary anymore. Back in the 1950s, as much as 25 percent of the labor force was unionized. Today, only about 13 percent of all wage and salary workers are union members. Clearly, unions have lost support. Their membership has been declining drastically because since the 1960s, more and more Americans have chosen not to be represented by unions.

So, it's obvious that the time has come for us to return to the notions that our country was based on: individual responsibility, individual initiative, and competition among individuals. These are the values that brought our country to its prominent place in the world, and if we are to maintain this position, we must restore them.

    a. What are the author's reasons for abolishing unions?

    b. Reread the third paragraph. What alternate causes for the declining strength of unions might the author have overlooked?

    c. What words or phrases contain a significant ambiguity?

B. *Learning the Basics*
Matching

1. ____ Wagner Act
          a. administrative agency charged with enforcing and interpreting the Wagner Act

2. ____ collective bargaining

b. nonviolent work stoppage for the purpose of obtaining better terms and conditions of employment under a collective bargaining agreement

3. ____ Taft-Hartley Act

c. forum in which workers communicate directly with upper management

4. ____ Landrum-Griffith Act

d. governs the internal operations of unions

5. ____ National Labor Relations

e. the first major piece of federal Board legislation designed to encourage the formation of labor unions

6. ____ Excelsior list

f. negotiations between a union and an employer over wages, hours and terms and conditions of employment

7. ____ quality circle

g. small group of workers who meet regularly on a voluntary basis to analyze work problems and to recommend solutions to management

8. ____ labor-management committee

h. list of the names and addresses of all employees eligible to vote in a representation election

9. ____ economic strike

i. refusal to deal with, purchase goods from, or work for a business

10. ____ boycott

j. prohibits unions from engaging in specified unfair labor practices, makes collective bargaining agreements enforceable in federal courts, and provides a civil damages remedy for parties injured by certain prohibited union activities

True or False

1. ____ Unions are currently much more powerful than they were in the 1950s.

2. ____ The Taft-Hartley Act and the Wagner Act are jointly known as the National Labor Relations Act.

3. ____ If a union loses a representation election, it may file an objection with the regional director of the NLRB.

4. ____ An employer's telling his employees that he thinks the company will go bankrupt if the union wins a representation election constitutes an unfair labor practice.

5. ____ Unions may picket for recognition whenever they wish to do so.

6. ____ Permissive subjects of collective bargaining include wages, rates of pay, hours of employment, and other terms and conditions of employment.

7. ____ The Secretary of Labor appoints the general counsel of the NLRB.

8. ____ Supervisors do not fall under NLRB jurisdiction.

9. ____ The first step in remedying an unfair labor practice is the filing of an unfair labor practice charge with the appropriate regional office.

10. ____ Union officials who are not employees of a company have the same rights as employees during a representation drive.

11. ____ An employee is still excluded from supervisor status under the NLRB if the "independent judgment" that he or she exercises is "ordinary professional or technical judgment in directing less skilled employees to deliver services in accordance with employer-specified standards."

Multiple Choice

1. The NLRB has jurisdiction over which of the following employers?

a. the Cuyahoga County Commissioner's office
b. Diaz Brothers Independent Contracting Co.

c. Williams & Williams Cattle Farm
d. none of the above

2. A union must demonstrate support of over ____ percent of its workers when petitioning for a representation election.

a. 30
b. 50
c. 75
d. 25

3. Both union representatives and employers are prohibited from making speeches to captive audiences within ____ hours of a representation election.

a. 20
b. 48
c. 24
d. 12

4. Which of the following is NOT an employer unfair labor practice?

a. telling employees that they will lose their coffee breaks if the union wins the representation election
b. prohibiting employees from passing out union pamphlets during work hours
c. recognizing a union that has the support of 45 percent of the employees
d. firing employee organizers

5. Mandatory subjects of collective bargaining include

a. wages paid
b. hours worked
c. capital structure of the business
d. both a and b

6. All of the following are unlawful strikes EXCEPT

a. jurisdictional strikes
b. unfair labor practice strikes
c. wildcat strikes
d. sit-down strikes

7. _____ occurs when one union wishes to protest an assignment of jobs to another union's members.

a. Organizational picketing
b. Jurisdictional picketing
c. Informational picketing
d. Signal picketing

8. In 1935, the _____ guaranteed the right of employees to bargain collectively.

a. Sherman Act
b. Landrum-Griffith Act
c. National Labor Relations Board
d. Wagner Act

9. Reports of corruption within some labor unions led to the passing of the _____.

a. Wagner Act
b. Taft-Hartley Act
c. Landrum-Griffith Act
d. both b and c

10. The NLRB is composed of ____ members.

a. five
b. fifteen
c. thirty-four
d. three

Short Answer

1. How are the Taft-Hartley Act and the Wagner Act related?

2. What is the *Cabot* rule and what are two exceptions to it?

CHAPTER 20
EMPLOYMENT DISCRIMINATION

This chapter introduces you to an extremely important area of law for the prudent business manager, employment discrimination law. To further your understanding of this vastly important and ever-expanding area in the legal environment of business, we will provide you with some more critical thinking exercises. Then, we conclude with objective questions.

A. More Critical Thinking

1. We'll begin by returning to the *Oncale v. Sundowner* case, which was mentioned briefly in your primary text. Read the following case excerpt before answering the critical thinking questions below.

Joseph Oncale v. Sundowner Offshore Services
United States Supreme Court
1998

Oncale was working for respondent Sundowner Offshore Services on a Chevron U.S.A., Inc., oil platform in the Gulf of Mexico. He was employed as a roustabout on an eight-man crew. Lyons, the crane operator, and Pippen, the driller, had supervisory authority. On several occasions, Oncale was forcibly subjected to sex-related, humiliating actions against him by Lyons, Pippen, and Johnson in the presence of the rest of the crew. Pippen and Lyons also physically assaulted Oncale in a sexual manner, and Lyons threatened him with rape. Oncale's complaints to supervisory personnel produced no remedial action; he eventually quit—asking that his pink slip reflect that he "voluntarily left due to sexual harassment and verbal abuse." Oncale stated, "I felt that if I didn't leave my job that I would be raped or forced to have sex."

Plaintiff Oncale brought a Title VII action against his former employer and against male supervisors and coworkers, alleging sexual harassment. The U.S. District Court granted summary judgment for defendants, and plaintiff appealed. The U.S. Court of Appeals affirmed. Plaintiff Oncale appealed to the U.S. Supreme Court.

Justice Scalia
[I]n the related context of racial discrimination in the workplace we have rejected any conclusive presumption that an employer will not discriminate against members of his own race. "Because of the many facets of human motivation, it would be unwise to presume as a matter of law that human beings of one definable group will not discriminate against other members of that group."

If our precedents leave any doubt on the question, we hold today that nothing in Title VII necessarily bars a claim of discrimination "because of ... sex" merely because the plaintiff and the defendant are of the same sex. [W]hen the issue arises in the context of a "hostile environment" sexual harassment claim, the state and federal courts have taken a bewildering variety of stances. Some, like the Fifth Circuit in this case, have held that same-sex sexual harassment claims are never cognizable under Title VII. Other decisions say that such claims are actionable only if the plaintiff can prove that the harasser is homosexual (and thus presumably motivated by sexual desire). Still others suggest that workplace harassment that is sexual in content is always actionable, regardless of the harasser's sex, sexual orientation, or motivations.

We see no justification in the statutory language or our precedents for a categorical rule excluding same-sex harassment claims from the coverage of Title VII. [M]ale-on-male sexual harassment in the workplace was assuredly not the principal evil Congress was concerned with when it enacted Title VII. But statutory prohibitions often go beyond the principal evil to cover reasonably comparable evils, and it is ultimately the provisions of our laws rather than the principal concerns of our legislators by which we are governed. Title VII prohibits "discriminat[ion] ... because of ... sex" in the "terms" or "conditions" of employment. Our holding that this includes sexual harassment must extend to sexual harassment of any kind that meets the statutory requirements.

Respondents and their amici contend that recognizing liability for same-sex harassment will transform Title VII into a general civility code for the American workplace. But that risk is no greater for same-sex than for opposite-sex harassment, and is adequately met by careful attention to the requirements of the statute. Title VII does not prohibit all verbal or physical harassment in the workplace; it is directed only at "discriminat[ion] ... because of ... sex." We have never held that workplace harassment, even harassment between men and women, is automatically discrimination because of sex merely because the words used have sexual content or connotations. "The critical issue, Title VII's text indicates, is whether members of one sex are exposed to disadvantageous terms or conditions of employment to which members of the other sex are not exposed."

Courts and juries have found the inference of discrimination easy to draw in most male-female sexual harassment situations, because the challenged conduct typically involves explicit or implicit proposals of sexual activity; it is reasonable to assume those proposals would not have been made to someone of the same sex. The same chain or inference would be available to a plaintiff alleging same-sex harassment, if there were credible evidence that the harasser was homosexual. But harassing conduct need not be motivated by sexual desire to support an inference of discrimination on the basis of sex. A trier of fact might reasonably find such discrimination, for example, if a female victim is harassed in such sex-specific and derogatory terms by another woman as to make it clear that the harasser is motivated by general hostility to the presence of women in the workplace. A same-sex harassment plaintiff may also, of course, offer direct comparative evidence about how the alleged harasser treated members of both sexes in a mixed-sex workplace. Whatever evidentiary route the plaintiff chooses to follow, he or she must always prove that the conduct at issue was not merely tinged with offensive sexual connotations, but actually constituted "discriminat[ion] ... because of ... sex."

And there is another requirement that prevents Title VII from expanding into a general civility code: the statute does not reach genuine but innocuous differences in the ways men and women routinely interact with members of the same sex and of the opposite sex. The prohibition of harassment on the basis of sex requires neither asexuality nor androgyny in the workplace; it forbids only behavior so objectively offensive as to alter the "conditions" of the victim's employment. "Conduct that is not severe or pervasive enough to create an objectively hostile or abusive work environment—an environment that a reasonable person would find hostile or abusive—is beyond Title VII's purview." We have always regarded that requirement as crucial, and as sufficient to ensure that courts and juries do not mistake ordinary socializing in the workplace—such as male-on-male horseplay or intersexual flirtation—for discriminatory "conditions of employment."

[T]he objective severity of harassment should be judged from the perspective of a reasonable person in the plaintiff's position, considering "all the circumstances." In same-sex (as in all) harassment cases, that inquiry requires careful consideration of the social context in which particular behavior occurs and is experienced by its target. A professional football player's working environment is not severely or pervasively abusive, for example, if the coach smacks him on the buttocks as he heads onto the field—even if the same behavior would reasonably be experienced as abusive by the coach's secretary (male or female) back at the office. The real social impact of workplace behavior often depends on a constellation of surrounding circumstances, expectations, and relationships which are not fully captured by a simple recitation of the words used or the physical acts performed. Common sense, and an appropriate sensitivity to social context, will enable courts and juries to distinguish between simple teasing or rough housing among members of the same sex, and conduct which a reasonable person in the plaintiff's position would find severely hostile or abusive.

Judgment reversed in favor of Plaintiff, Oncale.

a. What relevant rule of law does Justice Scalia note?

b. What additional information would help you to determine whether the harassment faced by Joseph Oncale was "because . . . of sex?"

c. Legal reasoning frequently relies on analogies. What parallel and different situations does Justice Scalia describe in the case? How appropriate are these comparisons?

2. Evaluate the following argument about affirmative action.

I am deeply disturbed by the path our government has taken in the past 30 years. Although the 1964 Civil Rights Act was passed to eliminate discrimination in the workplace, the opposite has occurred.

Affirmative action plans allow employers to select job applicants on the basis of race, sex, and national origin. Rather than choose the most competent person for the job, businesses are encouraged to choose the candidate that will help them meet their "goals" and "timetables."

Sometimes, the government even forces businesses to discriminate. Federal programs often offer contracts only to those employers who have instituted affirmative action programs that give unfair preferences to women and minorities. In these cases, the company has a choice: discriminate or go broke. What ought to be done is simple: The Civil Rights Act prohibits discrimination, so the government must enforce the Act by bringing the era of affirmative action to an end.

a. What important word in this argument is ambiguous?

b. Depending on which alternative definition of this ambiguous word, what alternative conclusions may be reached?

c. What ethical norm does the author of this passage elevate above the others?

3. Let's conclude our critical thinking exercises by assessing an argument about sexual harassment.

The courts have gone too far. By extending the definition of sexual harassment, they have made it possible for people to be sued because they told jokes. Such restraints on our First Amendment right to free speech are unthinkable. Thomas Jefferson would roll over in his grave if he knew how badly the courts were limiting our speech.

Furthermore, everybody makes jokes about sex. People are fascinated by sex, as they have been since the beginning of time. What's wrong with letting people talk about it openly?

Honestly, real problems would occur if people never mentioned sex. If they lacked talking and joking as outlets, they would be so overwhelmed by their sexual desires that they would be driven to commit serious crimes. Then we wouldn't worry about offending some secretary; we'd have to be concerned about sexual assaults occurring at the workplace!

a. What issue is the author attempting to settle? Be careful! This question is not as easy as it first appears.

b. What conclusion does the author give?

c. Identify the author's reasons for his conclusion.

d. What evidence does the author give for these reasons?

B. Learning the Basics

Matching

1. ____ employment-at-will doctrine

a. discrimination cases in which the employer's facially neutral policy has a discriminatory effect on employees that belong to a protected class

2. ____ Equal Pay Act of 1963

b. requires employers to make reasonable accommodations to the known disabilities of an otherwise qualified job applicant or employee with a disability, unless the necessary accommodation would impose an undue burden on the business

3. ____ Title VII

c. race, color, national origin, sex, and religion

4. ____ disparate treatment

d. prohibits wage discrimination based on sex

5. ____ sexual harassment

e. programs adopted by employers to increase the representation of women and minorities in their workforce

6. ____ Americans With Disabilities Act

f. unwelcome sexual advances, requests for sexual favors and other verbal or physical conduct of a sexual nature that makes submission a term of employment or that creates an intimidating, hostile, or offensive environment

7. ____ affirmative action plans

g. prohibits discrimination in hiring, firing, and other terms and conditions of employment on the basis of race, color, national origin, sex, or religion

8. ____ disparate impact cases

h. states that a contract of employment for an indeterminate time is terminable at will by either the employer or the employee

9. ____ protected classes

i. defense to a Title VII charge alleging that a person's membership in a protected class is necessary for the performance of the job in question

10. ____ bona fide occupational

j. discrimination cases in which the employer treats one employee less favorably than another because of that employee's membership in one of the five protected classes

True or False

1. ____ Because of the Equal Pay Act of 1963, women no longer have to worry about workplace discrimination.

2. ____ The employment-at-will doctrine concentrates power in the hands of the employee.

3. ____ The public policy exception to the employment-at-will doctrine is based on the theory that every employment contract, even an unwritten one, contains the implicit understanding that the parties will deal fairly with each other.

4. ____ No antidiscrimination laws were in place before the Civil Rights Act of 1964.

5. ____ In interpreting the Equal Pay Act, jobs are assumed to be equal if they are substantially the same in four factors: skill, effort, responsibility, and working conditions.

6. ____ When the plaintiff establishes a prima facie case in a Title VII claim, the burden of proof switches to the defendant, who must prove that the plaintiff was rejected for legitimate, non-discriminatory reasons.

7. ____ Hostile environment cases of sexual harassment occur when a supervisor makes sexual demands on someone of the opposite sex and these demands are perceived as a condition of employment.

8. ____ Bona fide occupational qualification, merit, and seniority systems are all defenses available to defendants in Title VII cases.

9. ____ State employers are not subject to the Age Discrimination in Employment Act.

10. ____ The Americans With Disabilities Act sometimes forces employers to hire people who are grossly unqualified.

Multiple Choice

1. The agency charged with administering employment discrimination laws is the

   a. EEOC
   b. SEC
   c. NAFTA
   d. EEO-1

2. Which of the following is NOT a defense to a Title VII charge?

   a. the employment decision was made on the basis of merit
   b. the employment decision was made on the basis of a seniority system
   c. bona fide occupational qualification
   d. intent

3. A successful plaintiff in a Title VII case is generally entitled to back pay for up to ___ years.

   a. seven
   b. five
   c. two
   d. one and a half

4. The Age Discrimination in Employment Act prohibits discrimination on the basis of age for those employees over ___ years of age.

   a. 18
   b. 35
   c. 40
   d. 55

5. Which of the following is NOT a protected class under Title VII?

   a. religion
   b. sex
   c. sexual orientation
   d. national origin

6. All of the following are covered under the Americans With Disabilities Act of 1991 EXCEPT

   a. current substance abusers
   b. epileptics

c. recovered cocaine addicts
d. cancer patients

7. Which of the following is an acceptable question to ask a job applicant?

a. Do you have cancer?
b. Have you used illegal drugs in the past two years?
c. How much alcohol do you drink during the average week?
d. How many days were you absent from work last year because of your disability?

8. Recent court decisions have determined that valid affirmative action plans must

a. end or change once the goal of remedying past discrimination has been met.
b. attempt to remedy past discrimination.
c. ensure that the workforce is racially balanced.
d. both a and b

9. _____ was the first law banning discrimination by state and local governments.

a. The First Amendment
b. Title VII
c. The Civil Rights Act of 1866
d. The Civil Rights Act of 1871

10. Which of the following is NOT a defense to a charge under the Equal Pay Act of 1963?

a. men are in short supply and therefore must be paid extra
b. a bona fide seniority system
c. a bona fide merit system
d. a pay system based on quality or quantity of output

Short Answer

1. Describe how the burden of proof shifts in an age discrimination case from the plaintiff, to the defendant, and back to the plaintiff. Be sure to note the "pretext-plus" argument and the accompanying Supreme Court case from your book.

2. Explain what is wrong with the following statement: "Title VII was unnecessary because the Civil Rights Acts of 1866 and 1871 were already in place."

Chapter 21

ENVIRONMENTAL LAW

This chapter will help you to sharpen your knowledge regarding environmental law. Ethical norms, such as freedom, security, and justice, underlying environmental positions are quite complex. While everyone wants a clean environment, they often do not agree on what society must do to achieve a clean environment. Your critical thinking skills will be particularly helpful when examining environmental issues.

A. More Critical Thinking

1. In the textbook, you learned about CERCLA. The following case helps to clarify some of the issues surrounding CERCLA that were raised in the text.

UNITED STATES

v.

BESTFOOD

1998

The United States brought this action under Sect. 107(a)(2) of the Comprehensive Environmental Response, Compensation, and Liability Act of 1980 (CERCLA) against, among others, respondent CPC International Inc., the parent corporation of the defunct Ott Chemical Co. (Ott 11), for the costs of cleaning up industrial waste generated by Ott II's chemical plant. Section 107(a)(2) authorizes suits against, among others, "any person who at the time of disposal of any hazardous substance owned or operated any facility." The trial focused on whether CPC, as a parent corporation, had "owned or operated" Ott II's plant within the meaning of Sect. 107(a)(2).

JUSTICE SOUTER The issue before us, under the Comprehensive Environmental Response, Compensation, and Liability Act of 1980 (CERCLA) is whether a parent corporation that actively participated in, and exercised control over, the operators of a subsidiary may, without more, be held liable as an operator of a polluting facility owned or operated by the subsidiary [emphasis added]. We answer no, unless the corporate veil may be pierced. But a corporate parent that actively participated in, and exercised control over, the operators of the facility itself may be held directly liable in its own right as an operator of the facility [emphasis added].

When (but only when) the corporate veil may be pierced, a parent corporation may be charged with derivative CERCLA liability for its subsidiary's actions in operating a polluting facility. It is a general principle of corporate law that a parent corporation (so-called because of control through ownership of another corporation's stock) is not liable for the acts of its subsidiaries. CERCLA does not purport to reject this bedrock principle, and the Government has indeed made no claim that a corporate parent is liable as an owner or an operator under Sect. 107(a)(2) simply because its subsidiary owns or operates a polluting facility. But there is an equally fundamental principle of corporate law, applicable to the parent-subsidiary relationship as well as generally, that the corporate veil may be pierced and the shareholder held liable for the corporation's conduct when, inter alia, the corporate form would otherwise be misused to accomplish certain wrongful purposes, most notably fraud, on the shareholder's behalf CERCLA does not purport to rewrite this well-settled rule, either, and against this venerable common-law backdrop, the congressional silence is audible. CERCLA's failure to speak to a matter as fundamental as the liability implications of corporate ownership demands application of the rule that, to abrogate a common-law principle, a statute must speak directly to the question addressed by the common law.

A corporate parent that actively participated in, and exercised control over, the operations of its subsidiary's facility may be held directly liable in its own right under Sect. 107(a)(2) as an operator of the facility. Pp. 11-20.

(a) Derivative liability aside, CERCLA does not bar a parent corporation from direct liability for its own actions. Under the plain language of Sect. 107(a)(2), any person who operates a polluting facility is directly liable for the costs of cleaning up the pollution, and this is so even if that person is the parent corporation of the facility's owner. Because the statute does not define the term "operate," however, it is difficult to define actions sufficient to constitute direct parental "operation." In the organizational sense obviously intended by CERCLA, to "operate" a facility ordinarily means to direct the workings of, manage, or conduct the affairs of the facility. To sharpen the definition for purposes of CERCLA's concern with environmental contamination, an operator must manage, direct, or conduct operations specifically related to the leakage or disposal of hazardous waste, or decisions about compliance with environmental regulations. Pp. 11-13.

(b) The Sixth Circuit correctly rejected the direct liability analysis of the District Court, which mistakenly focused on the relationship between parent and subsidiary, and premised liability on little more than CPC's ownership of Ott II and its majority control over Ott II's board of directors. Because direct liability for the parent's operation of the facility must be kept distinct from derivative liability for the subsidiary's operation of the facility, the analysis should instead have focused on the relationship between CPC and the facility itself i.e., on whether CPC "operated" the facility, as evidenced by its direct participation in the facility's activities. That error was compounded by the District Court's erroneous assumption that actions of the joint officers and directors were necessarily attributable to CPC, rather than Ott II, contrary to time-honored common-law principles. The District Court's focus on the relationship between parent and subsidiary (rather than parent and facility), combined with its automatic attribution of the actions of dual officers and directors to CPC, erroneously, even if unintentionally, treated CERCLA as though it displaced or fundamentally altered common-law standards of limited liability. The District Court's analysis created what is in essence a relaxed, CERCLA-specific rule of derivative liability that would banish traditional standards and expectations from the law of CERCLA liability. Such a rule does not arise from congressional silence, and CERCLA's silence is dispositive. Pp. 13-18.

Nonetheless, the Sixth Circuit erred in limiting direct liability under CERCLA to a parent's sole or joint venture operation, so as to eliminate any possible finding that CPC is liable as an operator on the facts of this case. The ordinary meaning of the word "operate" in the organizational sense is not limited to those two parental actions, but extends also to situations in which, e.g., joint officers or directors conduct the affairs of the facility on behalf of the parent, or agents of the parent with no position in the subsidiary manage or direct activities at the subsidiary's facility. Norms of corporate behavior (undisturbed by any CERCLA provision) are crucial reference points, both for determining whether a dual officer or director has served the parent in conducting operations at the facility, and for distinguishing a parental officer's oversight of a subsidiary from his control over the operation of the subsidiary's facility. There is, in fact, some evidence that an agent of CPC alone engaged in activities at Ott II's plant that were eccentric under accepted norms of parental oversight of a subsidiary's facility: The District Court's opinion speaks of such an agent who played a conspicuous part in dealing with the toxic risks emanating from the plant's operation. The findings in this regard are enough to raise an issue of CPC's operation of the facility, though this Court draws no ultimate conclusion, leaving the issue for the lower courts to reevaluate and resolve in the first instance.

Reversed, vacated and remanded for petitioner, United States.

a. What is the issue and conclusion in this case?

b. The court recognized the ambiguity of the word "operate" in CERCLA. How did the court resolve this ambiguity?

c. To decide whether CPC is considered an operator according to the definition set forth by the Supreme Court, what additional information would you need?

2. Examine the following letter.

Dear concerned citizen:

The Acid Rain control program has failed. We should simply end the program now before we waste any more money on it. The program has been in place since 1960, and we still have an acid rain problem. The program has had eight years to eradicate acid rain. We should try a different program that has the potential to solve the problem.

As citizens of a democracy, we should have a say in how the government is run. People do not want the acid rain program. A recent poll of over 10,000 Americans revealed that only 2 percent listed acid rain as one of the five major environmental problems facing the United States. No one listed acid rain as the most significant problem. Congress should listen to the people; it is clear they do not want the program.

Please join with those of us who truly care about the environment. Write your congressman and demand that the acid rain program be ended.

Sincerely, Thomas Jackson
Lobbyist for the New Acid Rain Permit Program (NARPP)

    a. What is the issue and conclusion of this argument?

    b. What are the reasons that the author offers? Do you see any problems with this reasoning?

    c. What evidence does the author offer for his reasons?

    d. What additional information would you like to know about the author?

B. Learning the Basics

Matching

1. ____pesticide

    a. any waste material that is ignitable, corrosive, reactive, or toxic when ingested or absorbed

2. ___ environmental impact

    b. a plan, required of every state, that explains how the state will meet federal air pollution standards

3. ___ point sources

c. any substance designed to prevent, destroy, repel, or mitigate any pest or to be used as a plant regulator or defoliant

4. ___ effluent limitations

d. a statement that must be prepared for every major federal activity that would significantly affect the quality of the human environment

5. ___ state implementation

e. precipitation with a high acidic content caused by atmospheric pollutants

6. ___ acid rain

f. distinct places from which pollutants are discharged into water

7. ___ hazardous waste

g. any chemical or mixture whose manufacture, processing, distribution, use, or disposal presents an unreasonable risk of harm to human health or the environment

8. ___ toxic substances

h. maximum allowable amounts of pollutants that can be discharged from a point source in a given time period

True or False

1. ___ Technology-forcing standards are set on the basis of health considerations.

2. ___ The primary device currently used for protecting the environment is the marketable discharge permits approach.

3. ___ The National Environmental Policy Act of 1970 (NEPA) is regarded as the country's most influential piece of environmental legislation.

4. ____ The environmental impact statement is part of the process of agency decision making.

5. ____ Primary national ambient air quality standards (PNAAQS) are stringent standards that protect the public welfare from any adverse effect associated with air pollution.

6. ____ Both conventional air pollutants and hazardous air pollutants pose serious risks to human health when even very tiny amounts are emitted.

7. ____ The Clean Air Act addresses both indoor and outdoor pollution.

8. ____ The best-known component of the Resource Conservation and Recovery Act of 1976 (RCRA) is its manifest program, which provides cradle to grave regulation of hazardous waste.

9. ____ CERCLA and Superfund are synonyms.

10. ____ Pesticides must be registered to be sold in the United States.

Multiple Choice

1. An environmental law case could be tried

a. through the tort of nuisance
b. through the tort of conversion
c. through the tort of negligence
d. both a and c

2. The Environmental Protection Agency

a. is the primary agency responsible for passing and enforcing environmental regulations
b. uses only civil sanctions to punish environmental offenders
c. creates self-auditing programs
d. all of the above

3. An environmental impact statement is required

a. if the action in question is federal
b. if the action in question is major

c.   if the action in question has a significant impact on human environment
d.   all of the above

4.   Water pollution is controlled by

a.   the Safe Drinking Water Act
b.   the Federal Water Pollution Control Act
c.   both a and b
d.   none of the above

5. The goal of the Federal Water Pollution Control Act

a. was to create fishable and swimable waters
b. was the total elimination of pollutant discharges into navigable waters
c. was to be achieved through a system of permits and effluent discharge limitations
d. all of the above

6. Which of the following does NOT control hazardous waste and toxic substances?

a. the Resource Conservation and Recovery Act of 1976 (RCRA)
b. the Pollution Prevention Act of 1990
c. the Federal Insecticide, Fungicide, and Rodenticide Act of 1972
d. the Comprehensive Environmental Response, Compensation, and Liability Act of 1980 (CERCLA)

7. Under CERCLA, potentially responsible parties include

a. present owners or operators of a facility where hazardous materials are stored
b. hazardous waste generators
c. past owners or operators of hazardous waste facilities
d. all of the above

8. International cooperation on environmental matters is necessary

a. because environmental problems do not stop at national borders
b. because many global resources are within no country's borders
c. because each nation's value of the environment is different
d. all of the above

9. The United States has played a role in establishing global environmental policies in the following ways:

a. research, conferences, treaties, and economic aid
b. research, history, executive orders, and military aid
c. executive orders, legislation, sanctions, and technology
d. technology, research, economic aid, and sanctions

10. Which of the following is NOT a way a nation can protect its environment?

a. subsidies
b. emission charges
c. discharge permits
d. none of the above (all can be used)

Short Answer

1. Why is the tort of nuisance not sufficient to control pollution?

2. NEPA requires that an EIS include a detailed statement of what items?

Chapter 22
RULES GOVERNING THE ISSUANCE AND TRADING OF SECURITIES

This chapter introduces you to the laws governing the buying and selling of securities, which have grown in importance due to the recent surge in the stock market and its multitude of new investors. As with the previous chapters, we begin by providing more opportunities to develop your critical thinking skills, and then move on to objective review questions.

A. *More Critical Thinking*

1. We will begin our review of this chapter by examining a recent case regarding an employee's purchasing stock options to help his company prevent a hostile takeover.

CAMPBELL v. NATIONAL MEDIA CORPORATION and TURCHI
1994

JUDGE DALZELL:

Plaintiff William H. Campbell brings this action under the Securities Exchange Act of 1934 against his former employer and its Chief Executive Officer for an alleged scheme to induce him to purchase stock of his corporate employer. Defendants move to dismiss and/or for summary judgment on the grounds that Campbell did not actually purchase any stock[.] We will deny the motion.

In January 1994, National Media, whose shares are traded on the New York Stock Exchange, was the target of a hostile takeover attempt by a competitor, ValueVision. According to Campbell, in order to entrench his control of National Media, defendant John J. Turchi, Jr., National Media's largest shareholder, Chairman of the Board, President and CEO, ordered Campbell to exercise the first two years of his stock options . . . Since Campbell did not have the funds required to exercise two years' worth of options at $ 5.125 per share, he executed a promissory note to National Media for $ 170,836.00 on January 13, 1994, and National Media, in turn, loaned him the money for the stock purchase.

Campbell alleges that he would not have exercised his options in January of this year but for Turchi's misrepresentations: "Defendant Turchi misrepresented that National Media would 'lend' Plaintiff the" money necessary to exercise his options, and "Defendant Turchi misrepresented to Plaintiff, in Defendant Turchi's office in Philadelphia, that if Plaintiff exercised these options at no cost to Plaintiff, that Defendant Turchi would direct National Media's Board of Directors to grant substantial stock options to Plaintiff, as well as further stock and cash consideration, for his loyalty to Defendant National Media after defeating ValueVision's hostile offer for control."

In April of 1994, ValueVision terminated its hostile takeover attempt. Two months later, Campbell demanded that Turchi and National Media grant him additional stock options for his loyalty to the company, as Turchi had previously promised. Rather than honor his demand, National Media allegedly wrote to Campbell advising him that they assumed he had resigned from National Media and that he would have to repay the money he borrowed in accordance with the promissory note he executed.

On July 28, 1994, Campbell brought this action seeking in excess of $1.3 million in compensatory and punitive damages. Count I alleges a violation of Securities Exchange Commission Rule 10b-5 and § 10(b) of the Securities Exchange Act of 1934 by Turchi and National Media for inducing Campbell to purchase stock in National Media through misrepresentations and omissions of material facts. . . . Turchi moved to dismiss Count I[.] National Media has joined Turchi's motion.

Defendants [argue] in their motion to dismiss and/or for summary judgment [that, among other things,] Campbell does not allege the purchase or sale of a security . . .

Section 10(b) of the Securities Exchange Act of 1934 prohibits the use of "any manipulative or deceptive" scheme "in connection with the purchase or sale of any security". Securities Exchange Commission Rule 10b-5 . . . forbids the making of "any untrue statement of material fact" in connection with the purchase or sale of securities. Both actions require a purchase or sale of a security as a predicate to an action.

The 1934 Act defines the terms in question: "the terms 'buy' and 'purchase' each include any contract to buy, purchase, or otherwise acquire." "The terms 'sale' and 'sell' each include any contract to sell or otherwise dispose of."

Defendants assert that the May 6, 1992, employment agreement, whereby National Media promised to issue to Campbell options to purchase 50,000 shares over three years pursuant to the company's 1991 stock option plan, does not constitute a "purchase" within the meaning of the Securities Exchange Act because Campbell did not offer any specific consideration for the granting of the options. They contend that the employment agreement merely gave Campbell the right to purchase shares in the company, but that Campbell was never required to exercise those options.

An employment contract whereby an employee exchanges his services in return for stock options has been held to constitute a purchase within the meaning of the 1934 Act. At this stage, we cannot on this record negate Campbell's employment contract, with option terms central to it, as a § 10(b) "purchase," given the elasticity of that term under the 1934 Act.

Defendants also claim that Campbell's exercise of his options to purchase shares in January 1994 does not constitute a "purchase". They assert that National Media, and not Campbell, provided the funds to purchase the shares and that Campbell merely signed a promissory note. Furthermore, since Campbell was free at any time . . . to tender his shares back to the company in full payment of the note, Campbell did not provide any consideration and thus cannot be considered a purchaser.

The Supreme Court has expressly held that a pledge of stock to secure a loan is a "sale" of securities. This is an unsurprising result since the statute on its face forbids fraud "in connection with" the purchase or sale of securities. Campbell alleges, and now has taken an oath, to the effect that he was duped into executing a $ 170,000 note to exercise options that gained him 33,334 shares of National Media common stock that he would not, but for the alleged fraud, have bought. This is a quintessential 10b-5 claim. The interposition of an option contract between a buyer and the later acquisition of shares does not change this underlying 10b-5 reality, and it is settled that fraud "in connection with" the exercise of options is actionable under § 10(b).

[I]t is hereby ORDERED that the motion is DENIED.

    a. Which primary ethical norm does the court elevate in this decision? Why is this ethical norm important in instances such as these?

    b. What ambiguous words lie at the center of the issue in this case?

    c. What reasons does the court give for its conclusion? In these reasons, did the judge omit any important information?

  2. Now, test your critical thinking skills in the following argument about securities fraud.

Our laws are far too easy on those who commit securities fraud. Ten thousand dollars and five years in prison are not penalties stiff enough for those who violate the public's trust in the stock market and thereby undermine our economy.

Because our economy is based on capitalism, our businesses are dependent upon outside sources of funding. If a company wishes to expand or to purchase another company, it needs access to outside funds. Additionally, people need to make money, and their prospects in today's job market are uncertain. Thus, people need to supplement their income. For this reason, they are willing to "loan" businesses money to expand by purchasing securities.

When people commit securities fraud, they cause two undesirable outcomes. First of all, they cause investors to lose their money. Many of these investors are counting on their investments to enable them to survive after retirement. By committing fraud, white-collar criminals wipe out the investors' savings and force them to work extra years. In this sense, these corporate con-artists are not just taking money away from the investors; they're taking away years of their lives.

Second, when the public hears about acts of securities fraud, they become afraid to invest. When people fail to invest, businesses are unable to raise the capital that they need. This lack of capital may cause them to lay off workers, to close down divisions, or possibly to close altogether. At any rate, lack of capital makes our economy run less efficiently, and when that happens, we all suffer.

Clearly, securities fraud isn't a small crime committed against a business. Instead, its effects are felt by companies, investors, and even workers all across the country. Because acts of securities fraud have such far-reaching effects, those who commit them must be subject to stiffer punishment.

   a. What reasons does the author give for harshly punishing those who use securities to defraud people?

   b. What evidence does the author provide for these reasons?

   c. What information would be helpful for you in evaluating the worth of the author's claims? (Refer to your previous answer in part b.)

   d. From the evidence presented, might a reasonable person draw different conclusions? What might they be?

   e. Which words or phrases are especially ambiguous?

B. Learning the Basics

Matching

1. ____ Securities and Exchange Commission

    a. investment banking firm that agrees to purchase a securities issue from the issuer with a view to eventually sell the securities to brokerage houses

2. ____ security

    b. procedure whereby large corporations can file a registration statement for securities it wishes to sell over a period of time rather than immediately

3. ____ underwriter

    c. federal administrative agency charged with the overall responsibility for the regulation of securities

4. ____ red herring

    d. a person engaged in the business of buying and selling securities for his or her own account

5. ____ shelf registration

    e. preliminary prospectus that contains most of the information that will appear on the final prospectus, except for the price of the securities

6. ____ letter of deficiency

    f. a tender offer that is opposed by the management of a target company

7. ____ dealer

    g. a person engaged in the business of buying and selling securities for others' accounts

8. ____ broker

 h. a stock or bond or any other instrument of investment of interest that represents an investment in common enterprise with reasonable expectations of profits derived solely from the efforts of those other than the investor

9. ____ tender offer

 i. Informal letter issued by the SEC indicating what corrections need to be made in a registration statement for it to become effective

10. ____ hostile bid

 j. a public offer by an individual or corporation made directly to the shareholders of another corporation in an effort to acquire the targeted corporation at a specific price

True or False

1. ____   The Securities and Exchange Commission is concerned only with whether potential investors are provided with adequate information to make investment decisions.

2. ____   A major task of the SEC is to determine whether a stock offering is meritorious.

3. ____   The 1933 Securities Act requires registration of securities any time they are sold.

4. ____   The Fourth, Fifth, and Sixth Amendment rights of witnesses at an SEC investigation are limited.

5. ____   The SEC was created by the Securities Act of 1933.

6. ____   "Interstate commerce" includes dealings between domestic and foreign corporations.

7. ____   The Foreign Corrupt Practices Act is enforced jointly by the SEC and FBI.

8. ____ Foreign corporations whose securities are traded on U.S. markets may be exempted from requirements of registration.

9. ____ Shelf registration allows a corporation to delay the sales of securities that it has already registered.

10. ____ The first attempts to regulate the trade of securities were in response to the stock market crash in 1929.

11. ____ EDGAR is an automated computer that performs collection, validation, indexing, acceptance, and dissemination of reports to be filed with the SEC.

Multiple Choice

1. Which of the following characteristics is used to determine whether an instrument or contract is a security?

a. expectation of profits
b. profit that is derived solely from the efforts of persons other than the investors
c. common enterprise
d. all of the above

2. In a takeover bid, the acquiring company seeks to purchase ____ percent of the target company's securities.

a. 10
b. 5
c. 50
d. 51

3. Oral offers, but not sales, are legal during the

a. waiting period.
b. prefiling period.
c. distributive period.
d. posteffective period.

4. Which of the following is NOT a type of exemption that, under the 1933 Securities Act, allows a transaction to go unregistered?

a. intrastate offering exemption
b. private placement exemption
c. executive dealing exemption
d. small business exemption

5. Which of the following is NOT a criterion that offerings must satisfy for the SEC to integrate and aggregate two otherwise exempt offerings?

a. The offerings are made for the same general purpose and at about the same level of pricing.
b. The offerings concern the same class of securities.
c. The issuing company will raise over $1.5 million through the offerings.
d. The offerings are part of a unitary plan or financing by the issuing company.

6. When the SEC finds evidence of a violation of securities law, it can do any of the following EXCEPT

a. immediately dissolve the issuing company
b. take injunctive action
c. recommend criminal prosecution to the Justice Department
d. take administrative action

7. Which Act prohibits a corporation's bribing a government or political official of another nation?

a. Securities Act of 1933
b. Bribery and Corruption Act
c. International Securities Enforcement Cooperation Act
d. Foreign Corrupt Practices Act

8. If MDM Corporation wants to purchase CW4 Corporation, but the latter company's management opposes the purchase, MDM's bid may best be labeled as a

a. proxy strategy
b. hostile bid
c. injunctive action
d. tender offer

8. Which division of the SEC is in charge of administering disclosure requirements?

a. Division of Enforcement
b. Division of Corporation Finance
c. Division of Investment Management
d. Division of Corporation Regulation

9. Any party that acquires over _____ of a corporation's registered securities must file with both the issuing corporation and the SEC.

a. 50 percent
b. 25 percent
c. 5 percent
d. 15 percent

10. The National Securities Market Improvement Act

a. limited regulation of investment companies to the SEC, and did away with most state authority
b. eliminated the SEC's regulation of purely intrastate corporations
c. both a and b
d. neither a nor b

11. Whether a firm may issue a free writing prospectus prior to the filing of the registration statement depends upon

a. the type of issuer
b. the issuer's history of reporting
c. the issuer's market capitalization
d. all of the above

Short Answer

1. Explain a relationship between the 1933 Securities Act and the Securities Exchange Act of 1934.

2. What are some arguments for and against the "full disclosure rule" of the SEC over securities analysts?

CHAPTER 23
ANTITRUST LAWS

This chapter provides an introduction into laws designed to ensure competition in our economy. We will help you to review this chapter with a series of matching, true-false, multiple choice and short answer questions, after the critical thinking practice.

A.   More Critical Thinking

1. The following antitrust case gives you an opportunity to practice your critical thinking and evaluation skills by reading the case and answering the questions that follow.

United States Postal Service

v.

Flamingo Industries

2004

JUSTICE KENNEDY

Flamingo Industries (USA) Ltd., a private corporation, and its owner and principal officer are the respondents here. Flamingo had been making mail sacks for the Postal Service, but then its contract was terminated. The respondents sued in United States District Court alleging that the Postal Service had sought to suppress competition and create a monopoly in mail sack production. (They also brought claims against the Postal Service under federal procurement law and state law, but those claims are not before us.) The District Court dismissed the antitrust claims, concluding that the Postal Service is not subject to liability under federal antitrust law. The Court of Appeals reversed. It held that the Postal Service can be liable but that it has a limited immunity from antitrust liability for conduct undertaken at the command of Congress. We granted certiorari to consider the question whether the United States Postal Service is a "person" amenable to suit under the controlling antitrust statute. We hold it is not subject to antitrust liability, and we reverse.

Under the PRA [Postal Reorganization Act], the Postal Service retains its monopoly over the carriage of letters, and the power to authorize postal inspectors to search for, seize, and forfeit mail matter transported in violation of the monopoly. It also retains the obligation to provide universal service to all parts of the country. The Postal Service has the power of eminent domain, the power to make postal regulations, and the power to enter international postal agreements subject to the supervision of the Secretary of State.   It has, in

179

addition, powers to contract, to acquire property, and to settle claims. As this brief summary indicates, the Postal Service has significant governmental powers, consistent with its status as an independent establishment of the Executive Branch. It was exempted from many, though not all, statutes governing federal agencies, and specifically subjected to some others. With respect to antitrust liability, however, the PRA neither exempts the Postal Service nor subjects it to liability by express mention. It is silent on the point.

The PRA waives the immunity of the Postal Service from suit by giving it the power "to sue and be sued in its official name." The first question we address is whether that waiver suffices by its own terms to subject the Postal Service to liability under the Sherman Act, as amended. We begin with a discussion of our precedents bearing on the inquiry.

In *Franchise Tax Bd. of Cal.* v. *Postal Service*, the underlying dispute concerned the obligation of the Postal Service to withhold unpaid state taxes from the wages of its employees. A unanimous Court held that the Postal Service was required to respond to an order to withhold the amounts, even though the process was a state administrative tax levy, not an order issued by a state court. The sue-and-be-sued clause, the Court held, must be given broad effect, and the Postal Service was required to respond to the administrative order even though it had not been issued by a judicial body.

The second case in which the Court considered the scope of the waiver effected by the PRA's sue-and-be-sued clause was *Loeffler* v. *Frank*. After the Postal Service had been found liable for damages from employment discrimination in an action brought under Title VII of the Civil Rights Act of 1964, the question arose whether it was subject as well to prejudgment interest. The Court allowed the interest, and in the course of its decision asserted, or repeated, formulations which indicate that the sue-and-be-sued clause effects a broad waiver of immunity. The Court also relied, however, upon the provisions of Title VII itself which, by specific amendment, extended the coverage under the Civil Rights Act to federal employees.

After *Loeffler*, this Court decided *FDIC* v. *Meyer*. In *Meyer*, the question was whether the Federal Savings and Loan Insurance Corp. (FSLIC), an agency of the United States, could be held liable in a so-called "*Bivens* action." A federal statute provided for a waiver of sovereign immunity in suits against the FSLIC, but the Court explained that the interpretation of the waiver statute was just the initial part of a two-part inquiry. Even though sovereign immunity had been waived, there was the further, separate question whether the agency was subject to the substantive liability recognized in *Bivens*. The *Loeffler* Court had not set forth the two-step analysis in the explicit terms *Meyer* used, but it did, as we have said, consult the statute as the source of the liability upon which the obligation to pay prejudgment interest depended.

The two-step analysis in *Meyer* applies here. We ask first whether there is a waiver of sovereign immunity for actions against the Postal Service. If there is, we ask the second question, which is whether the substantive prohibitions of the Sherman Act apply to an independent establishment of the Executive Branch of the United States.

When the Court of Appeals considered the instant case, it cited *Meyer* and seemed at the outset to follow *Meyer*'s two-step analysis. In our view, however, the ensuing discussion in the Court of Appeals' opinion was not consistent with the *Meyer* framework; for, having found that the Postal Service's immunity from suit is waived to the extent provided by the statutory sue-and-be-sued clause, the Court of Appeals relied on the same waiver to conclude that the Sherman Act applies to the Postal Service. This conflated the two steps and resulted in an erroneous conclusion.

As to the first step, as an "independent establishment of the executive branch of the Government of the United States," the Postal Service is part of the Government and that status indicates immunity unless there is a waiver. The sue-and-be-sued clause waives immunity, and makes the Postal Service amenable to suit, as well as to the incidents of judicial process. While Congress waived the immunity of the Postal Service, Congress did not strip it of its governmental status. The distinction is important. An absence of immunity does not result in liability if the substantive law in question is not intended to reach the federal entity. So we proceed to *Meyer*'s second step to determine if the substantive antitrust liability defined by the statute extends to the Postal Service. Under *Meyer*'s second step, we must look to the statute.

Some years before *Meyer* was decided, the Court of Appeals for the District of Columbia Circuit recognized the two distinct inquiries required when the question is whether the Government, or an entity it owns, is named as a defendant in a suit under the antitrust laws. That is the correct approach. Upon examining the Sherman Act, our decisions interpreting it, and the statutes that create and organize the Postal Service, we conclude that the Postal Service is not subject to antitrust liability.

The Sherman Act imposes liability on any "person." It defines the word. It provides that "'person' shall be deemed to include corporations and associations existing under or authorized by the laws of either the United States [or of States or foreign governments.]" It follows then, that corporate or governmental status in most instances is not a bar to the imposition of liability on an entity as a "person" under the Act. The federal prohibition, for instance, binds state governmental bodies.

Congress did not change the definition of "person" in the statute, but added a new section allowing the United States to sue. So, *Cooper*'s conclusion that the United States is not an antitrust "person," in particular not a person who can be an antitrust defendant, was unaltered by Congress' action; indeed, the means Congress used to amend the antitrust law implicitly ratified *Cooper*'s conclusion that the United States is not a proper antitrust defendant.

The remaining question, then, is whether for purposes of the antitrust laws the Postal Service is a person separate from the United States itself. It is not. The statutory designation of the Postal Service as an "independent establishment of the executive branch of the Government of the United States" is not consistent with the idea that it is an entity existing outside the Government. The statutory instruction that the Postal Service is an establishment "of the executive branch of the Government of the United States" indicates just the contrary. The PRA gives the Postal Service a high degree of independence from other offices of the Government, but it remains part of the Government. The Sherman Act defines "person" to include corporations, and had the Congress chosen to create the Postal Service as a federal corporation, we would have to ask whether the Sherman Act's definition extends to the federal entity under this part of the definitional text. Congress, however, declined to create the Postal Service as a Government corporation, opting instead for an independent establishment.

As we have noted, the PRA refers in explicit terms to various federal statutes and specifies that the Postal Service is exempt from some and subject to others. It makes no mention of the Sherman Act or the antitrust laws, however. The silence leads to no helpful inference one way or the other on the issue before us; but the other considerations we have discussed lead us to say that absent an express statement from Congress that the Postal Service can be sued for antitrust violations despite its status as an independent establishment of the Government of the United States, the PRA does not subject the Postal Service to antitrust liability.

Our conclusion is consistent with the nationwide, public responsibilities of the Postal Service. The Postal Service has different goals, obligations, and powers from private corporations. Its goals are not those of private enterprise. The most important difference is that it does not seek profits, but only to break even, which is consistent with its public character. It also has broader obligations, including the provision of universal mail delivery, the provision of free mail delivery to the certain classes of persons, and, most recently, increased public responsibilities related to national security. Finally, the Postal Service has many powers more characteristic of Government than of private enterprise, including its state-conferred monopoly on mail delivery, the power of eminent domain, and the power to conclude international postal agreements.

On the other hand, but in ways still relevant to the nonapplicability of the antitrust laws to the Postal Service, its powers are more limited than those of private businesses. It lacks the prototypical means of engaging in anti-competitive behavior: the power to set prices. This is true both as a matter of mechanics, because pricing decisions are made with the participation of the separate Postal Rate Commission, and as a matter of substance, because price decisions are governed by principles other than profitability. Similarly, before it can close a post office, it must provide written reasons, and its decision is subject to reversal by the Commission for arbitrariness, abuse of discretion, failure to follow procedures, or lack of evidence. The Postal Service's public characteristics and responsibilities indicate it should be treated under the antitrust laws as part of the Government of the United States, not a market participant separate from it.

The Postal Service does operate nonpostal lines of business, for which it is free to set prices independent of the Commission, and in which it may seek profits to offset losses in the postal business. The great majority of the organization's business, however, consists of postal services.

The Postal Service, in both form and function, is not a separate antitrust person from the United States. It is part of the Government of the United States and so is not controlled by the antitrust laws. The judgment of the Court of Appeals is reversed.

It is so ordered.

    a. What are the issue and conclusion of this case?

    b. What reasons does the Court provide to support its conclusion?

    c. What kind of evidence does the court primarily use to support its reasoning? Provide examples of this evidence in the case, and explain how this evidence contributes to the Court's reasoning.

2. Now apply your critical thinking skills to the following argument about antitrust law.

Our antitrust laws are far too weak. If you just take a look at the business world today, it is blatantly obvious that companies are gaining too much power.
Take, for example, Microsoft. This company is so big that its president, Bill Gates, has more power than the President of the United States. Microsoft controls over 90 percent of the market for computer operating system software, and it is showing no signs of losing any of its market share. Other companies are powerful, too. Consider Nike, a company that can pay its workers only

pennies per hour and then charge consumers hundreds of dollars for its products. Another example is General Electric. Not only is G.E. powerful in the electronics industry, it has also branched out into other industries as well. It owns NBC, a network that many Americans depend on for news. In the past, Americans could count on the news to give them an objective report of what's going on in our nation. Now, they hear only the stories that the corporate bigwigs want them to hear.

These corporations are so powerful and so impersonal that they'll just get up and leave if they think they can get more money elsewhere. New York City lost over a million jobs in the manufacturing industry between 1970 and 1984 because companies would rather put their factories in Third World nations than pay Americans a decent wage.

If our society is to return to its status as the greatest in the world, Congress and the courts need to broaden the scope of antitrust laws. We need to make sure that any corporation powerful enough to control public opinion or to ignore its obligations to society is broken up.

    a. What reasons are given for the author's conclusion?

    b. Evaluate the evidence given for these reasons.

    c. What important words or phrases in the passage are ambiguous?

B. Learning the Basics
Matching

1. ____ laissez-faire

    a. prohibits price discrimination, tying and exclusive-dealing arrangements, and corporate mergers that substantially lessen competition in interstate commerce

2. ____ Chicago School

    b. economic market in which one business has enough power to fix the price of goods and services

3. ____ Harvard School

    c. approach to antitrust policy based on the preservation of economic competition

4. ____ parens patriae suit

    d. merger between two or more companies producing the same or similar products and competing in the same geographic market

5. ____ class action suit

    e. suit brought by one member of a group on behalf of all members of the group

6. ____ Sherman Act

    f. concept that business should be able to compete without government intervention

7. ____ Clayton Act

    g. merger between two or more firms that have a supplier-customer relationship

8. ____ horizontal merger

    h. suit brought by a state's attorney general on behalf of citizens of the state

9. ____ vertical merger

    i. states that every combination, contract, or conspiracy that constitutes an unreasonable restraint on interstate trade is illegal

10. ____ monopoly

    j. approach to antitrust policy based on the goal of economic efficiency

True or False

1. ____ The Chicago School of antitrust policy favors tighter regulation of business than does the Harvard School.

2. ____ The Department of Justice and the Federal Communication Commission are responsible for enforcing antitrust laws in the public sector.

3. ____ Employees can be punished when a court rules that a company has violated antitrust law.

4. ____ The Sherman Act regulates only trade that occurs within a state's borders.

5. ____ Horizontal price fixing occurs when competitors collude to set prices for a product or service.

6. ____ The Sherman Act was passed to clarify the Clayton Act by advising businesspeople about which actions were lawful and which were not.

7. ____ The primary criterion used by courts to determine the relevant product market is cross-elasticity of demand.

8. ____ The Clayton Act allows individuals to bring suit against a company to recover injuries resulting from antitrust violations.

9. ____ The narrow language of the Federal Trade Commission Act of 1914 makes it virtually useless.

10. ____ All bank mergers must be approved by a federal banking agency before they occur.

Multiple Choice

1. Which of the following is NOT a primary goal of antitrust legislation?

a. the preservation of a large number of small sellers
b. government control of business
c. maximizing consumer welfare
d. prevention of concentrated market power

2. A consent decree

a. shuts a business down
b. enables businesses to perform an otherwise unlawful action
c. can be issued only by the President of the United States
d. binds a company to stop an allegedly illegal activity without its having to admit guilt

3. Identical actions taken independently, but nearly simultaneously, by the leading companies in an industry is

a. conscious parallelism
b. predatory pricing
c. vertical price fixing
d. a horizontal merger

4. Which of the following is NOT among the criteria used by the Supreme Court to determine whether a firm is a monopoly?

a. relevant product and geographic markets
b. overwhelming market power
c. intent
d. number of employee

5. If Ford purchased a steel plant, this acquisition would be a

a. horizontal merger
b. vertical merger
c. conglomerate merger
d. monopoly

6. The Hertindahl-Hirschman index

a. was developed by two Supreme Court justices
b. is used to determine when the Justice Department will challenge a horizontal merger
c. analyzes the post-acquisition market share of a recently-merged corporation
d. both b and c

7. All of the following are vertical restraints of trade EXCEPT

a. price fixing
b. clearance sales
c. tying arrangements
d. exclusive-dealing contracts

8. Which of the following is an example of antitrust legislation?

a. Sherman Act
b. Federal Trade Commission Act
c. Clayton Act
d. all of the above

9. Which of the following requires the plaintiff to prove only that the alleged offense took place in a case involving a business activity that is extremely anticompetitive in nature?

a. per se standard
b. parens patriae doctrine
c. reason of rule standard
d. nolo contendere plea

10. Horizontal division of markets

a. is legal in almost all instances
b. eliminates only price competition
c. eliminates all forms of competition
d. was outlawed by the Bank Merger Act of 1966

Short Answer

1. The Sherman Act requires three elements to constitute a violation. What are they?

2. When are tying arrangements illegal under antitrust law?

CHAPTER 24
LAWS OF DEBTOR-CREDITOR RELATIONS AND CONSUMER PROTECTION

This final chapter introduces you to the laws protecting each of us in our roles as consumers and borrowers. Following is a case and an argument designed to put your critical thinking skills to the test. Then, we conclude with a section of objective questions.

A.   More Critical Thinking

1. We have provided a formal opportunity for you to evaluate the Supreme Court's legal reasoning by including the following bankruptcy case.

KAWAAUHAU v. GEIGER
1998

When petitioner Kawaauhau sought treatment for her injured foot, respondent Dr. Geiger examined and hospitalized her to attend to the risk of infection. Although Geiger knew that intravenous penicillin would have been more effective, he prescribed oral penicillin, explaining in his testimony that he understood his patient wished to minimize treatment costs. Geiger then departed on a business trip, leaving Kawaauhau in the care of other physicians, who decided she should be transferred to an infectious disease specialist. When Geiger returned, he canceled the transfer and discontinued all antibiotics because he believed the infection had subsided. Kawaauhau's condition deteriorated, requiring amputation of her leg below the knee. After trial in the malpractice suit brought by Kawaauhau and her husband, the jury found Geiger liable and awarded the Kawaauhaus approximately $355,000 in damages. Geiger, who carried no malpractice insurance, moved to Missouri, where his wages were garnished by the Kawaauhaus. Geiger then petitioned for bankruptcy. The Kawaauhaus requested the Bankruptcy Court to hold the malpractice judgment nondischargeable under 11 U.S.C. § 523(a)(6), which provides that a "discharge [in bankruptcy] . . . does not discharge an individual debtor from any debt . . . for willful and malicious injury . . . to another." Concluding that Geiger's treatment fell far below the appropriate standard of care and therefore ranked as "willful and malicious," that court held the debt nondischargeable. The District Court affirmed, but the Eighth Circuit reversed, holding that §523(a)(6)'s exemption from discharge is confined to debts for an intentional tort, so that a debt for malpractice remains dischargeable because it is based on negligent or reckless conduct.

JUSTICE GINSBURG

Section 523(a)(6) of the Bankruptcy Code provides that a debt "for willful and malicious injury by the debtor to another" is not dischargeable. The question before us is whether a debt arising from a medical malpractice judgment, attributable to negligent or reckless conduct, falls within this statutory exception. We hold that it does not and that the debt is dischargeable.

Section 523(a)(6) of the Bankruptcy Code provides:

"(a) A discharge under Section 727, 1141, 1228(a), 1228(b), or 1328(b) of this title does not discharge an individual debtor from any debt

"(6) for willful and malicious injury by the debtor to another entity or to the property of another entity."

The Kawaauhaus urge that the malpractice award fits within this exception because Dr. Geiger intentionally rendered inadequate medical care to Margaret Kawaauhau that necessarily led to her injury. According to the Kawaauhaus, Geiger deliberately chose less effective treatment because he wanted to cut costs, all the while knowing that he was providing substandard care. Such conduct, the Kawaauhaus assert, meets the "willful and malicious" specification of §523(a)(6).

We confront this pivotal question concerning the scope of the "willful and malicious injury" exception: Does §523(a)(6)'s compass cover acts, done intentionally, that cause injury (as the Kawaauhaus urge), or only acts done with the actual intent to cause injury (as the Eighth Circuit ruled)? The words of the statute strongly support the Eighth Circuit's reading.

The word "willful" in (a)(6) modifies the word "injury," indicating that nondischargeability takes a deliberate or intentional injury, not merely a deliberate or intentional act that leads to injury. Had Congress meant to exempt debts resulting from unintentionally inflicted injuries, it might have described instead "willful acts that cause injury." Or, Congress might have selected an additional word or words, i.e., "reckless" or "negligent," to modify injury." Moreover, as the Eighth Circuit observed, the (a)(6) formulation triggers in the lawyer's mind the category "intentional torts," as distinguished from negligent or reckless torts. Intentional torts generally require that the actor intend "the consequences of an act," not simply "the act itself."

The Kawaauhaus' more encompassing interpretation could place within the excepted category a wide range of situations in which an act is intentional, but injury is unintended, i.e., neither desired nor in fact anticipated by the debtor. Every traffic accident stemming from an initial intentional act-for example, intentionally rotating the wheel of an automobile to make a left-hand turn without first checking oncoming traffic-could fit the description. A knowing breach of contract "could also qualify. A construction so broad would be incompatible with the "well-known" guide that exceptions to discharge should be confined to those plainly expressed."

Subsequent decisions of this Court are in accord with our construction. In *Mclatyre v. Kavanaugh*, a broker "deprived another of his property forever by deliberately disposing of it without semblance of authority." The Court held that this act constituted an intentional injury to property of another, bringing it within the discharge exception. But in *Davis v. Aetna Acceptance Co.*, the Court explained that not every tort judgment for conversion is exempt from discharge. Negligent or reckless acts, the Court held, do not suffice to establish that a resulting injury is "willful and malicious."

Finally, the Kawaauhaus maintain that, as a policy matter, malpractice judgments should be excepted from discharge, at least when the debtor acted recklessly or carried no malpractice insurance. Congress, of course, may so decide. But unless and until Congress makes such a decision, we must follow the current direction §523(a)(6) provides.

We hold that debts arising from recklessly or negligently inflicted injuries do not fall within the compass of §523(a)(6). For the reasons stated, the judgment of the Court of Appeals for the Eighth Circuit is **AFFIRMED**.

    a. What ambiguous phrase is of central importance to this case? How does each side define this ambiguous phrase? Why is this ambiguity so important?

    b. What reasons does the Court give for its conclusion?

    c. Examine the next-to-last paragraph (the one that begins, "Finally,..."). What ethical norm does the Court elevate here? With what other ethical norm might this norm conflict?

2. Now, critically evaluate this argument about children's advertising.

The FTC needs to set tighter standards with regard to children's advertising. The FTCA is supposed to protect consumers from deceptive advertising, and it is about time the FTC does its job and enforces the law.

Children are less sophisticated than adults, and they're unable to separate reality from fiction. Therefore, they are more susceptible to the cunning ploys of marketing and advertising wizards. These people show no shame, endlessly manipulating small children just to make money.

"How are our children being manipulated?" you ask. It's obvious. Every time they turn on the TV, they're subjected to a plethora of commercial advertisements. Many of the TV shows that kids watch are nothing more than half-hour advertisements for a particular toy. Additionally, the ads themselves mislead children. In the ads, toy companies show kids looking as happy and satisfied as possible while they play with the toys. The children who see these images are convinced that if they only had the toy, they would be just as happy. However, when they actually receive the toy, they find that it's fun to play with for a few hours, but not much longer. They never experience the continuing climax of joy that the advertisers make them think they will. Such disappointments are likely to harm the children psychologically, making them become cynical at a young age.

For these reasons, the FTC must step in to protect our children from these money-hungry marketers. To fail to do so is to jeopardize America's future: its children.

a. What primary ethical norm is downplayed by this argument?

b. In this argument, what is the relevant rule of law to which the author refers? (You'll need to refer to your primary text to find the actual words of this law.)

c. What are the reasons that the author gives for tighter control of advertising to children?

d. Examine your answers to b and c. What effect does this comparison have on your willingness to accept the argument?

e. What relevant information does the author leave out of this argument? Why is this information important?

B. Learning the Basics

Matching

1. ____ lien

    a. provision of the Bankruptcy Reform Act aimed primarily at financially-troubled businesses

2. ____ attachment

    b. exaggerated recommendation made to promote a product in a sales pitch

3. ____ garnishment

              c. party who borrows money or goods

4. ____ puffery

              d. party who lends money or goods in a transaction

5. ____ Regulation Z

              e. court-ordered judgment allowing a local officer of the court to seize property of a debtor

6. ____ Chapter 13

              f. order by a clerk of the court directing the sheriff to seize any of the debtor's property within the court's jurisdiction

7. ____ Chapter 11

              g. provision of the Bankruptcy Reform Act that provides a wage earner's plan

8. ____ writ of execution

              h. claim on a debtor's property that must be satisfied before any creditor can make a claim

9. ____ creditor

              i. an order of the court granted to a creditor to seize the wages or bank accounts of a debtor

10. ____ debtor

              j. requires lenders to disclose certain information to borrowers

True or False

1. ____ An artisan's lien is placed on the real property of a debtor when she fails to pay for work done by the creditor.

2. ____ If a garnishment order is granted, the creditor may seize the debtor's wages and bank accounts, but not the debtor's pension accounts.

3. ____ The Magnuson-Moss Warranty Act covers both oral and written warranties.

4. ____ In open-end credit transactions, all conditions of the loan must be agreed upon before the loan is given.

5. ____ Caveat emptor refers to the mindset that consumers may relax while the government regulates market transactions.

6. ____ Only businesses may file for bankruptcy under Chapter 11.

7. ____ Suretyships allow a third party to pay the debts of a debtor in the event that the latter does not pay the creditor.

8. ____ The freedom to contract doctrine holds that people can enter into only those contracts that have been pre-approved by the government.

9. ____ Most of the laws regulating credit are unnecessary because consumer credit is not important to our economy.

10. ____ The Uniform Consumer Credit Code was designed to create consistency in federal law with regard to consumer credit.

11. ____ Under the Fair Credit Reporting Act of 1970, an employer must obtain a job applicant's consent prior to requesting a credit report

Multiple Choice

1. A contract that allows a third person to become secondarily liable to a creditor for the debts of a debtor is a(n)

a. suretyship
b. foreclosure
c. lien
d. guaranty

2. The _____ Act amended the Federal Trade Commission Act to prohibit "unfair or deceptive acts or practices."

a. Taft-Hartley
b. Wheeler-Lea
c. Lanham
d. Customer-Protection

3.   The major enforcer of the Truth-in-Lending Act is

a.   the public
b.   the Chairperson of the Federal Reserve Bank
c.   the Secretary of the Treasury
d.   the Chairperson of the Federal Trade Commission

4.   What kind of legal actions might a violator of the Equal Credit Opportunity Act face?

a.   civil injunctive actions
b.   administrative actions
c.   civil suits
d.   all of the above

5.   Who may file for bankruptcy reorganization under Chapter 12?

a.   migrant workers
b.   farmers
c.   fishermen
d.   b and c only

6.   Under _____ of the Bankruptcy Reform Act a debtor's assets are sold so the proceeds can be used to pay off the creditor.

a.   Chapter 7
b.   Chapter 11
c.   the preamble
d.   Title IX

7.   Which of the following is not among the criteria used by the courts to determine whether an advertisement is unfair or deceptive?

a.   there is a misrepresentation or omission likely to mislead consumers
b.   intent to deceive consumers
c.   the misrepresentation is material
d.   consumers are acting reasonably given the circumstances

8.   A statement by a public figure professing the quality of some product or service is a(n)

a.   misleading advertisement
b.   testimonial
c.   material misrepresentation
d.   automatic violation of the Landham Act

9. Which of the following practices violate the FTC's regulations on telemarketing?

a. calling at 9:30 p.m.
b. failing to inform the person who receives the call that it is a sales call
c. both a and b
d. none of the above

10. Which Act seeks to make creditors disclose all terms of a credit arrangement before they enter into an agreement with a consumer/debtor?

a. Truth-in-Lending Act
b. Fair Credit Billing Act
c. Fair Credit Reporting Act
d. Equal Credit Opportunity Act

Short Answer

1. Explain a relationship between attachment and a writ of execution.

2. Can you explain the rationale for naming debts that cannot be discharged by Chapter 7, 11, 12, or 13 bankruptcy proceedings?

ANSWERS

Matching	True and False	Multiple Choice
1. d	1. False	1. b
2. a	2. True	2. d
3. f	3. False	3. d
4. c	4. False	4. a
5. g	5. False	5. c
6. h	6. False	6. b
7. e	7. True	7. b
8. b	8. True	
	9. False	
	10. False	
	11. False	
	12. False	

Short Answer

1. Critical thinking is the ability to recognize the structure of what people say (their reasoning) and then apply evaluative criteria to assess the quality of the reasoning offered in support of the conclusion.

2. Critical thinking is important for the legal environment of business because you will be faced with many ethical dilemmas as a future business manager. These dilemmas require legal analysis and ethical understanding guided by critical thinking. Furthermore, learning these critical thinking skills in the legal environment of business context will help you transfer these skills to your role as a business leader.

3. a. What are the facts?
   b. What is the issue?
   c. What are the reasons and conclusion?
   d. What are the relevant rules of law?
   e. Does the legal argument contain significant ambiguity?
   f. What ethical norms are fundamental to the court's reasoning?
   g. How appropriate are the legal analogies?
   h. Is there relevant missing information?

4. The primary ethical norms that can influence a judge's reasoning are the following: justice, security, efficiency, and freedom. We want to identify these norms because the interplay between the norms will provide direction for the laws governing business behavior. For example, if a judge values justice more than efficiency, she will be more likely to make a certain decision. Knowing the ethical norms help us to better understand the

judge's reasoning. Furthermore, if we know a judge's value preference, we may be able to predict her decision.

<u>Chapter 2</u>

More Critical Thinking

1. a. In this case, the Delaware Supreme Court was extremely concerned with the goals of the spousal immunity doctrine. The Court overturned precedent because the Court felt that the Doctrine no longer achieved its purpose of preserving family harmony and preventing fraud and collusion. Is there any evidence to support the Court's opinion about the Doctrine's ability to achieve its goals? Is there any evidence that spouses are more or less likely to stay married if they are able to bring suit against each other? Is there any evidence that spouses are more or less likely to commit fraud or engage in collusion if they are able to sue each other? If the Court does not have strong evidence about the Doctrine's ability to achieve its goals, then the Court relied on weak reasoning when overturning precedent.

   b. The Delaware Supreme Court cited *Plotkin* and *Alfree* for the purpose of overturning the precedent set by those cases. Given the American legal system's assumption that precedent should be followed, the Court in this case needs to somehow show that this case is different from *Plotkin* and *Alfree* to justify overturning the precedent. The Court claims that the goals promoted by the rulings in *Plotkin* and *Alfree* are no longer viable due to contemporary conditions; but, as discussed above, the Court does not provide convincing evidence. The Court's distinction between *Plotkin* and *Alfree*, and this case may not be appropriate.

   The Court also cites *Williams* as support for their decision in this case. There is one key difference between *Williams* and this case. *Williams* overturned the parental immunity doctrine; whereas, this case overturned the spousal immunity doctrine. Are there significant differences between the two doctrines and the purposes of each? Are there significant differences between the abilities of the two doctrines to achieve their purposes? Are there significant differences between parental and spousal relationships that affect the necessity of the doctrines? Without more information about the two doctrines, it is impossible to tell whether the Court's analogy to *Williams* was appropriate.

   c. The Court seemed to be heavily influenced by the fact that only four other states recognized the doctrine of spousal immunity. The Court also noted that, among all of the states that have overturned the doctrine of spousal immunity, not one has reenacted the Doctrine. The Court sees these facts as evidence of the appropriateness of overturning the

Doctrine; however, as discussed above, the quality of these facts is questionable.

2. a. The conclusion of the argument is that fairness requires election of judges. But fairness is quite complicated. For instance, the idea that one should be responsible for his or her actions is tied to fairness as earned award or blame. This form of fairness certainly is important. But its application is full of potential confusion. Fairness to the judges would require their being judged by their legal peers, the only group who has been trained to understand legal reasoning. Fairness to the recipients of legal reasoning, the voters, would require that the general public have some method of checking on their judges. So just what is fair in this case?

   Another instance of ambiguity is present in the person's reasoning that because judges "make the rules," they need to be checked. If we were to see that phrase as meaning that judges are all-powerful, then the author's argument is especially important. But if what judges do as they make laws is interpret what elected legislatures have done, the people already have a check on judges via their election of representatives.

   b. The reasons are that those affected by behavior should control that behavior, judges make the very rules that govern our behavior, and citizens are now powerless in the face of judicial rulings.

   c. (1) Citizens need to take a more active role in Congressional elections to voice their concerns about what kinds of judges should be appointed.
   (2) Congress should establish a review board to hold individual judges accountable to the people.
   (3) Public tax money should be used to sponsor an ombudsperson office to provide citizen feedback on the quality of judicial decisions.
   (4) Public polls about judicial performance should be commissioned and publicized to apply social pressure on judges.

3. a. The reader should become alarmed about the power and growth of administrative agencies. Every sentence in the argument leads to that viewpoint.

   b. Yes, in each case the person making the argument is concerned about potential abuse of power. The writers are seeking some avenue for assuring that power will be widely dispersed. The downside of this orientation, of course, is the resulting slowness of policy responses, as well as the yielding of power to those who may know little about the issues involved.

c. (1) What are the Congressional controls on the rulemaking by agencies? Perhaps there is already more control on the power of these agencies than the author seems to indicate.

(2) Does the Constitution <u>imply</u> that administrative agencies might have extensive powers? The author's argument is that something unconstitutional is occurring. But the Constitution is a relatively small document. Much of what it permits has been inferred from its broad guidelines.

(3) Have the needs met by the agencies "exploded"? If they have then what looks like abuse of power might instead be responsible governmental activity, meeting the needs of the society.

Learning the Basics

Matching	True and False	Multiple Choice
1. d	1. False	1. c
2. f	2. True	2. a
3. p	3. False	3. d
4. k	4. True	4. a
5. b	5. False	5. c
6. j	6. True	6. b
7. o	7. False	7. d
8. g	8. False	8. c
9. l	9. True	9. d
10. m	10. False	10. b
11. c	11. False	
12. i	12. True	
13. e	13. True	
14. a	14. True	
15. n	15. False	
16. h		

Short Answer

1. The legal environment of business includes the study of: legal reasoning, critical thinking skills, and ethical norms; legal and administrative law processes; selected areas of public and private law; relevant international dimensions.

2. a. Becoming aware of the rules of doing business
   b. Familiarizing yourself with the legal limits on business freedom
   c. Sensitizing yourself to potential misconduct of competitors
   d. Being able to communicate with your lawyer
   e. Making you a fully informed citizen
   f. Developing an employable skill

g. Providing a heightened awareness of business ethics
h. Exploring the complexity of business decisions
i. Discovering the excitement of the law and business

3. The positivist school relies on case precedent and statutory law to determine which direction the law should take. In contrast, proponents of the sociological school argue that human behavior or contemporary community values are the most important factors in determining the direction the law should take.

4. Both emphasize the influence of power relationships and law. Critical legal jurisprudence suggests that the elite have created a belief structure to rationalize their dominant power. Similarly, feminist jurisprudence suggests that the law is a means of men's expressing power over women.

5. In a civil case, the plaintiff must show the defendant's guilt beyond a preponderance of evidence. However, in a criminal case, the plaintiff must prove beyond a reasonable doubt that the defendant is guilty. Proof beyond a reasonable doubt is much more stringent than proof beyond a preponderance of evidence.

Chapter 3

More Critical Thinking

1. *Swidler v. Berlin* Case

   a. The court argues that it has been "generally, if not universally" accepted that the attorney-client privilege survives the death of a client. The burden of proof is on the Independent Counsel to suggest that disclosure should occur. Because the independent counsel did not demonstrate strong reasons for overturning this common law and thus meet their burden of proof, the court holds that the attorney-client privilege prevents disclosure. The court seems quite interested in maintaining the status quo.

   b. The court seemed overly concerned about preserving the status quo. In other words, it seemed very afraid to overturn a practice that was "generally, if not universally" accepted. A practice is not necessarily good or correct simply because it has been in practice for a long time and many people agree with it. However, the fact that it has been "generally, if not universally" accepted that the attorney-client privilege survives the death of a client seemed to be most persuasive to the court.

   c. The court states that if a client knows that the attorney-client privilege ends at his death, he may be less willing to disclose information relevant to his relationship with his attorney during his life. Consequently, the court would want to uphold the attorney client privilege after death for the same reasons that the attorney-client privilege holds through a client's life. This reason provides support for maintaining the common law and preventing disclosure after a client dies. The statement is an example of a reason that provides support for a larger reason.

2. Juries Argument

  a. Conclusion: Juries make biased decisions based on sympathy.

  b. Reason 1) Juries give excessive awards to "innocent" victims. Reason 2) Studies suggest that juries struggle to fulfill their roles. Because they are confused, they use their emotions to make decisions. Reason 3) Juries do not consider evidence. These reasons suggest that juries have problems making decisions in cases. However, the author concludes that juries make decisions because of sympathy. The only reason somewhat related to sympathy is Reason 1. The author offers no reason why he or she believes that sympathy causes jurors to make flawed decisions. Thus, the conclusion does not seem to make much sense with those reasons.

  An alternative conclusion would be the following: Jurors struggle to make reasonable decisions in the courtroom. This conclusion seems to make more sense with the reasons. It does not offer an explanation for why juries have problems making decisions. For example, the statistics regarding the jury's ignorance about the judge's rules support the conclusion that jurors have trouble performing their roles.

  c. "Juries" is an example of an ambiguous word. We do not know whether the author is referring to grand juries or petit juries. It is important to identify the ambiguity because we would probably be more concerned about the flaws in decisions made by the petit jury. The grand jury simply decides whether there is enough evidence to charge a defendant with a crime. However, a petit jury is the fact-finding jury; it decides a case. Therefore, because a flawed decision by a petit jury could mean harsh consequences (e.g., prison sentences, large fines, etc.), we would be more concerned about petit juries. Thus, we would be better able to assess the argument if we knew to which kind of jury the author was referring.

  d. What percentage of jury decisions are flawed, according to the author's definition of "flawed"? What percentage of jury decisions are accurate decisions? The answers to these questions would create a better understanding of jury decision making. We need to know more about the number of biased and unbiased decisions. The author of the argument may be persuaded by one or two cases. If the majority of juries are performing accurately, perhaps we do not need to be concerned about jury decision making.

How many cases have been reduced because of excessive damages? How do we know that these awards were not justified? Although the author claims that juries give excessive damage awards, what evidence does he have to support this claim? He mentioned the McDonald's coffee example. However, he provides only one example. Certainly, I could find an example of a jury decision that did not award excessive damages. Thus, we need a better idea of what a *typical* jury case is like.

Are the studies and statistics accurate? Who completed the studies? Was that person biased? For example, the author cites a study of actual jurors. How many jurors were questioned? If only 8 of 10 actual jurors said they were lost, we should be less persuaded than 800 of 1000 saying they were "lost" in the trial.

Finally, we need to know the types of cases that apply to jurors. For example, jurors may perform their role very well in certain types of cases and struggle in others. For example, a product liability case might be much more difficult to decide than a defamation case. Perhaps the jurors struggle as a result of the type of case rather than their inability to make unbiased opinions.

Learning the Basics

Matching	True and False	Multiple Choice
1. e	1. False	1. c
2. g	2. False	2. c
3. a	3. True	3. d
4. i	4. False	4. c
5. d	5. False	5. d
6. b	6. True	6. b
7. h	7. False	7. b
8. f	8. False	8. d
9. c	9. True	9. d
	10. False	

Short Answer

1. Although the adversary system has been in existence since the beginning of our nation, it is not necessarily the best way to achieve justice. The adversary system is good because both sides aggressively seek the truth while strict rules of admissibility govern the admissibility of evidence. However, the adversary system is problematic for several reasons. First, each side ignores evidence that might harm its position. Thus, the final ruling is not necessarily fair. Furthermore, the process is time consuming and expensive. Moreover, the adversary system favors the wealthy. Those

who have money can get better lawyers and can afford to litigate longer. Finally, the adversary system promotes winners and losers, and compromises are often the best way to resolve problems. Additionally, the system is not the best simply because it has been in place the longest. The length of the existence of the system tells us very little about the fairness or effectiveness of the system.

2. While both petit and grand juries are types of juries, there are distinct differences between the two. Petit juries are finders of fact for trial courts. A trial court could be a civil or a criminal case. However, grand juries issue indictments only in criminal cases. Grand juries determine whether there is enough evidence to justify charging a defendant with a crime. Thus, in a criminal case, you will have a grand jury and a petit jury. In civil cases, you will have only a petit jury.

3. Why does a court need both in personam and subject matter jurisdiction to decide a case? In personam jurisdiction, or jurisdiction over the person, is the power to make decisions affecting legal rights. The court gains this power over the plaintiff when the plaintiff files a complaint. The court gains this power over the defendant when the defendant is summoned or responds to the complaint. Subject matter jurisdiction is the power of the court to hear and render a decision in a particular type of case, and this power is predetermined by the Constitution. Subject matter jurisdiction is important because if a judge rules in a case where the court does not have subject matter jurisdiction, the decision is meaningless. Exclusive federal jurisdiction is given to cases involving admiralty, bankruptcy, copyrights, trademarks and patents, claims against the U.S. government, and federal criminal prosecutions. The state has subject matter jurisdiction over all cases not under exclusive federal jurisdiction. States and federal courts have concurrent jurisdiction over issues of federal questions and diversity of citizenship.

4. The Class Action Fairness Act of 2005 altered the rules surrounding class action suits, affecting the plaintiffs and defendants differently. For instance, the Act made it easier for plaintiffs to access the federal courts, but simultaneously made it easier for defendants to argue in federal courts, which are likely to award smaller damages. The Act restricted the amount of money that could be paid in fees to the plaintiffs' attorneys, but did not restrict the amount of money that could be paid to the defendants' attorneys. When these two factors are combined, the plaintiffs may actually be at a disadvantage because of the Act. Plaintiffs' attorneys cannot look forward to the same enormous legal fees at the end of a case, and the cases may increasingly be tried in a venue that awards smaller damages. Without strong monetary incentives to take on the work associated with a class action suit, talented plaintiffs' attorneys may be hard to find.

Chapter 4

More Critical Thinking

1. Trailmobile Case

   a. The Court defined the issue to be whether the arbitrator had the power to determine whether Wigginton had been terminated for "just cause." Trailmobile, however, thought that "just cause" was defined in the contract and that thus the arbitrator's only duty was to determine whether or not Wigginton had been involved in a fight.

   b. Judge Wollman noted that the contract provided that employees could be dismissed for "just cause" without defining the meaning of the phrase in the contract. Thus, although fighting is specifically mentioned as an offense penalized by dismissal in the employee handbook, submitting the matter to arbitration gave the arbitrator the power to determine whether the employee's cause of dismissal was indeed "just."

   c. Trailmobile might clarify or delete the "just cause" clause in its contract with employees, perhaps replacing it with a list of specified offenses that automatically qualify an employee for dismissal.

2. Private Jury Trial Argument

   a. The author comes to the following conclusion: Private jury trials include the benefits associated with litigation but remove the negative aspects of litigation.

   b. First, because the jurors may have previous experience with a party, such as a corporation or a business, they might be biased against that party. For example, pretend that a juror heard a tort case involving one company one year. The next year, the same juror hears a similar tort case involving the same company. Because the juror heard the earlier case, the juror might be more likely to believe that the company is at fault. Thus, jurors may have a greater chance of being biased by previous cases. Second, the jurors in the database may not be very diverse. They are probably relatively affluent people who are at least somewhat interested in the law. Consequently, a party may be disadvantaged by the lack of diversity.

   c. First, the author states that while jurors in litigation struggle to perform their role, private juries are more educated and more interested in the system. Consequently, the author claims that the private juries will make better decisions. Is there any evidence that private juries make better decisions? Furthermore, how many people use private juries? What kinds of cases are typically heard in private jury cases? This information is important because one type of case may be more successful in private jury trials. Moreover, the author seems to ignore the negative aspects associated with jury trials. Why should we NOT use jury trials? Are they fair?

    d. What do you mean by "better decisions"? Do you mean correct decisions? Do you mean decisions in which both parties are satisfied with the decision?

3. Litigation Argument

    a. Conclusion: Litigation is the best form of dispute resolution.
    Reason 1: Most parties that use an ADR method end up appealing the decision through litigation.
    Reason 2: ADR forces parties to compromise when they should not be expected to compromise.

    b. The author uses the phrase "alternative dispute method," but we do not know which ADR methods he is including in "alternative dispute method." In the third paragraph, the author seems to be describing mediation. However, he uses "alternative dispute method" as a blanket term. Therefore, because we do not know what he means by "alternative dispute method," we cannot accept his argument.

Learning the Basics

Matching	True and False	Multiple Choice
1. f	1. True	1. c
2. c	2. False	2. c
3. g	3. False	3. b
4. a	4. False	4. c
5. b	5. False	5. a
6. d	6. True	6. d
7. e	7. True	7. c
	8. False	8. d
	9. True	

Short Answer

1. There are several problems with the statement. First, the word "best" is ambiguous. No single method of dispute resolution is best for any type of case. The "best" method for resolving any kind of dispute would depend on the individual disputant's objectives and the circumstances surrounding the dispute. Often the "best" method from one party's perspective is not the "best" method from another party's perspective. When a party wants to set a precedent and it believes that its case arose in a jurisdiction where

the judge is likely to make a ruling that is favorable to its position, litigation is probably the best method for resolving its dispute. Litigation would also be preferable if the party wanted to generate publicity for its case. This party may even think that it will lose in court, but it might still drum up enough public protest to get the company it is suing to change the contested behavior. Furthermore, if the plaintiff is suing for damages, litigation with a jury might be preferable because juries are often more sympathetic and hand down bigger judgments. Arbitration is certainly not the least adversarial alternative dispute resolution method. In fact, it is almost as adversarial as litigation, but its informality makes it seem somewhat less adversarial, as does the fact that the arbitrator often will try to come up with a decision that gives both parties something.

2. Mediation is premised on the value assumption of cooperation over victory or collective responsibility over individual responsibility. Both parties take responsibility to give up something rather than go through arbitration or litigation to see what they are forced to give up. Other forms of alternative dispute resolution are more focused on clear winners and losers. Mediation is a much more collaborative process and allows both parties to come to their own decisions.

3. While ADR methods may be more efficient than traditional litigation, the value of justice may not necessarily be well-served by ADR methods. For instance, ADR may allow a corporation to hide its faults from the public, perhaps allowing them to do further harm to consumers. In some forms of ADR, like mediation, there is also a danger that a legally inexperienced or biased mediator might neglect the procedural rights.

Chapter 5

More Critical Thinking

1. *Black* Case

   a. The Supreme Court argued that the Supreme Court of Virginia misapplied the *R.A.V* precedent, as the state Supreme Court held that the Virginia statute was unconstitutional because it included content-based discrimination. In other words, the Virginia statute specifically applied to cross-burning, while not taking into account other types of behavior that might arouse anger. However, Justice O'Connor explained that *R.A.V.* was an applicable analogy in the *Black* case, but not for the reasons set forth by the state Supreme Court. Instead, O'Connor explained, *R.A.V.* does not suggest that all content-based discrimination is unconstitutional. While some types of content-based discrimination are unconstitutional, others are not. In the *Black* case, the U.S. Supreme Court argued that the Virginia statute was unconstitutional, not because the statute discriminated on the basis of content, but because the statute included a provision that made cross-burners guilty in almost every instance, even before violators were provided an opportunity to make a defense.

b. "Intent to intimidate," "unacceptable risk," and "suppression of ideas" are phrases that can have a variety of meanings. What are the criteria for determining whether there is intent to intimidate, whether an individual's conduct creates an "unacceptable risk," or whether such conduct leads to the suppression of ideas? The Supreme Court attempts to clarify some of this language, namely that an intent to intimidate involves the likelihood that particular behavior will lead to a violent response. However, the Court does not provide enough clarification for us to make an informative decision about the conclusion. Depending on the Court's definitions of these three phrases, our response to the Court's argument may change.

c. The Supreme Court, because it permits cross-burning activities in some instances, is promoting freedom, specifically with speech and other forms of expression. Although the Court acknowledges that freedom of speech is appropriately limited in some cases, cross-burning, while potentially creating much public anger, is not absolutely barred from First Amendment protection. The Court recognizes that cross-burning may at times be an expression of group ideology. Because the Court places an emphasis on freedom, security is restricted, as some individuals would take great offense and perhaps feel some degree of fear as a result of cross-burning activities, regardless of the degree to which an individual or group intended to intimidate another individual or group.

2. Fourth Amendment Argument

a. The author's conclusion is the following: We should change the Fourth Amendment to stop criminals from escaping punishment for their crimes. The only evidence that is offered is the example of the Jones case. We need to remember that this example is emotional; however, it is only one example.

b. We do not know if the Jones case is typical. It may simply be an unfortunate extreme example. Thus, we need more information about how many criminals are using the Fourth Amendment as a "loophole." Furthermore, what kinds of crimes are the criminals avoiding? In other words, what kinds of evidence are often improperly seized? Drugs? Evidence of crimes? If the government seizes the drugs, but the criminal is not prosecuted, the criminal is still somewhat punished because he lost his drugs. However, if evidence of murder is often inadmissible evidence due to improper search and seizure, we might be more willing to consider changing the amendment. The severity of the crime might influence our thought.

c. By using the word "criminal," she wants us to be sympathetic to her argument. When she says "criminals" are using the Fourth Amendment as a loophole, she suggests that the person (i.e., the criminal) is guilty. However, we do not *know* that the individual is guilty. Our justice system assumes that individuals are innocent until proven guilty. The author wants to use our emotions regarding "criminals" escaping punishment. Many people who are not guilty receive protection through the Fourth Amendment, and the author does not consider the protection needed to ensure that individuals are not falsely accused.

Learning the Basics

Matching	True and False	Multiple Choice
1. e	1. False	1. a
2. h	2. False	2. c
3. a	3. False	3. b
4. i	4. False	4. b
5. b	5. False	5. a
6. j	6. True	6. d
7. c	7. False	7. b
8. d	8. True	8. d
9. f	9. False	9. b
10. g		

Short Answer

1. The commerce clause, found in Article I of the Constitution, gives power to the federal government by allowing it to "regulate commerce with foreign nations, among the several states and with the Indian tribes." However, the commerce clause takes powers away from the government because the constitution was set up such that only the powers explicitly authorized to Congress or necessary to reach an authorized end are considered valid. Through the years, the interpretation of the commerce clause has varied.

   The commerce clause has severely limited the power of the state governments because of the broad interpretation it has been given by the courts. According to the constitution, any power not expressly given to the federal government is reserved for the state governments. According to the state's police powers, the states have authority to enact legislation to protect the health and safety of its citizens. However, if state legislation interferes with interstate commerce, by the doctrine of federal supremacy, the legislation will be struck down in the event of a challenge.

2. The federal government can regulate behavior by granting tax credits and subsidies to industries and citizens who perform certain desired actions, and denying those credits and subsidies to those who do not. As long as

taxation is related to the state's constitutional duty to collect revenue, such behavior is constitutional.

3. The Supremacy Clause declares that federal laws are the supreme law of the land. Federal preemption is used to strike down state laws that attempt to regulate in an area in which federal legislation is so pervasive that it is evident that Congress intended only federal regulation in that general area. Thus, the link between the Supremacy Clause and federal preemption is that the Supremacy Clause provides the basis for federal preemption. Because the federal laws are supreme (established by the Supremacy Clause), we want to strike down state laws that attempt to regulate an area in which Congress wanted only federal regulation (federal preemption).

Chapter 6

More Critical Thinking

1. *Diamond Rio* Case

   a. The issue is whether the Diamond Rio MP3 player is a digital audio recording device under the Audio Home Recording Act.
   b. There is a key ambiguity surrounding the word "indirectly"; the Court needs to determine whether it modifies the word "transmission" or the phrase "digital music recording." The Court decided that "indirectly" modifies "digital music recording," because under the opposing reading only the indirect copying of transmissions (and not the direct copying of said transmissions) would be covered under the statue, an implausible reading of the statute given its legislative history and common sense.
   c. These services do not fall within the ambit of the AHRA; although copyright violations might be taking place, Napster's servers are not digital audio recording devices and are not designed for individual use (as the statute specifies.)

3. Napster argument

   a. It is crucial that the ability of music exchange services like Napster to operate be preserved.
   b. R1) The right to free speech endangered by shutting down Napster outweighs the intellectual property rights of record property owners. R2) Unknown bands can get their names out at a low cost using Napster.
   c. This author seems to prefer freedom over the other ethical norms, as evidenced in his reason citing freedom of speech as a primary concern.
   d. Is the impact on the recording industry accurately depicted by a "record company CEO having one fewer suit?" It may be that Napster could cause such staggering losses to the industry that it would no longer be profitable to produce and distribute music. Also, are songs "ideas" in

need of protection? Will the copyright of songs prevent the free exchange of ideas?

Matching	True and False	Multiple Choice
1. b	1. False	1. a
2. c	2. True	2. b
3. d	3. False	3. a
4. a	4. False	4. b
5. f	5. False	5. a
6. i	6. True	6. d
7. e	7. False	
8. g	8. False	
9. h	9. True	

Short Answer

1. Allowing private firms to subpoena the names of users of on-line services might violate the privacy of those firms' employees, creating a chilling effect on free speech.

2. A company can be held liable for its employee's behavior on-line if it is determined that the forum in which the questionable action takes place is an extension of the workplace and that the company derives substantial benefit from that forum.

Chapter 7

More Critical Thinking

1. *N.O.W.* Case

    a. The issue in this case may be stated, "Must an 'enterprise' have an economic goal in order to be subject to prosecution under RICO?"

    b. R1) An "enterprise," by the statutory definition, can affect interstate commerce without seeking a profit
R2) Even if the protesters do not seek a profit, they still "drain money from the economy by harming businesses."
R3) In *U.S. v. Turkette*, the Supreme Court decided that businesses that were not legitimate were included in the definition of "enterprise."
R4) The Department of Justice's guidelines were amended to
include organizations with "other [noneconomic] identifiable goal[s]"in its definition of "enterprise."

c. "Enterprise," "pattern of racketeering activity," and "affect interstate commerce" are all ambiguous. Notice, however, that Chief Justice Rehnquist clarifies what exactly the Court meant when it used two phrases by offering statutory and dictionary definitions of these words or phrases. Because of these clarifications, the phrases are no longer ambiguous in the sense that an uncertainty over their intended meaning prevents us from being able to evaluate the Court's argument.

2. Argument about Sentencing

a. R1) Street crime is more traumatic to victims than is white-collar crime.
R2) Blue-collar criminals are more likely to commit crimes again after being caught.
R3) Street crime violates not only a victim's property, but also her rights.

b. Several alternative conclusions could be drawn from the reasons given by the author. For example, a reasonable person could conclude "We need to impose stiffer penalties on street criminals." This conclusion, however, does not negate the possibility of imposing harsher penalties on white-collar criminals as well. Another possible conclusion is "Those people found guilty of street crimes should undergo extensive counseling and rehabilitation to prevent them from committing more crimes." "We need legalization that gives more rights to the victims of street crimes," and "We should increase our taxes to hire more police," are also reasonable alternative conclusions.

c. Actually, the author provides no evidence for his claims. He states that street crime is more traumatic, but does nothing to prove this assertion. If the author stated how trauma was measured and cited a study that demonstrated that street crime is harder on victims than is white-collar crime, then it would be easier for readers to accept his conclusion.

Additionally, the author says that white-collar criminals stop committing crimes after they are caught once. Yet, there is no evidence to justify this claim. The author might support it by offering statistics that compare the rates of recidivism for both street criminals and white-collar criminals.

d. Some important ambiguities are present in this passage. For example, "ability to feel secure" could mean "freedom from any fear of harm" or "ability to walk down a city street in broad daylight without fear of being murdered." Depending upon which definition we choose, our willingness to accept the author's argument would vary. More specifically, if we chose the first definition, we'd probably reject the author's reasoning because almost nobody has that strong of an "ability to feel secure." Therefore, it is impossible for a street criminal to take it away (because the victim never had it in the first place).

212

Another important ambiguity is "rights." The author states that white collar crime harms only property, while street crime harms one's rights. Which rights does the author mean? The right to vote? The right not to be physically injured by other people? The right to property? If we choose the first or last definition, we'd be much less prone to accept the author's reasoning than we would be if we chose the middle definition. Street crime has no effect on our right to vote. Thus, the first definition makes little sense in the context of this passage. Additionally, the last definition contradicts the author's reason. The author states that white-collar crime harms people's property, not their rights. But if the right to property is included in the definition of rights, then white-collar crime also harms people's rights.

e. The issue is "Should white-collar criminals receive stiffer sentences than they currently receive?" Yet, the author's reasons discuss street criminals, not white-collar criminals. In this sense, the author's argument does not adequately address the issue. Instead, he gets sidetracked and focuses his entire argument on a topic that is only indirectly related to the issue at hand.

Learning the Basics

Matching	True and False	Multiple Choice
1. d	1. True	1. c
2. h	2. True	2. d
3. f	3. True	3. c
4. i	4. False	4. b
5. b	5. True	5. d
6. e	6. False	6. c
7. c	7. True	7. d
8. a	8. False	8. a
9. g	9. True	
	10. False	

Short Answers

1. Eight reasons why a corporate culture can encourage white collar crime are:
   1. a lack of job security
   2. inadequate pay
   3. a lack of recognition for outstanding work
   4. perceived inequities among salaries of employees
   5. poor promotion opportunities
   6. inadequate expense accounts or unreasonable budget expectations
   7. poor training
   8. poor communication practices

213

Some methods that a manager can use to discourage white-collar crime include:

1. assigning specific high-level individuals to oversee compliance with the standards and procedures
2. installing monitoring and auditing systems designed to detect criminal conduct.
3. not delegating authority to individuals who the organization knows have a propensity to engage in illegal activities
4. communicating standards and procedures to all employees and agents through training programs and printed materials
5. reinforcing standards through appropriate disciplinary mechanisms

2. Arguments in favor of holding corporations criminally liable:
   a) Imposing financial sanctions against corporations will result in lower stockholder dividends which will prompt shareholders to try to make sure that the corporation is behaving legally.
   b) If the crime is an omission, the responsibility for performing the certain duty is not assigned to any one individual. If the corporation cannot be held responsible, there is no one to blame.
   c) Because there are many potential suspects at each corporation, it is much less time consuming to hold the entire corporation responsible.
   d) Because many decisions come from committees, it is hard to hold one person responsible. Consequently, it would make more sense to hold the entire corporation responsible.
   e) Holding one individual responsible does not necessarily impact the corporation. If a manager commits an illegal act and we hold him responsible, the manager may be blamed, but the corporation benefits from his act.
   f) It isn't fair to punish one or two individuals when the illegal behavior is probably common to the entire corporation.
   g) If we do not hold the corporation responsible, shareholders will benefit from illegal actions.
   h) If we hold the corporation criminally responsible, the public will link the crime with the corporation, not an individual. Thus, consumers will be better able to make informed decisions about interacting with this corporation.

   Arguments against holding corporations criminally liable:
   a) Imposing fines on the corporation isn't a good deterrent. The corporation will simply pass the cost of the fines to the consumers by raising their prices. Thus, the corporation isn't being punished.
   b) Because shareholders may not have a lot of influence over the behavior in the corporation, it is unfair to reduce their dividends by holding corporations criminally responsible.

214

© 2009 Pearson Education, Inc. publishing as Prentice Hall

Because the crimes are not necessarily well publicized, holding corporations criminally responsible may not negatively impact the corporation's image. Corporations have public relations personnel to counteract the negative publicity.

Chapter 8

More Critical Thinking

1. *In Re Krogh* Case

   a. The court elevates the ethical norm of justice. Here, we mean justice in the sense that if a person commits a crime, that person ought to be punished

   b. The court's decision relies heavily on the fact that lawyers have an elevated knowledge of the law. Because of this elevated understanding, the court rules out the potential excuse of ignorance of the law. It also states that such conduct from an attorney is unacceptable because lawyers should be the ones to dissuade their superiors from violating the Constitution.

   c. R1) Krogh acted without considering the morality or legality of his actions. He merely did what his superiors told him to do. "Such an attitude . . . manifests . . . a fundamental unfitness to serve as an officer of the courts."
   R2) Krogh had reason to know that his actions were illegal.
   R3) Because Krogh is schooled in the law, he should be able to dissuade others from engaging in actions that violate the Constitution.
   R4) The reputation and honor of lawyers in general have been harmed as a result of his actions.

2.

   a. Under a rule utilitarian ethic, the court's reasoning could be explained by saying that requiring warnings of potentially fatal consequences on products *as a rule* produces more happiness for society than any other rule, such as stating only "Do not breathe spray" and forcing individuals to accept responsibility for product misuse. On the other hand, an act utilitarian would say that, in this case, requiring warnings of potentially fatal consequences produces more social benefit; yet, the act utilitarian would argue, future cases should be assessed independently.

   b. A humanist would argue that requiring the warnings of potentially fatal consequences on products enhances human capabilities by promoting greater intelligence among consumers that consumers might not otherwise have.

c. Using Kant's standard of universalizability as our deontological rule, the court's decision could be justified by saying that the court's ruling instead for Lane in this case would potentially lead to the harm of more individuals in similar situations. The court must have seen this harm, resulting from less-informed consumers, as undesirable, because the court could not accept warnings label void of information about potentially fatal consequences as a universal standard.

Learning the Basics

Matching	True and False	Multiple Choice
1. c	1. True	1. d
2. e	2. False	2. d
3. h	3. True	3. b
4. a	4. False	4. c
5. f	5. False	5. d
6. d	6. False	6. a
7. g	7. False	7. c
8. b	8. False	8. a

Short Answer

1. It seems likely that Reynolds subscribed to the "profit-oriented" theory of corporate responsibility, given that they defended their advertising on (among other explanations) the grounds that it and other cartoon-oriented ad campaigns were effective business practices among adults, and also seemingly mislead investigators into their advertising to defend the market advantage that it provided them. Their actions were not reflective of the long-term relationships that the corporation would have to maintain with Congress and consumers, ruling out a managerial theory of responsibility.

2. The Court, in ruling out the argument that advertising would adversely affect the quality of service provided, said that:

"In sum, we are not persuaded that any of the proffered justifications rise to the level of an acceptable reason for the suppression of all advertising by attorneys. As with other varieties of speech, it follows as well that there may be reasonable restrictions on the time, place, and manner of advertising.

"The constitutional issue in this case is only whether the State may prevent the publication in a newspaper of appellants' truthful advertisement concerning the availability and terms of routine legal service."

If Bates and O'Steen were making false claims, the issue at hand would be different and the Court might well uphold a law restricting their untruthful ads.

Chapter 9

More Critical Thinking

1. *Breard v. Greene Case*

   a. If an international treaty conflicts with a national procedure rule, which of the two is supreme? Specifically, if the Vienna Convention on Consular Relations conflicts with the procedural default doctrine, which is trump?

   b. The court offered two reasons for its conclusion. First, the court said that it is "recognized" in international law that the procedural rules of a state govern the implementation of the treaty in that state. Second, the court stated that while treaties are recognized as the supreme law of the land, the same status applies to constitutional provisions. The Vienna Convention confers the right of consular assistance following arrest. However, the Antiterrorism and Effective Death Penalty Act (AEDPA) says that a petitioner who claims he is held in violation of a treaty of the U.S. must develop a factual claim in state court.

   c. The court emphasizes security, in the sense that it wants to ensure that the laws of the U.S. are supreme and consistent. The court also seems to emphasize efficiency because it does not want to encourage additional claims to flood the court system. Part of the court's ruling insisted that factual basis of claims must be made in the state court for a petitioner to receive evidentiary hearings. This holding helps reduce the number of appeal cases.

2. PNTR with China Argument

   a. The author comes to the following conclusion: We should not allow Permanent Normalized Trade Relations with China. She offers the reason that trade with China, which is imbalanced, will bankrupt the American economy. She also indicates that American businesses will lose from the illegal copying of intellectual property that will increase if trade is increased with China.

   b. The author offers the qualitative evidence that establishing PNTR with China eliminates the bargaining tools that the U.S. has to extract concessions with China. One might thus infer that any trade with China would be unfavorable to the United States. However, no quantitative evidence is offered to support this author's conclusion.

c. This evidence is not particularly convincing. There is nothing to indicate that trade with China would be any worse for the U.S. than it would be for China; we have no information about what concessions that the Chinese have made, nor any statistical information about the balance of trade with China, et cetera. It is thus difficult for us to evaluate the validity of the claims that this author makes.

d. As we noted above, the concessions that China made to the United States would be helpful in determining how fair U.S./Chinese trade is. Furthermore, statistics describing the balance of trade between China and the U.S would be useful in our evaluating the fairness of trade between the U.S. and China.

Learning the Basics

Matching	True and False	Multiple Choice
1. g	1. False	1. a
2. d	2. False	2. c
3. a	3. True	3. d
4. j	4. False	4. d
5. b	5. True	5. c
6. k	6. False	6. b
7. h	7. True	7. a
8. c	8. False	8. c
9. f	9. True	9. d
10. e		
11. i		

Short Answer

1. Common law is typical in the United States, England, and former British colonies. Case law is the primary source of law, and decisions rely on case precedents. Courts can declare statutory law unconstitutional. In contrast, countries with Romano-Germanic Civil Law Systems organize their legal system around legal codes rather than around statutes, regulations, and precedents as the common law systems do. Generally, the high court cannot declare laws of parliament unconstitutional.

2. Trade is considered the least risky means of doing international business because it demands little involvement with a foreign buyer or seller. However, it is not necessarily the best method because it is least risky. International trade is often complex; many nations and products are involved, and political factors are often more potent than economic factors.

Chapter 10

More Critical Thinking

1. *The Private Movie Company, Inc. v. Pamela Lee Anderson, et al.*

   a. The judge concluded that there was no oral or written contract between the plaintiff and Pamela Lee.

   b. First, the judge said that oral and written preliminary negotiations may occur, but they are binding only when all of the essential terms are definitely understood. He concluded that "nudity and sexual conduct" are material points that must be clearly understood. Pamela Lee asserted that she never agreed to the nudity and sexual conduct in the script. However, the rewritten script included three or four scenes that depicted simulated sex. Therefore, the judge ruled that there was no contract.

   c. According to the judge's reasoning, this additional information would not change the decision. The judge looked to see if each element of the contract was fulfilled. He decided that mutual consent did not exist. Therefore, there was no contract.

2. Contracts argument

   a. Courts should change to recognize more mistakes in contracts.
   b. The author provides a long-winded story about the potential sale of a house that demonstrates the complexity of contracts. He believes that this example shows that our society would be better without such explicit contract law.
   c. The evidence actually demonstrates the need for complex contract law. The story about Jerry and Elaine also highlights the need for security in contracts. Jerry tried to create numerous contracts for the same object. Without complex contract law, we would probably not be able to sort through the mess of facts provided in the story. The author thought his evidence supported his conclusion. However, it better supports the following alternative conclusion: Courts need to continue to use strict standards when examining contracts.

Learning the Basics

Matching	True and False	Multiple Choice
1. g	1. False	1. d
2. c	2. True	2. d
3. a	3. False	3. a
4. i	4. False	4. c
5. b	5. True	5. c
6. d	6. True	6. b
7. j	7. False	7. a
8. f	8. False	8. b
9. e	9. True	9. b
10. h	10. True	

Short Answer

1. This statement is false because for a valid contract to exist all six elements (only one of which is the offer) must be present. The six elements of a valid, enforceable contract are a legal offer, legal acceptance, consideration, genuine assent, competent parties and a legal object. A legal offer must demonstrate objective intent by the offeror/promisor, use definite terms, and be communicated to the offeree/promisee.

2. Both fraud and duress are conditions such that if they occur, then the requirement of genuine assent is not met. Fraud is the misrepresentation of a material fact, made with intent to deceive the other party, who is injured because she believes the misrepresentation. Duress is any act or threat negatively influencing a person's decision to enter into a contract or preventing a person from doing so. Thus, if fraud or duress is present, there is no genuine assent and the contract is void.

3. The statement is problematic because *all* contracts can be classified as executed (all terms have been completed) or executory (all terms have not been completed). All contracts can be classified as express contracts or implied contracts. Express contracts are exchanges of written or oral promises that are enforceable in a court of law. Implied contracts are contracts established by the conduct of a party rather than by oral or written words. Furthermore, all contracts can be classified as unilateral or bilateral. A unilateral contract is an exchange of a promise for an act. A bilateral contract is an exchange of one promise for another. Thus, all contracts can be classified as express or implied, unilateral or bilateral, and executed or executory.

Chapter 11

More Critical Thinking

1. *Thomas v. I.NS.* Case

    a. Issue: Is the INS bound by a cooperation agreement made by the United States Attorney?
    Conclusion: Yes, the INS is bound.

    b. The court quickly decided that the cooperation agreement was meant to bind the INS. To determine whether the agreement actually bound the INS, the court determined that a United States Attorney's authority to commit the government not to oppose a motion for relief from deportation as part of a plea bargain comes from his statutory authority to prosecute crimes.

    c. The court seems to be emphasizing security. It is ensuring that the United States follows through with its agreement. This ethical norm is evident is the last statement in the opinion. "We shall not invent an excuse for the government to break its promise. If they have an excuse, let them prove it."

2. Punitive damages argument

    a. Conclusion: Judges should award punitive damages for breach of contract cases.
    Reason 1: Too many cases of breach of contract are occurring.
    Punitive damages would serve as a good deterrent for individuals to breach a contract.
    Reason 2: Parties are losing faith in the security of a contract.
    Awarding punitive damages will cause fewer parties to breach the contract thus increasing faith in contracts.

    b. First, the survey included a small number of people. Second, can business *students* accurately communicate how businesspeople treat contracts in business? How do these first-year students know what businesspeople think about contracts?

    c. The author states that 8,000 cases of breach of contract occurred last year. Did all these cases go to trial? Perhaps a party breached a contract but simply compensated the "injured" party. What type of damages does the typical party in a breach of contract case receive? As long as an injured party receives compensatory damages, do we really need punitive damages? What evidence does the author have that imposing punitive damages will deter parties from breaching contracts?

Learning the Basics

Matching	True and False	Multiple Choice
1. f	1. False	1. d
2. c	2. False	2. <u>d</u>
3. h	3. True	3. d
4. a	4. True	4. d
5. g	5. False	5. b
6. d	6. False	6. c
7. e	7. True	7. b
8. b	8. False	8. c
9. j	9. False	9. b
10. i		

Short Answer

1. If an unforeseeable event makes a promisor's performance objectively impossible, the contract is discharged by impossibility of performance. "Objectively impossible" is defined as meaning that no person or company could legally or physically perform the contract.

   Commercial impracticability is a situation where performance is impracticable because of unreasonable expense, injury, or loss to one party. A situation that was not foreseeable occurs that makes performance of the contract unreasonably expensive or injurious to a party.

   Thus, in a situation of commercial impracticability, a person or company could legally or physically perform the contract, unlike an objectively impossible situation.

2. Legal remedies involve money being awarded to one of the parties because of the other party's failure to complete the terms of the contract. Examples of legal remedies are compensatory, punitive, nominal, and liquidated damages.

   Equitable remedies are nonmonetary awards given to parties injured as a result of a contract. These two types of remedies are the only remedies that can be sought when contracts are violated or when one party is harmed by contract. Examples of equitable remedies include rescission, reformation, injunction, and specific performance.

Chapter 12

More Critical Thinking

1. *Ramsey* Defamation Case

   a. The court's reasoning in this case is relatively clear. The court established several elements, including the following: (1) The broadcast's mentioning that the Ramseys were successful in several defamation cases suggests that the family has been falsely accused of participating in the crime; (2) the "recent major development" in the broadcast was that the Ramseys were no longer being accused or suspected of committing the crime; (3) Fox did not need to exonerate the Ramseys to avoid their making defamatory statements. These three reasons led the court to conclude that Fox had not made any defamatory statements in its broadcast about the Ramseys.

   b. There are two facts that are very important in the court's reasoning. First, the court refers to the broadcast's mentioning that the Ramseys successfully sued mainstream media and tabloids for defamation. This fact suggests that the Ramseys have been falsely accused of the crime, which does more to exonerate the Ramseys than to imply guilt. Second, the court references remarks made by the Plaintiffs' lawyer, which refer to the "recent major development," of which the Ramseys are no longer considered suspects in the criminal investigation, as District Attorney Keenan took over the investigation. The court believed that these two reasons persuasively dismissed the allegations of defamation.

   c. The court places a high degree of importance on the ethical norm of freedom, particularly with regard to freedom of speech. Although the broadcast may have been able to more convincingly portray the Ramseys as not guilty, the court ruled that preserving and promoting "robust" debate is essential, especially on matters of public concern.

2. Oprah Argument

   a. Nikki provides evidence regarding Oprah's Book Club. Nikki states that Oprah's suggestion to read one book resulted in three million additional copies being printed. Nikki believes that this increase in number of books printed is evidence of Oprah's influence on her audience.

   b. While Oprah's Book Club certainly accounts for some of the sales of the book, how do we know that she is responsible for the sale of over three million copies? Perhaps the book club selections are more

223

visible (*i.e.*, near the store entrance) in the bookstore because the stores believe that people will buy books suggested by Oprah. Because the books are more visible, people may be more likely to buy them. They may not buy the book because Oprah suggested it. Rather, they bought it because they saw it near the front of the store. We don't know the consumers' reasons for buying the book.

c. Additional causes that could explain the drop in the beef industry include environmental factors (weather conditions such as a flood or a drought) and increasing cost of caring for cows (increase in cost of feed). Furthermore, there is a lot of information about the health considerations of eating red meat. Individuals could be paying more attention to their health by eating less red meat.

d. First, has the beef industry experienced a similar drop in the past few years? In other words, is it typical for the beef industry to experience a large drop at certain times in the year? Second, did the beef industry stay low or did sales increase? If viewers were truly persuaded by what Oprah said, the sales probably would not experience a large increase soon after the drop. Third, is there reason to be concerned about the dangers of red meat? Was the guest correctly describing dangers? If the statements were true, should we reward the beef industry for wanting to sell the public something that is harmful to their health?

Learning the Basics

Matching	True and False	Multiple Choice
1. i	1. False	1. b
2. a	2. True	2. d
3. f	3. True	3. b
4. b	4. True	4. b
5. g	5. False	5. d
6. c	6. False	6. b
7. j	7. False	7. d
8. d	8. False	8. c
9. e	9. True	
10. h	10. False	

Short Answer

1. No single element of negligence is most important. You must prove every element to have a case. The first element you must prove is the duty that the defendant owed to the plaintiff. You must show how a reasonable

person in the defendant's position would act so as to not subject the plaintiff to an unreasonable risk of harm.

Next you must demonstrate that the defendant breached his duty. His behavior did not meet that standard of care. Third, you must show that the breach of duty caused the plaintiff's harm. There are two types of causation: actual cause and proximate cause. Actual cause is a factual question. In other words, if the defendant had not breached his duty of care, the plaintiff would not have incurred the harm she suffered. Proximate cause is a policy question. Proximate cause differs depending on whether you are in a majority or minority rule state. The final element is damages. You must show that the plaintiff suffered some actual, compensable injuries. Thus, because you need every element to recover, no element is most important.

2. The goals of tort law include compensating injured persons, discouraging private retaliation by injured persons ("taking the law into their own hands"), and deterring future damages to the property and persons of others.

3. Assault is the intentional placing of someone in fear of an immediate offensive bodily contact. Battery is any intentional, unwanted offensive bodily contact. Assaults are frequently followed by battery. Assault is determined, to a large degree, by the victim's perception whereas battery is determined by the tortfeasor's action.

Chapter 13

More Critical Thinking

1. *Welge v. Planters Lifesavers Company* Case

   a. Judge Posner concluded that if a kind of accident occurs that would not have occurred but for a defect in the product, and if it is reasonably plain that the defect was not introduced after the product was sold, the accident is evidence of the defect. This conclusion can be reworded to respond to the facts of the case. Richard Welge did not need to exclude possible causes of the accident other than a defect introduced in the manufacturing process.

   b. Posner states that testimony of Karen Godfrey and Richard Welge excludes all reasonable doubt that the defect was introduced after the jar left the shelf in the store. First, Welge testified that he used no more than the normal force one exerts in snapping a plastic lid onto a jar. Because of this uncontradicted testimony, Posner concluded that the jar must have been defective. Furthermore, Karen Godfrey testified that the jar was not "jostled, dropped, bumped, or otherwise subjected to stress" beyond that of normal use. Because of this testimony, Posner concluded that the defect must have been introduced when the defendants had possession of the jar.

c. Posner seems particularly influenced by justice, in the sense that when an individual is injured by another's action, it is fair that the individual should receive compensation.

d. Asking that question would not produce any additional information. Judge Posner essentially responds to this question in his opinion. The District Court said that the plaintiff failed to rule out other causes of the broken bottle. However, Posner states that the "Plaintiff is not required to rule out every possibility, however, fantastic or remote, that the defect which led to the accident was caused by someone other than the defendants." A plaintiff is not required to completely rule out all causes of the accident to bring a product liability case. Thus, Judge Posner tells us that this critical thinking question is not necessary in this case.

2. Breast Implant Argument

a. Conclusion: Breast implant manufacturers should be liable for the harm their products cause to women.
Reason 1: Breast implants cause disease.
Reason 2: Breast implant manufacturers have admitted their guilt by making a $4.25 billion class-action settlement.
Reason 3: The breast implant cases are just like the DES cases, which allowed women to recover damages because DES can cause cancer.
Reason 4: So many women with health problems cannot be wrong about the connection between disease and breast implants.

b. The author offers little evidence. She offers no concrete evidence that breast implants cause disease. However, she states that some research studies have found no link between implants and illness. This acknowledgment is important; she cites no research supporting her conclusion. However, there is research that suggests an alternative conclusion about implants and illness. The author tries to suggest that because juries have given large damage awards for women with implant-related illness, the award somehow proves that the illness exists. Juries might have given a large award for many reasons. The fact that they gave a large award to one woman does not prove that the disease exists.

The author is further convinced that the large number of women who claim to experience illness is evidence of the disease. However, the author states that these women claim to experience the disease; there is no proof that they actually have a disease. Perhaps they became involved with implant litigation because they thought they could receive money. The large number of women who claim to experience illness is the most persuasive piece of evidence the author offers; yet, this evidence is not extremely convincing because I can think of alternative reasons why women might claim to have the disease.

c. Before I could decide to agree or disagree with the statement, I would need answers to the following questions: First, what is the evidence regarding the link between disease and implants? The author is not clear. If research studies and legal scholars are skeptical about the existence of the link between implants and disease, it is important to examine more research studies. Furthermore, is this research trustworthy? Who conducted the research? How was the research carried out? Have the results been replicated? These questions help to assess the quality of the research. Consequently, they help me to make a better decision about the link between breast implants and disease.

Second, who is the writer of the argument? The writer is quite sympathetic to women with breast implants. Perhaps she has implants herself or is close to someone who has implants. Knowledge of the biases of the writer is important to acknowledge. Third, exactly how many women who have implants claim to have disease? Is there any evidence of their disease?

d. This analogy is flawed because we are more certain about the link between DES and cancer than we are about the link between implants and illness. The author highlights the controversy about breast implants-related illness; we do not know for sure that the implants cause disease. However, scientific research has demonstrated the link between DES and cancer. Because the link is unclear in the breast implant cases, this analogy is problematic.

Learning the Basics

Matching	True and False	Multiple Choice
1. c	1. True	1. d
2. d	2. False	2. d
3. f	3. True	3. a
4. b	4. True	4. b
5. a	5. False	5. c
6. h	6. True	6. d
7. e	7. False	7. b
8. g	8. True	8. c

Short Answer

1. The good:
   a. must pass without objection in the trade under contract description
   b. must be of fair or average quality within the description

227

c. must be fit for the ordinary purpose for which the goods are used

d. must run, with variations permitted by agreement, of even kind, quality, and quantity within each unit and among all units involved

e. must be adequately contained, packaged, and labeled as the agreement may require

f. must conform to any affirmations or promises made on the label or container

2. The two tests are the Consumer Expectations Test and the Feasible Alternatives Test. The Consumer Expectations Test asks, "Did the product meet the standards that would be expected by a reasonable consumer?" Thus, the Consumer Expectations Test relies on knowledge of the ordinary consumer; no expert testimony is needed.

The Feasible Alternatives Test, also called the risk utility test, looks at the following seven factors:

a. the usefulness and desirability of the product--its utility to the user and to the public as a whole

b. the safety aspects of the product--the likelihood that it will cause injury, and the probable seriousness of the injury

c. the availability of a substitute product that would meet the same need and not be as unsafe

d. the manufacturer's ability to eliminate the unsafe character of the product without impairing its usefulness or making it too expensive to maintain its utility

e. the user's ability to avoid danger by the exercise of care in the use of the product

f. the user's anticipated awareness of the dangers inherent in the product and their avoidability, because of general public knowledge of the obvious condition of the product or of the existence of suitable warnings or instructions

g. the feasibility, on the part of the manufacturer, of spreading the loss by adjusting the price of the product or carrying liability insurance

In the consumer expectations test, if the plaintiff applies the knowledge of the ordinary consumer, recognizes a danger and can appreciate that danger, the plaintiff cannot recover for injuries resulting from that danger. The Feasible Alternative Test differs from the consumer expectations test because it allows plaintiffs to recover for any injury resulting from a recognized danger if the utility of the product is outweighed by the danger that the product creates.

Chapter 14

More Critical Thinking

1. *Qualitex* Case

   a. R1) Because lighting affects the way people perceive colors, allowing color to be a trademark will result in an abundance of court cases that cannot be resolved with any reasonable degree of certainty.
   R2) There are a limited number of colors, and competing businesses might use up all of them.
   R3) Past Supreme Court cases forbade companies to use color as a trademark.

   R4) Color may be used as part of a trademark. Thus, there is no reason for color alone to qualify as a trademark.

   b. R1) Courts have been able to decide cases involving similar words and symbols. By analogy, if courts can determine between other similar symbols, then they can determine between colors as well.
   R2) Should all possible colors be used, the functionality doctrine will forbid them from being used as trademarks. Thus, competitors will not be put at a disadvantage because of a lack of remaining colors.
   R3) The cases cited by Jacobson were all decided before the Lanham Act, which loosened the requirements of trademarks, was passed.
   R4) Placing a symbol on the product might be difficult for the firm.

   c. The Court elevates freedom in the sense of allowing businesses to choose from a vast range of symbols the one that they wish to represent their company.

2. Argument about Property Rights

   a. Issue: Should federal administrative agencies be allowed to regulate the use of private property?
   Conclusion: No.

   b. The author compares the relationship between the government and its citizens to the relationship between a business and its customers. The government-citizen relationship is similar to the business-consumer relationship in that the latter party in both instances transfers money to the former party for some combination of goods and services. The relationships are different in several ways. First of all, customers are able to choose which goods and services they want, and then pay accordingly. In this sense, the business-consumer relationship is based upon individual choice. Conversely, customers are compelled to pay taxes to the government. They do not choose which government goods and services they wish to receive or which ones they pay for. Instead, the government makes those choices for the citizens. In this sense, the government-citizen relationship is based upon collective choice. People collectively decide (indirectly) which goods and services they want when they vote. Another difference between the two relationships is the difference in the power gap. Governments are much more powerful than citizens. Certainly, businesses are more powerful than customers also, but businesses lack the power to put customers in jail for failing to buy their products. Governments, on the other hand, can imprison their constituents if the citizens fail to pay taxes. In this way, the power differential between governments and citizens is much greater than that between businesses and customers. Because of these important differences, we can conclude that the author's analogy is not very appropriate.

c. Several elements of important information are missing from this argument. For instance, the author fails to inform us as to how typical it is for the government to deprive a property owner of use of her property. The more common such occurrences are, the more willing we would be to accept the author's argument. Additionally, the author fails to answer the question "In what ways do we all benefit from such regulations?" For example, regulations protecting the kangaroo rat may maintain the present food chain. It is possible that if the kangaroo rat falls victim to extinction, species that depend on it for food (e.g., hawks) will also die. Because of the absence of these predators, other species (such as sewer rats) may move into the area and flourish. Then towns would be overrun by these other species. If this case is true, then we all benefit greatly from such regulations, and we'd be less likely to accept the author's reasoning.

Learning the Basics

Matching	True and False	Multiple Choice
1. i	1. True	1. c
2. c	2. False	2. d
3. g	3. False	3. c
4. f	4. False	4. b
5. a	5. True	5. b
6. h	6. True	6. d
7. b	7. False	7. a
8. j	8. True	8. a
9. e	9. True	9. b
10. d	10. True	10. c

Short Answer

1. Both trade secrets and patents serve to protect a company's or person's right to exclusivity for a product, process, or method of operation. Thus, both give such companies or people a competitive advantage. The two are different in that patents give inventors, developers, etc. the exclusive rights to their development for a set period. Trade secrets, on the other hand, are not public knowledge like patented items are. Thus, the government protects the developer's rights to exclusivity for as long as its product or process goes undiscovered.

2. The ambiguity of the phrase "public purpose" is perhaps best demonstrated by the Trump Plaza example used in your book. While a "public purpose" might mean "things that are directly used by the public and do not enrich a particular consumer or firm, such as roadways," it might also mean "things intended for the proprietary use of a firm that incidentally enrich the public through increased business prosperity." This difference would be significant to someone considering the validity of an exercise of eminent domain who was concerned about the possible masking of private enrichment under the cloak of public good.

Chapter 15

More Critical Thinking

1. *Faragher* Case

   a. The primary issue in this case is "Are supervisors who harass their employees acting within the scope of their employment?" The more general issue in this case may be stated as "Should employers be liable for harassing acts committed by their managers?"

   b. The relevant rule of law is, "A master is subject to liability for the torts of his servants committed while acting in the scope of their employment." The phrase "the scope of their employment" is significantly ambiguous. In fact, it is this ambiguity that is at issue in this case. The disputants differ over whether harassing conduct is within a supervisor's scope of employment.

   c. The Court gives two primary reasons for holding employers liable for the discriminatory acts of supervisors. First of all, the Court states that harassing behavior is easier for supervisors to get away with because they have more power over employees than would coworkers. In this sense, the Court concludes that harassing behavior falls within the scope of the supervisor's employment. The second reason the Court offers for holding employers liable is that the employer has a greater opportunity to guard against harassing behavior by supervisors.

2. Argument on Agency Relationships

    a. The first analogy offered by the author is that agency relationships are like contracts. The two items stated in this analogy (agency relationships and contracts) are similar in that agency relationships are a type of contract. However, they are different because the laws governing them are different. (Actually, the author is arguing against this difference.)

    A second analogy is that agency by implied authority is like two people who speak different languages trying to negotiate a contract. These two situations are similar in that full understanding is not reached in either case. However, they are different because most aspects of agency relationships are understood in a relationship of agency by implied authority. Conversely, in the latter scenario, it is unlikely that the two parties would be able to achieve *any* understanding of the contract's terms.

    A third analogy in this argument is that agency by ratification or estoppel is the same as saying that you're engaged to someone in order to coax that person into marrying you. These situations are similar in that both originate with a false statement. However, the similarity ends there. A significant way in which they are different is that they carry extremely different consequences. If one ratifies a previously false agency relationship or is stuck in a relationship by estoppel, they will not have to live with or share resources with the other person, as they would have to in a marriage. Because the differences in these analogies are more significant than the similarities, we can conclude that the analogies offered are not very appropriate.

    b. The author concludes that only agency relationships originating with agreement should be legally binding. He supports that conclusion with three primary reasons. First of all, he argues that agency by implied authority is plagued by uncertainty. Secondly, he argues that accepting agency by ratification or estoppel motivates people to lie. Finally, the author claims that allowing relationships created without an explicit agreement results in too many lawsuits.

    c. Other than the analogies, which we have already determined are weak, the author provides no evidence for his reasons.

    d. The author failed to provide readers with a lot of evidence that would help them evaluate his argument. For example, how many relationships created by ratification or estoppel originate with intentional lies as opposed to innocent misstatements? Additionally, how often and how severely are people hurt by entering into agency relationships lacking an explicit contract? Finally, how many lawsuits are caused by such relationships relative to the number arising out of relationships that are explicitly agreed upon?

e. The ethical norm of security plays a major role in this argument. However, because the ethical norms themselves are ambiguous, we must clarify what kind of security we're talking about. In this instance, we mean that the author is advocating security in the sense that when a relationship between two people exists, both parties will know what to expect from that relationship.

Learning the Basics

Matching	True and False	Multiple Choice
1. g	1. False	1. b
2. i	2. False	2. a
3. a	3. True	3. c
4. e	4. True	4. d
5. h	5. False	5. c
6. c	6. True	6. b
7. f	7. False	7. d
8. b	8. True	8. c
9. d	9. True	9. c
10. j	10. True	10. b

Short Answer

1. Principal-agent relationships are the most basic agency relationships, and employer-independent contractor relationships are based upon the former. The two types of agency relationships are different in the sense that the agent in a principal-agent relationship may perform more tasks for her principal. An agent in a principal-agent relationship is granted both expressed and implied authority (meaning that the agent can perform tasks that the principal did not specifically tell her to do), whereas independent contractors are hired to perform a specific job.

2. This statement assumes that when an agent commits a crime on behalf of a principal, it was as much the agent's idea to break the law as it was the principal's. Additionally, it assumes that agents and principals have equal power in the agency relationship. This assumption is not valid because agents are dependent upon principals for employment, and therefore it is often difficult for them to say "no" to their principals.

Chapter 16

More Critical Thinking

1. *Safford* Case

   a. The fact that PaineWebber employed Safford as a stockbroker was especially important in shaping the court's reasoning. The nature of this employment does not involve acting for Safford's benefit "so that [PaineWebber] must be faithful to [Safford's] financial or business interests." Had Safford been one of the company's lawyers or had the company been one of Safford's clients, the relationship would have been substantially different.

   b. The relevant rule of law in this case is, "One is said to act in a fiduciary capacity when the business which he transacts 'is not his own or for his own benefit, but for the benefit of another person, as to whom he stands in a relation implying and necessitating great confidence and trust on the one part and a high degree of good faith on the other part.' "

   c. The plaintiff provides legal analogies to support his case. More specifically, the plaintiff cites *Plaquemines Par. Com'n Council v. Delta Development Co., Inc.; ODECO v. Nunez;* and *United Companies Mtg. v. Estate of McGee.* The court responds to this evidence by assessing the appropriateness of each analogy. It points out ways in which the issue in each case cited by the plaintiff is substantially different from the issue in the case at hand. Because these differences exist, the court rejects the plaintiff's argument that the decision of the case at hand should mirror the decisions in these previous cases. In this sense, the court assesses the analogies in a critical thinking manner.

2. Argument on Corporations

   a. The author gives three primary reasons for abolishing corporations. First of all, the author argues that corporations cause social problems such as pollution and sweatshops. In addition, they harm the public with some of their products, such as cigarettes. Secondly, the author argues that corporations treat their workers poorly. The third reason that the author gives is that the economic philosophy upon which our economy is based (capitalism) assumes that businesses competing in the market will be small ones.

   b. The author omits a lot of important information from his argument. First of all, the author states that corporations pollute the environment, but fails to state how pervasive this problem is. Furthermore, the author fails to cite statistics that support his claim that corporations are the sole parties guilty of pollution.

Moving on, the author omits a lot of information that would aid readers in evaluating the third paragraph. Where did the survey and the study that he cites come from? How did the survey measure "unhappiness"? How happy are the people who work for partnerships in relation to those who work at corporations? What percentage of the workforce works in corporations? After all, if 87 percent of the workforce works in corporations, then we would expect 87 percent of accidents to occur in corporations. By failing to answer these questions, the author makes it more difficult for readers to feel that his reasons are supported by adequate evidence.

Finally, the author omits ways in which corporations have helped people. He asserts that corporations have harmed society more than they have helped it, but only provides information on how corporations are harmful. Because of this omission, readers cannot assess the validity of his "comparison." Certainly, we would not expect any form of business to be all good or all bad. Instead, we must search for ways in which each form is both good and bad. Should we decide that the good things that corporations do (e.g., hiring more workers, providing more benefits, producing better goods, keeping prices low, etc.) outweigh the bad things, then the author's conclusion (that corporations should be outlawed) seems foolish.

c. While the author cites numerous examples of how corporations can be harmful, his reasons do not automatically lead to the conclusion that they should be banned. A reasonable conclusion that a reader might make after examining the author's reasoning is "Our society needs to place tighter restrictions on corporations."

d. This argument suffers from a tremendous lack of evidence. The author blames corporations for sweatshops, old-boy networks, and poor pay, but provides no evidence to support these claims. The author's claim that sole proprietorships and partnerships do not harm society suffers the same problem. Again, the author's assertion that the United States is run by corporations has no evidence to support it. Because of the author's failure to provide evidence, readers are unable to determine how valid his reasons are.

The evidence that the author does provide is, for the most part, incredibly weak. Most of his evidence consists of single examples. Such evidence is flawed because readers have no way of knowing whether these examples are typical. For example, the author uses cigarette companies for evidence that corporations provide the public with harmful products. Certainly, cigarettes are harmful, but are most of the other products produced by corporations harmful? Probably not. The author's argument would be better supported if he would include statistics demonstrating that the problems he describes are typical.

Learning the Basics

Matching	True and False	Multiple Choice
1. d	1. False	1. c
2. e	2. False	2. c
3. j	3. False	3. c
4. b	4. True	4. b
5. g	5. False	5. a
6. c	6. True	6. d
7. i	7. False	7. b
8. a	8. True	8. a
9. h	9. True	9. c
10. f	10. False	10. A
	11. False	

Short Answer

1. A Limited Liability Corporation disperses liability in a way similar to publicly held corporations; each owner of the firm is liable only up to his or her individual capital contribution. They are, however, generally much smaller than public corporations; further, the individual owners (and not the corporation) are taxed after profits are divided.

2. Cumulative preferred stock prevents the preferred shareholders from losing their rights to a dividend during a year in which no dividends are paid. Participating preferred stock enables the preferred shareholders to share remaining income with the common shareholders after dividends have been paid off. Liquidation preferred stock guarantees its holders to receive either the par value of their stock or a specified monetary amount in the instance of liquidation. These payments are to be made before the common shareholders share pro rata in the remainder of the assets. Finally, convertible preferred stock may be exchanged, at a stated ratio, for common stock at the shareholder's request.

<u>Chapter 17</u>

More Critical Thinking

1. *Hecla* Case

   a. "Final agency action" is the ambiguous phrase that is of central importance to both parties in this case. Hecla Mining Co. and the EPA disagree as to whether the agency's actions constitute a "final" action. Thus, the issue of this case may be phrased, "Do the actions that the

236
© 2009 Pearson Education, Inc. publishing as Prentice Hall

EPA took in adding the South Fork of the Coeur d'Alene River and the Lucky Friday Mine to Idaho's C list constitute a final agency action?"

b. The only reason offered by the court is that listing decisions are preliminary steps, not final decisions in the NPDES permit process.

c. The reason given by the court really isn't a reason at all. It's just a restatement of the conclusion! The court's reasoning is the following:
Issue: Do the actions that the EPA took in adding the South Fork of the Coeur d'Alene River and the Lucky Friday Mine to Idaho's C list constitute a final agency action?
Conclusion: No.
Reason: Listing decisions are not final decisions; they're preliminary steps. Such a reason does nothing to support the conclusion; instead it merely repeats the conclusion.

2. Argument about Formal and Informal Rulemaking

a. This argument downplays the ethical norm of efficiency. Because the rules governing informal rulemaking are less expansive than those governing formal rulemaking, informal rulemaking is more convenient and it allows rules to be made more quickly. By arguing that these benefits are unimportant, the author expresses that he values other ethical norms more than he does efficiency.

b. Despite the length of this argument, the author provides only two reasons for allowing only formal rulemaking.
R1) Formal rulemaking does a better job of ensuring that the agency listens to the thoughts and desires of the public, which is an essential element of democracy.
R2) Formal rulemaking provides the public with an opportunity to make sure that the agency's reasoning is sound.

c. The major problem with this author's evidence is that there is none. Both of the reasons that the author gives make sense, but they are not backed up by any facts that support them. Because of this lack of evidence, we cannot be sure that agencies really pay more attention to the public during formal rulemaking procedures. From what the author says, it would make sense for them to do so, but we cannot be sure if that's what really happens.

d. How common is it for agencies to ignore printed statements that they receive during the informal rulemaking process? To what extent do agency officials pay attention to the testimony of interested parties during formal rulemaking sessions? How easy is it for interested parties to make it to the testimony sessions of formal rulemaking? Due to difficulties in arranging and paying for transportation, might it be easier for people to give their testimony through the mail (as is done in the informal rulemaking process)? Is the reasoning behind current agency decisions any more valid under formal rulemaking than it is under informal rulemaking?

Learning the Basics

Matching	True and False	Multiple Choice
1. a	1. False	1. c
2. c	2. False	2. a
3. f	3. True	3. c
4. h	4. True	4. d
5. d	5. True	5. b
6. b	6. False	6. d
7. g	7. False	7. c
8. e	8. True	8. b
	9. True	9. a
	10. False	

Short Answer

1. The first step in both informal and formal rulemaking is to publish the proposed rule in the Federal Register. In informal rulemaking, the next step is for interested parties to submit written arguments regarding the proposed rule. Finally, the agency publishes the final rule in the Federal Register. The second step in formal rulemaking is for the agency to hold a public hearing. Witnesses at this hearing are cross-examined, and an official transcript is created from this hearing. The agency publishes the formal findings resulting from the hearing. The last step is for the agency to publish the final rule in the Federal Register.

2. The legislative branch has the following checks over administrative agencies:
   a. oversight power
   b. investigative power
   c. power to terminate an agency
   d. gives consent to President's nominations for head of agency

   The executive branch has the following checks over administrative agencies:
   a. power of President to appoint heads of agencies
   b. power of the Office of Management and Budget to recommend a fiscal year budget for each agency
   c. presidential executive orders

Chapter 18

More Critical Thinking

1. *Rambo* Case

   a. The Court's decision supports the ethical norm of justice. In this sense, two alternative forms of justice are accented. First of all, the Court expresses its value of justice in the sense that people who are injured at work and unable to earn the same amount of money they did before the accident ought to have their previous condition restored. Additionally, the Court recognizes justice in the sense of not paying exorbitant sums of money to people who do not need it. Because this latter definition of justice is related to the allocation of a scarce resource (money), it could also be evidence of the Court's valuing efficiency.

   b. R1) Disabilities that do not adversely affect a person's capacity to work now may reduce her capacity to work in the future.
   R2) Failure to continue to compensate victims of accidents would prevent them from receiving compensation in the future, should they need it then.
   R3) Such a decision is consistent with the position of the Director of the Office of Workers' Compensation Programs.

   c. Information on how typical it is for the wages of an injured worker to remain the same following the accident and then decline would help readers to determine if this decision was even necessary. Additionally, it would help readers to know why the Director of the Office of Workers' Compensation Programs favors such an approach. If he supports this approach for poor reasons, then the Court's third reason is not very valid.

2. Argument about Paid Parental Leave

   a. The issue of this argument is, "Should the United States adopt a policy of guaranteeing new parents the right to paid leave from work so they can care for their children?" The author's conclusion is "Yes."

   b. The second paragraph mentions that spending time with newborns has a "profound effect" on their development. What does the author mean by this phrase? Does he mean that the amount of time spent with children predicts their life chances and future earnings with 90 percent accuracy? Does he mean that children whose parents do not spend time with them are never able to become productive citizens? Does he mean that most people who assume positions of leadership in our society were blessed with parents who spent a lot of time with them? Until this phrase is clarified, readers cannot be sure whether they agree with the author's contention.

The phrases "poorly socialized" and "psychological problems" also suffer from ambiguity. To which psychological problems is the author referring? If he is referring to paranoid schizophrenia, we'd be much less likely to accept his reasoning than if he is referring to mild cases of poor self-esteem.

A final important ambiguity arises in the author's last paragraph, where he states that the Swedish system "works." In what sense does it "work"? Does he mean that it works in the sense of providing new parents with a way to spend time with their child? In the sense of eliminating poverty? Providing Swedish children with a firm foundation for their future? Readers will react differently to the argument when different definitions are chosen.

c. Before deciding that Sweden presents a model for our society to follow, it would help us to know more about other aspects of life in Sweden. How is parental leave in Sweden funded? How high are their taxes? Would such tax rates be desirable to Americans? How large is the nation of Sweden, and does its size make it easier to implement such policies there? Would it even be feasible for a large nation to model its policies after those of a smaller nation?

Additionally, it is difficult for us to know how to react to the second paragraph without some additional information on the evidence presented. For example, who performed these studies? When? Were the sample sizes large enough for us to generalize from their results? Until we are provided with some additional information, we should withhold judgment on the argument to avoid making a premature determination that paid parental leave is or is not a good policy for our society to implement.

d. The ethical norm of justice (in the sense of providing every child with the opportunity to experience parental affection regardless to the economic status of the parents) is elevated here. Conversely, the ethical norm of efficiency (in the sense of allowing businesses to implement only those policies that will aid them in maximizing production and profits) is downplayed in this argument.

Learning the Basics

Matching	True and False	Multiple Choice
1. d	1. False	1. d
2. f	2. True	2. b
3. e	3. False	3. d

4. b	4. True	4. c
5. c	5. False	5. c
6. a	6. True	6. c
	7. False	7. b
	8. True	
	9. False	

Short Answer

1. Advantages -
   a. guaranteed recovery for on-the-job injury

   b. no need to hire a lawyer to recover for employee's own negligence

   c. negligence of other workers does not bar recovery

   Disadvantages -

   a. employees give up the right to bring a negligence action, which might have yielded a much larger recovery

   b. because employers do not have to fear large damage awards to workers who suffer substantial injuries, they may be less concerned about safe working conditions

2. The birth of a child
   The adoption of a child
   The placement of a foster child in the employee's care
   The care of a seriously ill spouse, parent, or child
   A serious health condition that renders the employee unable to perform any of the essential functions of his or her job

3. The safety and health inspector arrives at the plant and asks to meet with the plant manager as well as a union representative. The inspector then examines the plant records of accidents. If the number of accidents in that plant is lower than the average for the industry, the inspection is ended. However, if the number of accidents is higher, the inspector tours the plant to examine the safety conditions. After the inspection, the inspector discusses what was found with the firm and asks them to address the problems.

Chapter 19

More Critical Thinking

1. *Allentown Mack* Case

    a. The relevant rule of law in this case is that when an employer conducts an internal poll of employee support of a union, this act constitutes an unfair labor practice unless the company has a good-faith reasonable doubt regarding the union's majority support. This rule of law is not part of a statute; instead it is an agency rule (created by the NLRB).

    b. The phrase "good-faith reasonable doubt" is extremely ambiguous. It is also the point of contention in this case. The employer argued that it had a "good-faith reasonable doubt" that the union still had majority support. Conversely, the NLRB argued that the company's information was not strong enough to constitute such a doubt.

    c. The Court gave two primary reasons for reversing the decision of the Circuit Court. First of all, it stated that the ALJ made a mistake by failing to regard the testimony of other employees. This testimony gave the company sufficient reason to doubt that the union had majority support of the company's workers. The second reason the Court gave was based on math and the testimony mentioned before. Considering the ALJ's admission that 7 of the 32 employees were anti-union, the union would need support from 17 of the remaining 25 workers in order to maintain its majority support. The union's enjoying that support among the remaining workers is extremely unlikely, especially when the previously mentioned testimony is considered.

2. Argument about Unions

    a. The author gives four primary reasons for abolishing unions. First of all, unions undermine competition. Secondly, allowing workers to bargain collectively, but forbidding corporations to do so imposes a double standard. The third reason is that unions' membership is declining because people don't want to be represented by unions. The fourth reason is somewhat tricky because it is implicit in the author's words. It is that unions run contrary to the individualistic principles upon which our nation was founded.

    b. The author states that the reason union membership has declined so sharply is that people no longer wish to be represented by unions. However, he fails to consider alternate causes of this drop in union membership. Could the decrease have been caused in part by differences in the way labor laws were enforced between 30 years ago and today? Could there have been a shift in management's attitude and policy toward unions? Might the drop in union support be due to the fact that many traditionally-union jobs (e.g., factory jobs) have been moved abroad by factories in America shutting down? By failing to consider rival causes, the author makes his argument more difficult to accept.

c. Several words used by the author are especially ambiguous. For example, in the first paragraph the author states that collective bargaining "undermines" the economy. However, he fails to tell us what he means by "undermine." Does he mean "to prevent from reaching maximum efficiency"? Does he mean "to cause severe problems for"? Does he mean "to completely ruin"? Each of these phrases is a possible definition of "undermine," yet our willingness to accept the argument differs significantly depending on which definition we select. Another important ambiguity is located in the second paragraph. The author claims that corporations must clear "endless legal hurdles" to work together. What do these "hurdles" consist of? How long is "endless"? Additionally, the author says that unions are "hardly necessary" anymore. Note that he doesn't answer the question "hardly necessary for what?" If he means that they're hardly necessary for getting a Democratic candidate elected, we'd probably be more likely to agree than if he means unions are hardly necessary to ensure working people with decent benefits and job security. Finally, the last paragraph speaks of the United States' "prominent place in the world." For what? Is the author proud of our "prominent place" as the nation with the highest rate of television viewing? Is he referring to our high GDP per capita? Our military strength? Depending upon which definition he chooses, we may be more or less likely to agree with his reasoning.

Learning the Basics

Matching	True and False	Multiple Choice
1. e	1. False	1. d
2. f	2. True	2. a
3. j	3. True	3. c
4. d	4. False	4. b
5. a	5. False	5. d
6. h	6. False	6. b
7. g	7. False	7. b
8. c	8. True	8. d
9. b	9. True	9. c
10. i	10. False	10. a
	11. False	

Short Answer

1. The Taft-Hartley Act amended the Wagner Act. It was passed in 1947 in response to the public perception that unions' power had grown too drastically. The Taft-Hartley Act cut down on unions' power by making it illegal for them to engage in certain activities and by giving employees the right not to engage in collective activity.

2. The *Cabot* rule states that employee committees formed by an employer are labor organizations, and are therefore illegal in shops already represented by a union. Two exceptions to the rule are committees that include all employees (because then they do not "represent" the employees) and committees that perform functions that are typically carried out by management. In the latter case, the committees are considered management, and therefore are not a competing labor organization.

Chapter 20

More Critical Thinking

1. *Oncale* Case

   a. Justice Scalia repeatedly cites Title VII's prohibition of "discriminat[ion] ...because of...sex" in the "terms or conditions" of employment.

   b. To determine if Oncale's sex was the cause of the harassment, it would be helpful to know if there were any female workers above the oil platform on which Oncale worked. If there were women working in the same area, and they were not subjected to the same type of harassment that Oncale was, these facts would strengthen Oncale's claim that he was harassed "because . . . of [his] sex."

   c. In the opinion, the Court is forced to determine when harassing behavior becomes pervasive enough to constitute altering the terms or conditions of an employee's work environment. Justice Scalia compares the behavior of Oncale's coworkers to a football coach's slapping his players on the buttocks. He then compares it to a football coach's slapping his secretary's buttocks.

   Both of these analogies are similar to the facts of the case at hand in that a potentially abusive act occurs in both situations and in the facts of the case at hand. The difference lies in perception. The latter analogy is more appropriate than the first because it is likely that a player would interpret the slap on the buttocks as a pat on the back, whereas a secretary would probably be offended by the same act. Because Oncale was offended by the harassing acts of his coworkers, his perception mirrors that of the secretary, not that of the football player. Justice Scalia concludes that the latter comparison is more appropriate in the case at hand for the same reason.

2. Argument about Affirmative Action

   a. "Discriminate" is ambiguous. For example, "discrimination" could mean "treating people of different backgrounds differently." It could also mean "any practice that produces fewer people from a particular group than would be reasonably expected." Depending upon which definition of discrimination we select, our willingness to accept the author's conclusion that affirmative action programs are discriminatory, and therefore illegal, will vary.

   b. If we define "discrimination" as "treating people of different backgrounds differently," then we would agree with the author that affirmative action is discriminatory. Conversely, if we define discrimination as "any practice that produces fewer people from a particular group than would be expected," then affirmative action would be seen as a device used to end discrimination. In this case, we would reject the author's argument.

   c. By expressing concerns that affirmative action prevents companies from hiring the "most competent" people, the author elevates the ethical norm of efficiency. In this sense, we mean the efficiency that results when each job is filled with the most qualified individual available for it.

3. Argument about Sexual Harassment

   a. The author of this passage does not express the issue explicitly. So, we must search for the issue in the author's ideas rather than his words. The issue could reasonably be stated as, "What balance should exist between the First Amendment right to free speech and the right of employees not to be subjected to sexual harassment?" It might also be stated as, "Which actions should be included under Title VII's prohibition of sexual harassment?"

   b. Depending upon how the issue is stated, the conclusion may vary. The reason for this variance is that the author does not explicitly state the issue and the conclusion. Regardless of the issue you stated, however, the author's conclusion should be something similar to "The current definition of sexual harassment prohibits some activities that ought not be prohibited."

   c. R1) The current definition of sexual harassment violates our right to free speech.
   R2) People are fascinated with sex and therefore should be allowed to

talk about it.

R3) If sex were never talked about, people would be unable to control their sexual urges.

d. The author gives no evidence to support these reasons. The author could have provided evidence for the first reason by quoting experts on Constitutional law or Supreme Court cases that discussed the limits of free speech and concluded that people's right to say what they wish is greater than others' rights not to hear offensive words or ideas. Additionally, the author could have provided evidence for the third reason by citing a study finding that people who are sexually repressed are more likely to be sex offenders. Because the author failed to provide such evidence, we cannot tell whether his reasons are any good.

Learning the Basics

Matching	True and False	Multiple Choice
1. h	1. False	1. a
2. d	2. False	2. d
3. g	3. False	3. c
4. j	4. False	4. c
5. f	5. True	5. c
6. b	6. True	6. a
7. e	7. False	7. b
8. a	8. True	8. d
9. c	9. True	9. d
10. i	10. False	10. a

Short Answer

1. The plaintiff must first prove that he or she belongs to the protected age group, was qualified for the position, and was terminated under circumstances that lend themselves to the inference of discrimination. The defendant must then establish that there was a legitimate, non-discriminatory reason for the discharge to defeat the charge. If the defendant can establish this non-discriminatory reason for the discharge, the plaintiff must then show that the defendant's explanation is a mere pretext for the age discrimination. Some courts have held that a "pretext-plus" standard is necessary for the plaintiff to recover in these cases, but the Supreme Court ruled that establishing that the explanation was a pretext (in the determination of the jury in the case) is sufficient for the plaintiff's case to succeed.

2. The Civil Rights Acts of 1866 and 1871 prohibited only discrimination in the ability to form contracts and acts of discrimination by state and local governments. Additionally, they were poorly enforced. For these reasons, a

statute that forbade discrimination in employment was necessary, and Title VII became that statute.

Chapter 21

More Critical Thinking

1. *CERCLA* Case

   a. Issue: When can a parent corporation be held liable as an owner or operator of a polluting facility owned and operated by a subsidiary? Conclusion: If a parent corporation participated in and exercised control over the *operations of a subsidiary*, the parent corporation is not liable. However, if the parent corporation actively participated in and exercised control *over a polluting facility*, the parent corporation is liable. (The court has emphasized the parent corporation's relationship with the facility, not the subsidiary.)

   b. The court stated that an operator "must manage, direct, or conduct operations specifically related to the leakage or disposal of hazardous waste, or decisions about compliance with environmental regulations." This definition is directly related to the court's conclusion about when a parent corporation is responsible. The court's definition of operator creates a link with the polluting facility instead of the subsidiary.

   c. We need evidence that CPC did or did not exercise control over the facility. The court ruled that CPC would be liable if it had control over the polluting facility. However, if the U.S. cannot demonstrate that CPC exercised control over the facility, CPC is not an operator and thus not liable.

1. Acid Rain Argument

   a. Issue: Should we continue the Acid Rain Control Program? Conclusion: No, we should end the Acid Rain Control Program.

   b. First, the author claims that we still have an acid rain problem even though the program has been in place since 1990. Because we have not completely solved the acid rain problem, he suggests that the program should be ended. However, the author ignores the fact that we may never be able to completely eradicate the acid rain problem. He wants a perfect solution to the problem, but a perfect solution may not be available. He does not consider any evidence about the effectiveness of the program of reducing acid rain. Perhaps the program has not *solved* the acid rain problem, but maybe the program has helped to *reduce* the level of acid rain.

Second, the author suggests that the American people do not want the program. Because we are a democracy, he believes we should listen to what the people want. Instead of evaluating the merits of the program, he tries to convince us that if the people want something we should comply. How many American citizens want to pay taxes? If they do not want to pay, should we end the tax system? The fact that the people do not want the program is not necessarily a good reason for ending the program.

   c. As evidence for the second reason, the author uses a survey about environmental problems the American people believe are most important. Because acid rain was not high on the importance list, the author claims that people do not want the program. However, perhaps the people are uneducated about the problem of acid rain. Even if acid rain is not one of the top five environmental problems, perhaps its effects are severe enough that we *should* be concerned–even if we are more concerned with other environmental problems. Alternatively, they might not think acid rain is a problem because they believe the Acid Rain Control Program is effective.

   d. Why is the author so adamant about ending the Acid Rain Control Program? What is the New Acid Rain Permit Program? Would the author benefit if the Acid Rain Control Program were ended?

Learning the Basics

Matching	True and False	Multiple Choice
1. c	1. True	1. d
2. d	2. False	2. a
3. f	3. True	3. d
4. h	4. True	4. c
5. b	5. False	5. d
6. e	6. False	6. b
7. a	7. False	7. d
8. g	8. True	8. d
	9. False	9. a
	10. True	10. d

Short Answer

1. First, courts will not necessarily use their authority to issue an injunction to stop polluting behavior even when they find that a nuisance exists. Second, an individual plaintiff has standing to sue only when the nuisance is a private nuisance. Most nuisances are public; thus, only a public official can file a suit for a public nuisance. Public officials are often hesitant to anger businesses that have created nuisances because the officials worry that the

business will close down and move to another area. For these reasons, the tort of nuisance is not adequate to control pollution.

2. The EIS must include a detailed statement of:

    a. the environmental impact of the proposed action;

    b. any adverse environmental effects that cannot be avoided should the proposal be implemented;

    c. alternatives to the proposed action;

    d. the relationship between local short-term uses of the human environment and the maintenance and enhancement of long-term productivity; and

    e. any irreversible and irretrievable commitments of resources that would be involved in the proposed activity should it be implemented.

Chapter 22

More Critical Thinking

1. *Campbell* Case

    a. The court's opinion elevates the ethical norms of justice and security. Both norms in this sense refer to being assured that when you enter into contracts with other people, those contracts will be upheld. Thus, the court is valuing security in the sense that you can feel sure that others will do what they promise. Similarly, the court's opinion values justice in the sense that people will be required to do what they previously promised to do.

    b. The ambiguous words are "purchase" and "sale." Two primary issues in this case are "Does the transfer of stock in employee stock options qualify as a sale/purchase?" and "Does a stock transfer in which the recipient did not pay for the stock with his own money qualify as a sale/purchase?"

    c. The court concluded that the company's transfer of stock to Campbell did constitute a sale/purchase. Its reasons follow:
        R1) "An employment contract whereby an employee exchanges his services in return for stock options has been held to constitute a purchase within the meaning of the 1934 Act."
        R2) "The Supreme Court has expressly held that a pledge of stock to secure a loan is a sale of securities."

These reasons lack relevant information that would assist readers in determining how good the judge's conclusion is. The first reason fails to answer important questions such as, "That conclusion has been reached by whom? Why has such an employment contract been held to constitute a sale? How similar were the facts in those cases to the facts in this case?" By stating only the conclusions of other courts and leaving out their facts and reasons, the judge makes it difficult to determine whether we should accept his conclusion. After all, if the reasoning of these cases does not support their conclusions, then it would be foolish to transfer those conclusions to the case at hand.

Similarly, the court's second reason fails to let readers know *why* the Supreme Court determined that a pledge of stock to secure a loan is a sale of securities. It is difficult for readers to weigh the value of the judge's conclusions when the judge merely restates the conclusions of others.

2. Argument about Securities Fraud

   a. The author gives two reasons for stiffer punishment for those guilty of securities fraud. First of all, securities fraud causes investors to lose money. Secondly, acts of securities fraud cause the economy to run less efficiently.

   b. The author provides no evidence whatsoever for these reasons.

   c. In order to determine if acts of securities fraud really take enough money away from investors to warrant stiffer penalties, it would be helpful for readers to know how much money a typical act of securities fraud takes away from investors. Additionally, how many people have been forced to work extra years because of money they have lost due to securities fraud?

   In order for readers to evaluate the author's claim that securities fraud causes the economy to run less efficiently, the author might answer the following questions: How typical is it for a business to reduce its workforce because it cannot raise capital? Are acts of securities fraud common and severe enough to prevent people from investing?

   d. A reasonable alternate conclusion for the author's reasons is "The SEC should do a better job monitoring the trade of securities." Another possibility is "We should vote for a tax increase that would enable the SEC to hire more investigators." A third alternative conclusion that could be reached is "Businesses ought to find a source of funding that is not as subject to fraud as the issuance and sale of securities."

   e. One major ambiguity in this argument is "securities fraud." The author describes how bad securities fraud is, but he does not describe exactly what he means by securities fraud. Does he mean all acts of securities fraud? Only acts that defraud investors out of more than $3 million? Readers' willingness to accept his conclusion that acts of securities fraud need stiffer punishment is dependent upon which acts of securities fraud the author means.

Another important ambiguity is actually found in the author's conclusion. While this passage argues for "stiffer punishment," the author never tells us what he means by that phrase. Does he mean life imprisonment? Larger fines? Death by firing squad? Torture? Certainly, we'd be more likely to accept his argument if he means "larger fines" than if he means "the death penalty."

Learning the Basics

Matching	True and False	Multiple Choice
1. c	1. True	1. d
2. h	2. False	2. d
3. a	3. False	3. a
4. e	4. True	4. c
5. b	5. False	5. c
6. i	6. True	6. a
7. d	7. False	7. d
8. g	8. True	8. b
9. j	9. True	9. c
10. f	10. False	10. a
	11. True	11. d

Short Answer

1. Both Acts were passed in response to the stock market crash of 1929 and the ensuing Great Depression. Together, they regulate the issuing and sale of securities. The major purpose of the first Act is to ensure full disclosure on new issues of securities. The latter Act's purposes were to regulate the trading of securities and to create the Securities and Exchange Commission to oversee the securities market.

2. The full disclosure rule makes the market fairer by eliminating the information advantage that securities analysts had before the rule. However, the market also becomes less stable as the analysts can no longer make as accurate a prediction of the value of a stock.

Chapter 23

More Critical Thinking

1. *Postal Service* Case

   a. Issue: "Is the United State Postal Service subject to antitrust liability?" Conclusion: "The United States Postal Service is not subject to federal antitrust laws."

   b. The Court proffers the following reasons to support its conclusion: (1) the Postal Service is part of the United States government, which cannot be held liable under federal antitrust laws; (2) Congress does not explicitly state that the Postal Service could be subject to antitrust laws; (3) the powers of the Postal Service are very limited compared with most for-profit corporations, as the Postal Service does not set prices or attempt to generate profits (apart from some limited profit-generating activities to curb losses).

   c. The Court relies heavily on analogies to support its reasoning, citing several relevant precedents. First, the court refers to *Franchise Tax Bd. of Cal.* v. *Postal Service,* a case in which the Postal Service was required to comply with a state tax law, from which the clause developed that the Postal Service could sue and be sued. Similarly, in *Loeffler* v. *Frank,* the Postal Service was responsible for damages related to discrimination that violated employees' rights under Title VII.

   However, the most important precedent was *FDIC* v. *Meyer.* This case established a two-prong test for determining whether a governmental entity was liable in a particular case. The first prong considers whether a governmental entity has sovereign immunity, and if not, whether the entity could be liable under the substantive law. The Supreme Court clarified and applied this two-prong test in *Postal Service,* as the Court simultaneously rejected the Court of Appeal's "erroneous" conclusion, while explaining the more proper interpretation of the *Meyer* precedent. With regard to the first prong of the *Meyer* test, the Court held that the Postal Service did not always have sovereign immunity, consistent with the precedent previously mentioned in *Franchise Tax Bd. of Cal.* v. *Postal Service,* from which the Postal Service could sue and be sued.

   But the second prong occupied the majority of the Court's attention. After concluding that the Postal Service could sue and be sued, the Court here addressed the issue of whether the Postal Service was subject to antitrust liability, as set forth in the Postal Reorganization Act and the Sherman Act. Accordingly, the Court held that the Postal Service is not a "person" as defined under the Sherman Act, just as the United States is not considered a "person" with respect to its being subject to antitrust laws. The Supreme Court's reasoning, as discussed in Question B of this section, focused on this second prong of the *Meyer* test, leading to the Court's conclusion that the Postal Service is not subject to antitrust laws.

2. Argument about Antitrust Laws

   a. The author offers two reasons for his conclusion:
      R1) Corporations are too powerful
      R2) Corporations are impersonal

   b. The author supports his first reason with examples of three powerful corporations. Such evidence is weak because readers have no way of knowing if these corporations are typical. If G.E., Nike, and Microsoft are not typical, then it is quite possible that corporations in general are not powerful. If this were the case, then we would be hesitant to accept the author's argument.

      The author also supports his claim that corporations are powerful by playing on the public's fear that their news may be flawed. Yet, the author does nothing to justify his assertion that G.E. taints the news that people watch. Thus, we cannot be sure whether there is any evidence for this claim or if the author is just making outrageous statements.

      A major problem with the evidence provided for the second reason is that readers are given no way to determine whether the job loss that New York City experienced was typical of other cities across the nation. Furthermore, the author does nothing to demonstrate that the jobs were lost as a result of the impersonal nature of corporations. They could have been lost for a number of other reasons (recession, the city's raising its tax rate, etc.).

   c. Several phrases in this passage are ambiguous. First of all, in the second paragraph, the author claims that Bill Gates has more power than the President of the United States. What kind of power is he talking about? While Bill Gates may have more purchasing power than the President of the United States, George Bush has diplomatic powers that Bill Gates could never employ.

      Additionally, in the fourth paragraph, the author states that corporations do not wish to pay Americans a "decent wage." What does this mean? Does it mean enough money to afford to eat steak every day? Just enough to keep a two-person family out of poverty? Depending upon the author's definition of "decent wage," readers might agree or disagree with the author's statement.

Finally, in the last paragraph, the author talks about our nation's former status as "the greatest in the world." However, he does not tell readers what he means by that phrase. Does he mean "the nation with the most advanced social safety net?" Or perhaps, "the nation with the highest rate of television ownership in the world?" Depending upon the author's definition of great, readers might conclude that it is undesirable to restore or maintain our position as "the greatest in the world."

Learning the Basics

Matching	True and False	Multiple Choice
1. f	1. False	1. b
2. j	2. False	2. d
3. c_	3. True	3. a
4. h	4. False	4. d
5. e	5. True	5. b
6. i	6. False	6. d
7. a	7. True	7. b
8. d	8. True	8. d
9. g	9. False	9. a
10. b	10. True	10. c

Short Answer

1. The Sherman Act requires three elements for a violation: (1) a combination, contract, or conspiracy; (2) a restraint of trade that is unreasonable; and (3) a restraint that is involved in interstate, as opposed to intrastate, commerce.

2. Tying arrangements have generally been adjudged per se illegal if the manufacturer of the tying product has a monopoly on the tying product either by virtue of a patent or as a result of a natural monopoly situation. If the tying arrangement does not exist in a monopoly situation, it may still be an illegal vertical restraint of trade if the following three conditions are present:

   1. The manufacturer or seller of the tying product has sufficient economic power to lessen competition in the market of the tied product.
   2. A substantial amount of interstate commerce is affected. If the manufacturer and lessor of a product, through a tying agreement, have little impact on the market of the tied product, the courts will not consider this agreement to be per se illegal and, using a rule-of-reason approach, will dismiss the case.
   3. Two separate products or services are involved.

In the Microsoft case in the chapter, we also saw that the Court ruled out most per se analysis of tying in the computer software industry: "Our reading of the record suggests merely that integration of new functionality into platform software is a common practice and the wooden application of per se rules in this litigation may cause a cloud over platform innovation in the market for PCs, network computers, and information appliances."

Chapter 24

More Critical Thinking

1. *Kawaauhau* Case

   a. "Willful and malicious injury" is an ambiguous phrase that is of paramount importance to this case. The plaintiff's definition of "willful and malicious injury" includes all injuries that resulted from intentional acts. On the other hand, the defendant's definition includes only injuries that another party intended to cause. This ambiguity is actually the issue of the case. The issue can be stated, "Does malpractice constitute willful and malicious injury?"

   b. The Court offers several reasons for its conclusion:
   R1) Congress intended for only intentional injuries, not those injuries that resulted from willful conduct, to be included in the exception to the rule of discharging debts. Had Congress intended to include the latter, it could have included such words in the legislation.
   R2) If the opposite conclusion were reached, then almost any intentional act that caused an unintended injury would enable the injured party to collect despite the other party's bankruptcy.
   R3) In a previous case (*Davis v. Aetna*), the Court held that negligent actions are not necessarily "willful and malicious."

   c. The final paragraph elevates the ethical norm of security. In this instance, we are referring to security in the sense that the law will be preserved as Congress wrote it (this is an example of judicial restraint). In this way, the Court seeks to remove the gray area where one branch of government's duties end and the next branch's begin under our system of separation of powers.

   This ethical norm conflicts with efficiency. Because the legislative process is long and tedious, a much more efficient way for the law to be changed would be for the Court to interpret it differently (this would be an example of judicial restraint). Thus, the Court's changing the law through its interpretation would lead to a much more efficient changing of the law than would the legislative process.

2. Argument about Children's Advertising

    a. This argument downplays the ethical norm of freedom. In this case, we mean freedom in the sense that advertisers ought to be free to create whichever advertisements they wish to create as long as they are not outright lies. We also mean freedom in the sense that consumers should choose which products and services they want without the government's regulating what they see.

    b. The Federal Trade Commission Act gives the FTC the authority "to cover . . . advertising deception." To demonstrate unlawful advertising, the FTC must show that

        1. there is a misrepresentation or omission in the advertising likely to mislead consumers;

        2. consumers are acting reasonably under the circumstances; and

        3. the misrepresentation or omission is material.

    c. The author gives three main reasons:
R1) children need more protection because they are less sophisticated than adults.
R2) Ads aimed at children manipulate them.
R3) Due to the manipulative nature of these ads, children stand to be hurt by reality. Such a situation could lead to children's becoming disillusioned.

    d. The author argues that if properly applied, the FTCA would not allow many of the practices in children's advertising. However, the reasons given in his argument are different from the relevant rule of law's requirements for a violation. Thus, the reasons that the author gives do not support his conclusion. Perhaps they would better support the following conclusion: The FTCA should be amended to outlaw many current practices in children's advertising.

Learning the Basics

Matching	True and False	Multiple Choice
1. h	1. False	1. d
2. e	2. True	2. b
3. i	3. False	3. a
4. b	4. False	4. d
5. j	5. False	5. <u>d</u>
6. g	6. False	6. a
7. a	7. True	7. b
8. f	8. False	8. b

9. d	9. False	9. c
10. c	10. False	10. a
	11. True	

Short Answer

1. Both attachment and a writ of execution are court-ordered judgments that enable an officer of the court (often a sheriff) to seize the property of a debtor. The difference between the two is a matter of timing. Attachment usually occurs before the judgment. On the other hand, a writ of execution is issued after the debtor has lost in court and is unable to pay the creditor. Once the debtor's property is seized, it will be sold in order to pay off the creditor.

2. The nondischargeable debts are:
   a. certain taxes and customs duties and debt incurred to pay such taxes or custom duties;
   b. legal liabilities resulting from obtaining money, property, or services by false pretenses, false representations, or actual fraud;
   c. legal liability for willful and malicious injuries to the person or property of another;
   d. domestic support obligations and property settlements arising from divorce or separation proceedings;
   e. student loans unless excepting the debt would impose undue hardship;
   f. debts that were or could have been listed in a previous bankruptcy in which the debtor waived or was denied a discharge;
   g. consumer debts for luxury goods or services in excess of $500 per creditor, if incurred by an individual debtor on or within 90 days before the order for relief;
   h. cash advances aggregating more than $750 obtained by an individual debtor under an open-ended credit plan within 70 days before the order for relief;
   i. fines, penalties, or forfeitures owed to a governmental entity.

Think about the types of debts listed as being nondischargeable. You may have listed multiple reasons why these debts should not be discharged during bankruptcy proceedings. A few possible reasons are listed below.

Debts (g) and (h) refer to debts that would be incurred if the individual filing for bankruptcy went on a shopping spree in anticipation of the bankruptcy proceedings. By forcing individuals to pay the debts incurred during any such spending sprees, the court is discouraging reckless spending that would be, in essence, a theft (if the individual buys goods knowing that he or she will not actually pay for the goods due to bankruptcy proceedings).

The rationale behind debt (f) is fairly straightforward. If a prior court has ruled that a debt was nondischargeable, then the individual cannot have the debt discharged during a second bankruptcy proceeding.

Debts (b) and (c) refer to debts incurred as a result of willful wrongdoing. If an individual has incurred debts by committing fraud or harming another person or property, then the individual should not be able to discharge those debts by filing for bankruptcy. If the individual were able to discharge the debts, then the victims of the individual's wrongdoing would never receive restitution.

The rationale behind debts (a), (d), (e), and (i) is not as clear as the others. If an individual owes money to the government or to an individual such as an ex-spouse or child, then the individual should have to repay those debts for reasons similar to those in the prior paragraph. If the individual can discharge debts owed to the government or ex-spouses, then the government and ex-spouses will never receive the debts owed them. Unlike businesses, the government and private individuals are not well prepared to suffer the loss of the debts owed them by an individual filing for bankruptcy.